Supervisory
and
Executive Development

A MANUAL FOR ROLE PLAYING

NORMAN R. F. MAIER
University of Michigan

ALLEN R. SOLEM
University of Maryland

AYESHA A. MAIER

Supervisory and

NEW YORK · JOHN WILEY & SONS, INC.

Executive Development

A MANUAL FOR ROLE PLAYING

London

MAY 1965

THIRD PRINTING, SEPTEMBER, 1962

Library of Congress Catalog Card Number: 57–5925

PRINTED IN THE UNITED STATES OF AMERICA

"Seeing's believing
            but
                  feeling's the truth"

Preface

Experience with human relations training and executive development programs is making it more and more clear that the learning of the principles of human behavior has little value unless it is supplemented with skill practice. Just as in learning golf, book learning and demonstrations are needed, but they will never replace practice. The best kind of practice is performing under competent supervision. The greatest need in all training programs that involve the ability to relate with other people is opportunity to practice without getting hurt or without hurting anyone.

The present volume is designed to give two kinds of practice. In the first place it permits role playing, and this method furnishes an opportunity to practice a human relations incident in a lifelike setting. The cases incorporate conflicts, differences in power and responsibility, and practical considerations. Participants soon discover how real and lifelike these situations become. Because they are play situations, participants can experiment and try out new methods without running the risks that such experimenting entails in real life.

In the second place the present volume is a casebook, and this approach to human relations invites practice in discussing and analyzing crucial issues. Discussion stimulates a group to actively explore a problem from many points of view. What may be passed over quickly in reading can become an issue that participants in a discussion find to be basic to their everyday jobs. Discussion also reveals varied attitudes and these can become clarified, evaluated, and modified through group discussion; reading, with no discussion, may have little or no influence on attitudes. Finally, a discussion permits persons to compare their thinking with that of other members of a group. It is important for each person to know how his views compare with those of others, if he is to effectively relate with people in a community or organization.

Both role playing and discussion methods approach human relations issues as problems, and the emphasis is on skills in solving and preventing problems. These methods differ from the lecture and textbook approach in which emphasis may be placed on principles and determining the "right" answer. The answer approach is so ingrained in our educational and training methods today that participants insist on the teacher's giving the answer. This interest in the answer does not mean that it will be accepted and utilized in the future. Quite the contrary: giving answers arouses arguments and stimulates people to think about what is wrong with the answer. Disagreements of this sort lead to face-saving problems, and new conflict issues are introduced.

This volume proposes to avoid giving answers. Some principles and facts may be introduced, but basically the aid that may be supplied is in the form of raising questions and exploring issues. With these aids a group of persons should come up with good answers, and as training proceeds the answers should become better. Improvement, not perfection, then becomes the goal.

The book can be used as a training manual for supervisory and executive training and requires no highly skilled leader. Certainly no leader should feel that he must supply answers. It can also serve as a training manual for a group of persons who wish to form a study group and have no designated trainer or leader (see page 16f). By inviting wives to participate, the role playing can become an interesting game. Since human relations problems arise in the home and in the community as well as in industry, the interest and value of these cases is quite universal.

NORMAN R. F. MAIER
ALLEN R. SOLEM
AYESHA A. MAIER

December 1956

Contents

Descriptive Chart

Case	Procedure in Role Playing	Type of Problem	Participants Needed
1.	Multiple	Group	6 per group
2.	Multiple	Individual	2 per group
3.	Multiple	Group	7 per group
4.	Multiple	Individual	3 per group
5.	Multiple	Group ·	4 per group
6.	Multiple	Individual	3 per group
7.	Multiple and Single	Group	6 per group
8.	Multiple	Group	7 per group
9.	Single	Group	13 role players
10.	Single (skit completion)	Individual	6 role players
11.	Single	Group	7 role players
12.	Multiple	Individual	4 per group
13.	Single (dramatized)	Individual	3 role players
14.	Single	Individual	2 role players
15.	Single	Individual	2 role players
16.	Single	Individual	2 role players
17.	Single	Group	8 role players
18.	Single	Individual	2 role players
19.	Single	Individual	2 role players
20.	Single	Group	4 role players

Introduction

THE INTEGRATION OF ROLE PLAYING AND CASE STUDIES

The case study approach to human relations was initiated at Harvard,[1] and it made a unique contribution to the educational process. Cases force one to think in terms of particulars. Whether a theory or broad generalization is sound can only be determined by applying it to a specific set of facts. When placed in an institutionalized setting, the facts must be considered in relation to power structure, given personalities, and time pressures.

The case-study approach assumes group discussion and the cases are sufficiently involved and detailed to produce a wide range in opinion concerning (*a*) who was to blame, (*b*) what caused a person to behave as he did, and (*c*) what is the best corrective action to take.

The fact that a group of persons with similar backgrounds and aspirations should disagree in simple behavior matters often comes as a surprise to participants. Since a case merely contains a description of a series of samples of events, each stating what someone said or did and how others reacted, it soon becomes apparent that there is a big gap between practical and theoretical thinking.

The more important contributions of the case method to training include the following:

[1] H. Cabot and J. A. Kahl, *Human Relations: Concepts and Cases in Concrete Social Science.* Vol. II, *Cases.* Harvard Univ. Press, Cambridge, Mass., 1953.

J. D. Glover and R. M. Hower, *The Administrator: Cases on Human Relations in Business* (2nd ed.), R. D. Irwin, Inc., Homewood, Ill., 1952.

1

1. It discourages the making of snap judgments about people and behavior.

2. It discourages believing in, or looking for, the "correct" answer.

3. It graphically illustrates how the same set of events can be perceived differently.

4. It destroys any smug generalizations one might have about right vs. wrong answers, management prerogatives, the attitude of labor, best methods of discipline, the younger generation, the place of women in management, and many other issues.

5. It trains one to discuss with others, and experience the broadening value of interacting with one's equals.

6. It keeps the thinking in a practical setting, so that such considerations as costs, convenience, deadlines, attitudes of top management, and the morale of other persons involved prevent solutions from taking on an idealistic character.

7. It causes doubt as to whether there really are basic human relations principles.[2]

Although human relations principles may exist, it is well not to come into a program with pat conclusions. If a program is well handled, some general principles should develop in the process of training.

The technique of role playing is an outgrowth of the work of Moreno [3] who initially developed the method in connection with his work with the mentally disturbed. The purpose of the technique was to give the patient insight into some of his relationships with others by having him play the role of these other persons. Thus a patient might be asked to act out his father's behavior while the clinical assistant plays the part of the patient. The scene portrayed might be that of the son asking the father for the use of the family car. The technique is becoming recognized and accepted as a training method in interpersonal relationships, and it is being modified and extended in a variety of ways to suit many specific purposes.

The unique values of role playing include the following:

1. It requires the person to carry out a thought or decision he may have reached. For example, a conferee may conclude from a case study that Mr. A should apologize to Mr. B. In role playing, A would be asked to go to B and apologize. Role playing experience soon demonstrates the gap between *thinking* and *doing*.

---

[2] F. J. Roethlisberger emphasized the need for more skill and less talk about verbal principles in his article, Human Relations: Rare, Medium or Well Done, *Harvard Business Review*, Jan. 1948, 107.

[3] J. L. Moreno, *Who Shall Survive?*, Beacon House, Inc., Beacon, N. Y., 1953.

2. It permits the practice of carrying out an action and makes it clear that good human relations require skill in the same sense that playing golf requires skill.

3. Attitude changes are effectively accomplished by placing persons in specified roles. It becomes apparent that a person's behavior is not only a function of his personality, but also of the situation in which he finds himself.

4. It trains a person to be aware of, and sensitive to, the feelings of others. This information serves as a feedback of the effect his behavior has on other people.

5. A fuller appreciation of the important part played by feelings in determining behavior in social situations is developed.

6. Each person is able to discover his own personal faults. For example, the person who enjoys making wisecracks may discover how these often hurt others.

7. It permits training in the control of feelings and emotions. For example, a person can be given practice in not becoming irritated by complaints since he can be repeatedly placed in the role of a supervisor.

In combining role playing with the case method one goes beyond giving practice in a segment of behavior. Instead, a situation is created that contains practical considerations beyond those involved in the interpersonal relationship. For instance, the question of whether or not a foreman can take time off to listen to an employee under a given set of conditions involves not only the matter of how to deal with an employee's request, but also other demands that the situation makes on the supervisor at the time. In this way practical considerations and good human relations skills must be integrated. It is the hope that the integration of role playing and the case method will yield the combined advantages of the two methods. There is no reason to believe that any of them must be sacrificed by this merger. Rather, it is probable that new insights will be achieved because of the new relationships that are created. Certainly the values of the discussion of how something was said or done in role playing can lead to insights into skill requirements as well as to better planning on what should or should not be done. Discussions of case studies, at best, remain at the intellectual level and this is the great deficiency that role playing can correct.

In using different types of role playing and by placing persons in new and strange situations, further training values are achieved. One learns not to act the role of another, but to act one's own part in varied situations and under many conditions. In this manner the role playing of cases comes very close to practicing actual industrial problems.

SELECTION OF CASES

All of the cases have been experimentally tested with various management groups and college student classes, and a large number of them have been used extensively for training and demonstration purposes. The role playing participants have included all levels of management in large and small companies, representing many different industries. Similarly, the college student participants represent various levels of academic training and many different areas of study.

In the selection of the cases for this manual, an important consideration was the previously demonstrated effectiveness of the cases for reproducing the conditions of a life situation with a minimum amount of detail. To the degree that this is accomplished the participants do not attempt to portray other individuals but instead are themselves and experience motivations and feelings similar to those in real life. Under these favorable conditions role playing experiences frequently have considerable impact on a person's perception of a problem so that the new attitudes and behaviors experienced in the scene tend to carry over into everyday life situations.

Much of the training value of a case depends on the breadth of the generalizations that can be drawn from the results obtained. For this reason an important factor in screening the cases was the extent to which each of the separate cases typified a broad range of management problems and, in addition, illustrated and highlighted the methods and principles for dealing with the problems.

A third factor in the selection of a case was the interest value and the kind of challenge it offered. Role playing may become somewhat boring if the cases used lack conflict and variety in viewpoint.

In addition to the other considerations, each case has been selected for its unique contribution to an over-all training program in human relations. The present selection is aimed toward providing a comprehensive coverage of human relations problems in industry with a relatively small number of cases.

It is sometimes felt that cases should be based upon instances taken from the company in which the training is given. It is the experience of the writers that this can be done successfully only after there has been a considerable amount of training with general cases. When cases are based upon company experiences, a number of unfavorable conditions may be created:

1. Irrelevant and extraneous facts tend to be introduced and these disrupt discussion as well as role playing.

2. Defensive behavior for persons involved in the company situation often is shown.

3. Persons who know the company situation may disagree on the basic issues in the conflict.

4. Participants become *solution minded* rather than *process minded* and hence speculate on whether the company made a mistake.

5. Company cases may be imbedded in a complex situation so that the human relations issues are colored by other practical or defensive factors.

Once the group becomes accustomed to role playing, has acquired a familiarity with the basic skill principles, and appreciates the constructive interaction that occurs in group discussion, it is good practice to try to role play company situations. It is best, however, to use problems that have not been resolved, both because face-saving difficulties and the betrayal of confidences are not involved, and also because the insights gained in the role playing can be utilized in solving the problem. When a group is ready to role play company problems, different members of the group should present their own case data for the group's consideration.

SEQUENCE OF CASES

There has been some attempt to introduce variety by mixing group and individual cases, but in general the order of presentation of the cases follows a developmental sequence of principles and skills. Each case tends to involve the use of partially new and increasingly complex abilities, but at the same time it should be understood that any of the cases may be made more difficult merely by raising the degree of competence expected. The Multiple Role Playing Procedure is emphasized at the outset because it is somewhat easier to handle and discuss. However, this fact made it necessary to feature cases that readily lend themselves to Multiple Role Playing in the first half of the book. The transition to Single Group Role Playing is made via Cases 9 through 13.

There is no content or special knowledge in the cases that requires that the sequence in the manual be followed. Rather, the order and number of the cases used may be determined by the requirement of a particular training problem. Thus in one program there may be a need for practice in a particular skill such as interviewing in connection with evaluation; in another, the desire to demonstrate and practice the principles of group decision may be in order; and in still a different instance there may be a wish to stimulate discussion on methods of handling a particular problem, such as clarification of coffee privileges. Often there are limitations imposed on the use of all of the cases. Lack of sufficient time, of suitable space, or an insufficient number of group members to play the roles in some of the cases may require selectivity. In such instances the problem is one of making the most appropriate and complete use of the material that is possible under the circumstances. Frequently these and other initial obstacles can be overcome with little difficulty after a few of the cases have been tried out.

When there is no need to follow a different order or to limit the number of cases, it is recommended that the cases be used in the sequence in which they appear. This order illustrates a progression that has been found useful for general training both at various levels in management and in many different industries.

PLAN OF CASE ORGANIZATION

All of the cases are presented in accordance with the same basic plan of organization. Each is divided into four general sections and given the same major headings. Beyond this point minor variations in form are made in order to meet the unique demands of a particular case. It is hoped that this consistency in the plan of presentation will facilitate the use of the role playing procedures in the different cases and make for convenience in locating and identifying the various parts of the cases.

The four major headings and the general nature of the contents under each one are as follows:

I. Focusing the Problem: This is the introductory section and contains a description of the general class of problem illustrated by the case. Some indication of the primary training functions as well as the nature or degree of skill required by the trainees is also given in order to establish a favorable mental set.

II. Role Playing Procedure: In this section the recommended role playing procedure is indicated and a step by step description is presented for setting up the role playing scene. Additional instructions are provided for conducting the role playing process. Questions and discussion topics are provided for facilitating the subsequent analysis of the developments in the role playing and for highlighting the applications of the new learning to problems on the job.

III. Materials: Background information on the role playing problem for all group members is furnished in this section as are the individual roles for the participants. Special instructions are provided for group members who act as observers in some of the cases. When the role playing procedure makes provision for the collection of data and comparison of results from several groups of participants there are sample tables provided which illustrate the method for recording the results.

IV. Comments and Implications: Under this heading there is discussion of the types of errors most likely to be made and the usual consequences of these errors. However, the main purpose of this section is to point up the principles involved in the case and the kinds of skills required for dealing with related problems. These aspects of the case are presented within the framework of an effective approach to the type of problem that the case illustrates. In this manner generalizations of the new learning can be made to other job problems.

Figure 1. Diagram of design of a case.

Taken together, the four sections conform to the design shown in Figure 1. A particular general problem issue, such as "how to be fair to all employees," is raised in Section I. In order to test the adequacy of principles or points of view, one must go from conceptual thinking to a particular set of circumstances. Communication between people is best when one deals with specifics and one cannot escape the inadequacy of an idea by speaking about exceptions. When one particular case is under consideration there are no exceptions. This process of funneling the thinking from a *broad* classification of problems to a *particular* one is shown on the left portion of the figure.

Since the role playing experience and the discussion that follows are concerned with a particular situation and set of facts (background and role instructions), Section II and Section III are shown as the narrow middle part of the diagram. This is the stage in which ideas, skills and viewpoints are tested. It may also include discussion of the best way to handle the particular problem.

Once there is clarification of the problem, it is interesting to speculate on the ways in which the skills, the attitudes, and the thinking about a specific case may be transferred to other situations. This generalization is of a different sort than the one discussed in Section I in that remedies and techniques rather than problems are generalized. It is possible that the boundaries for transferring techniques might be quite different from those for classifying problems. Section IV tends to bridge the gap between the lessons learned in the particular case and the development of human relations principles.

It is felt that communication between participants established in the discussion of particulars will facilitate the communication of the generalized principles. It is in the conceptual area of thinking that communication is most faulty. However, when a group has carefully discussed a particular situation, it is hoped that they will be in a favorable condition to understand each other when an attempt is made to generalize the findings.

TYPES OF ROLE PLAYING PROCEDURES

Two role playing procedures are featured in this casebook. Approximately half of the cases are set up for the Multiple Role Playing Procedure (MRP) [4] and for the remaining half, the Single Group Role Playing Procedure is prescribed.

The use of the two procedures for role playing has an important advantage over confining the training to either one of the procedures because different kinds of training objectives are achieved by each.

When the MRP procedure is used, the entire audience is formed into role playing groups, the size of the groups depending on the number of participants required for the particular case. This procedure requires that all groups role play simultaneously. There are several advantages to this method.

1. The Multiple Role Playing Procedure is a particularly effective way for training by doing because it maximizes practice opportunities for the members of the audience to try out new attitudes and behaviors.

2. It provides data from each of the several groups so that comparisons of the results can be made. Discussion of the findings and relating them to various actions of the leader are especially convincing because the conclusions are based upon the group's own experiences. Since the roles are the same for all groups, differences in outcome are the product of variations in group interactions.

3. The Multiple Role Playing Procedure is a markedly effective way of getting all members of an audience involved in a problem. This in turn quickly dispels any initial feelings of shyness or self-consciousness among

[4] N. R. F. Maier and L. F. Zerfoss, MRP: A Technique for Training Large Groups of Supervisors and Its Potential Use in Social Research, *Human Relations*, 1952, 5, 177–186.

members who have not role played previously. When all persons are involved in a similar activity no one feels that he is being observed. Instead, the spirit of interacting has a contagious effect so that one group tends to stimulate rather than inhibit the performances of others. Embarrassment and face-saving problems are entirely eliminated.

When the main purpose of the training is to develop skill in sensitivity to the feelings of others, the Single Group Role Playing Procedure is most effective. This procedure is preferable for intensive training or advanced work with small groups and for certain types of demonstrations. Because the procedure permits only one role playing group to perform, all other members of a class can participate as observers during the role playing. A minor variation of the method is to have the observers function as consultants to the role playing leader or interviewer. Thus when no progress is being made, the role playing can be interrupted for a brief discussion and consultation. After the interruption the action is resumed.

After the scene has been completed, discussion methods are used to create opportunities for analysis and evaluation. There are several advantages to Single Group Role Playing.

1. Since all persons observe a single performance, it is possible to discuss the details that led to a particular effect. For example, the group can discuss the first appearance of defensive behavior on the part of one role player and then attempt to determine what behavior on someone else's part caused it.

2. Participants in the role playing profit from the analytical discussion of their behaviors since they often are unaware of the effect their actions produce on others.

3. Observers can develop sensitivity to the feelings of participants. If one person in the role playing indicates that he will improve his work, can the observers tell whether or not he means it? Since the role players can report on their true feelings it is possible to check the keenness of the sensitivity of observers.

It should now be apparent that one of these two procedures is not preferable to the other, but that they perform different training functions. These functions effectively complement each other in the development of all-around proficiency in human relations. It follows, therefore, that the decision to use one procedure or the other on a particular occasion should be determined by the specific training objectives and by the size of the group.

Within the framework of both procedures a number of variations are possible. In Case 10, the Skit Completion Method [5] is illustrated. This

[5] N. R. F. Maier, *Principles of Human Relations: Applications to Management,* John Wiley & Sons, New York, 1952.

variation uses a skit to create the situation and carry developments to a specific conflict area. Role players must pick up the action from this point and complete the interrupted action. This approach serves to control events up to a certain stage, thereby controlling the type of conflict situation more carefully.

Another variation is the Dramatized Case Method [6] in which a previous incident is furnished by means of written dialogue. From this point on the subsequent contacts are role played. This type of approach is illustrated in Case 13.

Both the Skit Completion Method and the Dramatized Case Method supply background data in a more interesting and dramatic way than can be achieved by role instructions. The description of a conflict situation may affect different role players in a unique manner but when previous lines are supplied the kind of emotion established in a role player is more effectively controlled. It is possible therefore to increase as well as control the range of problems and emotions that can be incorporated in a role playing episode.

TYPES OF ROLE PLAYING PROBLEMS

Generally speaking, it is possible to divide human relations problems into two general types, those having to do with individuals and those having to do with a group. Giving a job assignment, correcting an individual, interviewing a person, dealing with a complaint, and calming an emotionally upset employee are examples of face-to-face relationships with individuals. These require skills in interpersonal relations on the part of the supervisor.

When more than one person reports to a supervisor, he not only has multiplied his face-to-face relationships but he must deal with an additional problem: the relationships that each employee has with the others. Problems of favoritism, discriminatory practices, face saving, fairness of assignments, and regimentation fall in this category. Insofar as the supervisor is in charge of a group he is a leader and certain leadership skills are demanded of him.

In some cases it is difficult for the supervisor to know whether he is dealing with a group or an individual problem. Problems in safety may reflect group attitudes [7] so that an individual's violation of a rule may

[6] N. R. F. Maier, Dramatized Case Material as a Spring Board for Role Playing, *Group Psychotherapy*, 1953, *6*, 30–42.

[7] In a large power plant the safety department had great difficulty in getting electricians to wear hard hats for protection. Finally, it was discovered that electricians re-

actually involve the entire group. One of the skills of a supervisor is his ability to make the correct diagnosis of the type of problem that confronts him. It is also important that he be ready to change his diagnosis if new and relevant factors are disclosed.

The descriptive chart on page xi shows the division of the cases into group and individual problems. It will be noted that both types of problems are represented about equally often and that both the Single and the Multiple Role Playing Procedures are used with each type of problem. In a few instances the problem of diagnosing is raised and it will be seen that both individual and group approaches seem to be adequate yet yield very different results.

The cases that contain group problems are primarily aimed toward training in various conference leadership skills. There is considerable research evidence that indicates the effectiveness of certain leadership attitudes and participation techniques. Important leadership functions can determine whether or not a group will work together, accept improvements, and try to develop better ways of doing a job.

The cases concerned with problems and dealings with individuals focus attention on the practice and outcomes of various interpersonal relations procedures and skills. These include ways for creating an atmosphere in which an individual feels his supervisor is a willing helper rather than a judge; procedures for discovering an individual's needs, aspirations, and attitudes; opportunities to practice avoiding defensive behavior; training in responding to feelings rather than facts; and ways to improve the effectiveness of interviews.

It is not within the scope of this volume to present an adequate discussion of the principles in group leadership and interpersonal relationships with individuals. Those who desire to explore further into these areas and other aspects of human relations are referred to related publications.[8]

MINIMUM NUMBER OF ROLE PLAYERS REQUIRED

The number of participants needed for role playing varies with the case and the role playing procedure. Many of the cases require only two role players while the largest number requested is thirteen.

sisted because hard hats made them look like construction workers. Thus the underlying difficulty was a class status problem. The simple solution was to provide different hard hats for the various groups of workers.

[8] N. R. F. Maier, *Principles of Human Relations: Applications to Management,* John Wiley & Sons, New York, 1952; *Psychology in Industry* (2nd ed.), Houghton Mifflin Co., Boston, 1955.

The number of participants needed to play the roles in each of the cases is shown in the descriptive chart on page xi.

In addition to the persons who role play, provision is made in the cases for other group members to participate as observers when Single Group Role Playing is used, and to form additional role playing groups when the Multiple Role Playing procedure is followed. Special instructions and details for involving all class members are provided separately in each of the cases and, in some instances, suggestions are supplied for role playing a case with fewer than the minimum indicated.

Although cases may be used when only the minimum number of persons required is present in class, this should not be regarded as the optimum condition. Observers perform a valuable group function as critics. Because they are not emotionally involved, they can be objective in their observations and evaluations. Everyone should have the opportunity to serve in both capacities since the learning of observers is different from that of role players. Observers readily increase their sensitivity to feelings because they can devote full attention to watching and need not be concerned with responding.

HOW TO ROLE PLAY

All people are good actors when they make up their own lines. This is one of the most impressive facts one experiences in working with role playing. One can completely dispense with any consideration of training participants in voice intonation and gestures. The role player remains himself and must merely behave in the situation described. If he is placed in the role of a union steward, he should consider himself to be the steward for the group specified and not act the way he thinks a union steward behaves. In addition to finding himself in a specific position, the role player may be expected to accept certain facts about his length of service, sex, family ties, friends, and previous experiences. He should adopt these as his own and let his feelings and attitude change as these imagined events or factors seem to require.

All of us conduct ourselves differently depending on the situation in which we find ourselves. As a supervisor on the job, one's conduct is likely to be very different than when at home with the family. Similarly, appropriate behavior at a party is quite unlike accepted conduct at the movies. This does not imply that personality changes, but rather that behavior is altered in response to the situation while the person remains himself.

The role playing instructions describe the setting in which a particular frame of mind will be formulated. Because they set up a state of mind that serves as a point of departure, the roles should not be reexamined by the players once the interaction has begun. It is important to realize that the initial attitude adopted by a role player need not remain static. Subsequent events or experiences, as they occur in the process of role playing, may alter these attitudes and create pleasant or unpleasant feelings. As a result, the persons involved may have some of the same emotional experiences that occur in real life situations. This emotional arousal is one of the most important values of role playing and makes it a form of rehearsal for practical problems. With experience in role playing situations, persons learn to feel the part; to the extent that this occurs, role playing behavior becomes more and more authentic. The fact that role playing can simulate real life situations makes it possible for one to try new ways of handling problems without suffering any serious consequences if the methods fail.

In the process of role playing, questions may be raised in the discussion that are not covered by the instructions to the participants. When this occurs the person questioned should feel free to make up facts or experiences that are appropriate to the circumstances. For example, if the foreman in a case asks a worker a question about the health of his children, he may answer it in any one of several ways without altering the spirit of the case. However, the player should not go out of his way to make up experiences or facts that are inconsistent with his role.

In conclusion it is perhaps worthwhile to repeat points that have already been stated in order to warn against two common mistakes in role playing.

1. Do not consult your role while playing a part. This practice tends to make an attitude a static condition and not subject to alteration. Real attitudes are dynamic forces and are subject to change in direction as well as in intensity.

2. Do not behave the way you feel a person in the position described in your role should behave. This ability to play the part of another person is perhaps a requirement for acting in a play, but it is a distinct disadvantage in successful role playing. A good role player need not be an accomplished actor.

USE OF BOOK AS A TRAINING MANUAL

Role Playing Supplies. All role playing supplies and instructions are contained in the manual. Since most of the contents of the book concern the class members and the instructor to a similar degree it has been unnecessary to prepare separate books for instructor and students. If serious study is undertaken it is desirable for each person to have his own copy of the book, not only to furnish him with the needed introductory and concluding sections, but also to facilitate the role playing process.

Recommended Sequence. Since the cases selected for the volume are diversified, taken together they sample a wide range of human relations principles. Unless the objective of a training program is selective or specialized it is suggested that the cases be used in the order that they appear in the book. If time is not available for using all of the cases, the selection still can be made in a forward order.

Previous Experience. No special previous training is required of the trainer or of the participants. If the trainer has had previous experience with role playing it is suggested that he refrain from attempting to explain it. Groups accept and get the feeling for role playing with a minimum amount of indoctrination. As a matter of fact, too much to-do about role playing often frightens participants. The only preliminaries necessary are (*a*) those explanations required to cover the company viewpoint or policy on training and (*b*) a warmup period during which each participant rises, introduces himself, tells a little about his background, and briefly describes his present position. Even when participants know each other, a little discussion of the latter two items may serve a valuable purpose.

Size of Group. The size of the group may range from 10 to 50. The ideal size for single group role playing is smaller than for multiple group role playing; it is around 12 to 15 for the former and between 25 and 50 for the latter. However, the skill of a leader and the type of room facilities are variable factors. When these are adequate, interest can be maintained in individual group role playing with classes as large as a hundred persons; and in multiple role playing successful and spirited participation has been achieved with an audience made up of 650 executives.

Rank Differences. In general it is not a good practice for a company to mix persons of different rank in a training class. Face-saving problems may be created by status differences and the greater the spread in rank, the more difficult this problem becomes. However, this problem is not serious in small companies where each supervisor knows all of the management personnel and they react to the personalities of each other, rather than to their positions. The extent of the problem of mixing rank will, of course, depend upon the attitudes of the higher officials and the skills of the trainer. When in doubt, it is best to play safe and avoid the status problem.

Mixing Departments. The mixing of supervisors from different jobs, departments, and divisions is highly recommended. It permits the attainment of such training byproducts for supervisors as:

1. Discovery that others have difficulties and problems similar to their own.

2. A fuller knowledge of the way work in other units relates to their own.

3. The acquisition of friends in several departments.

These byproducts improve communication, help in the development of a broader view of company functions, and ease the process of lateral transfers. There is no need to separate men and women supervisors since each can take the role of either sex in role playing.

The Class Room. The room need be no larger than is required to accommodate the size of the group. It is unnecessary to supply extra space for discussion groups since, even in multiple role playing, the noise of adjacent groups tends to stimulate the business of role playing rather than act as a distraction.

It is best if chairs or movable seats are furnished so that members can form groups of varying size with comfort and ease. However, auditoriums with fixed seats can be used by having persons in one row turn around to discuss with persons immediately behind. Inadequate facilities should not be a reason for avoiding role playing.

Furnishings. Necessary furnishings are a table and a few chairs that can be moved to the front of the room when the directions request it. A card table and chairs will serve this need. Also needed for multiple role playing are two portable blackboards or two large easels. It is desirable that trainers use these visual aids as much as possible, even when they are not specifically required in the instructions. The use of a blackboard effectively slows down discussion, supplies a more permanent record of the group's thinking, and requires that ideas be efficiently and briefly stated.

Class Assignments. The question of previous preparation for each case should be left to the instructor. He may wish to make reading assignments in order to give the group a background of related principles. However, this is not a requirement for the use of the cases.

In developing the procedure it has been assumed that the case has not been assigned ahead of time. However, it is desirable for the instructor to read over the material so that he will be familiar with the procedure and the points in the discussion. He should not study ahead in order to be prepared to supply the answers to problems raised. His role is to assist the group in executing the role playing and to direct the discussions.

The last three cases in the book have rather complex role assignments. In these instances it is suggested that the role players study their roles in advance. These instructions are supplied in connection with the case.

USE OF BOOK BY SMALL GROUP WITHOUT A TRAINER

A teacher or trainer is available to persons only when an educational institution or a company develops or sponsors the human relations or executive development program. Since the psychological aspects of this training and development are of relatively recent origin, the desired training facilities may not be available to all persons who wish them.

Companies often have difficulty motivating some of their employees to develop or grow and by the same token there will be a similar number of individuals who wish to develop at a pace more rapid than the company facilities afford. Then, too, there are people whose occupations do not offer training along these lines.

The instructions in this section are intended for those who have similar or diversified interests in human relations that go beyond the available facilities in the company or community. Dealing effectively with people and obtaining satisfaction from these relationships may be goals of a great number of men and women. In addition to supervisors and executives in business and industry these are important goals for ministers, teachers, parents, social workers, doctors, nurses, committee chairmen, and community leaders. Since both men and women are included in this list of interested persons, mixed groups can meet together and participate in role playing. The aspects of drama and the conflicts in views stimulated by the case situations will make for a lively and entertaining evening. The fact that there are important practical gains associated with the sociability of the procedure should not be misleading.

Since the case material is placed in an industrial setting, it is desirable to spend time at the end of each case to apply the principles discussed to related problems found in the experiences of the group members. If the case under consideration deals with a problem of "fairness," for example, each person in the group may be asked to describe a similar problem in his or her own experience. The fact that different occupational groups have problems with similar or identical human relations elements will serve to enrich the meaning of these elements and facilitate understanding of each other's situation. This is particularly true of married couples.

The procedures described should be fully adequate for use with groups having no teacher or trainer. Since the instructions are directed to various participants and role players as well as to the instructor, it is only necessary that someone in the group take charge of coordinating the activity. Cases set up for multiple role playing may be limited to one or two groups on some occasions, but there are enough gains to offset this disadvantage.

In order to obtain more examples of solutions, the role players may wish to exchange roles and repeat the role playing process. This exchange in roles will usually result in a different solution and it has a distinct value in itself. A person gains a fuller appreciation of the part a man's position plays in determining his outlook and his behavior if he can view the same conflict from different points of reference.

USE OF CASES FOR EXECUTIVE SELF-DEVELOPMENT

The special merits of discussion and role playing for training in human relations have already been enumerated. Since discussions require groups, this means that an individual interested in improving his ability to relate with people would be denied the values of discussion. For some time the authors have been interested in developing a method whereby a single person, studying by himself, might gain some of the training values that are available in a discussion.

It is hoped that the present case book will partially satisfy this need. To accomplish the benefits, however, the volume must be used in accordance with the instructions. If the individual reader agrees that he wishes to derive the values of both role playing and discussion from this volume, he must set a block of one to two hours aside for each case and carry out the assignments described below. Shortcuts or scanning of materials ahead of time or using the book to fill short intervals of leisure will not accomplish the objective.

Since all cases are divided into similar sections the procedure outlined below will apply to all of them. Once the individual reader gets into the spirit of the method he will be able to visualize some of the interplay that takes place in group interaction.

The first section, Focusing the Problem, will cause no difficulty, since it is a straightforward presentation of a problem and requires only careful reading. The second section sets the stage for role playing. This part should be studied with an attempt to visualize the setting and individuals involved. When the instructions call for a reading of background materials and instructions (parts of Section III), the reader should study these as do regular role players. He should then return to Section II and proceed with any further steps in arrangements.

The reader should assume that he is to play the role of the leader in *group* cases and of the interviewer in cases dealing with an *individual*. He should then study his specific role carefully and prepare himself for the conference or the interview. The roles for other participants should not be read at this time. As the leader or interviewer he would not know what was on another person's mind until it was revealed in a discussion.

After studying his role, the reader should write out his opening remarks in detail. Once he begins writing he should not alter what he has already written. Any changes should be made as corrective statements and hence be in the form of additions rather than erasures. As is the case with the spoken word, the imaginary role player must be required to cope with his previously expressed remarks.

When the introductory statement has been completed, the reader should read it aloud and then imagine the reactions he would get from typical group members or interviewees, as the case may be. A few sample reactions should be noted on a pad, each followed with the response he would give. The brief exchanges should be evaluated by noting whether the imagined reactions he obtained were of a constructive nature and whether or not he handled the reactions satisfactorily.

Another important phase of human interaction is the acceptance of a line of action. The reader should write out a plan or solution to the problem that he feels will be acceptable to the group or the interviewee. Reasons why the plan or solution should be adopted may be noted in the margin so that they can be checked later against the role instructions.

One of the other roles should now be studied. The reader should assume that he has taken this role and then reread his previous introductory remarks from this new vantage point. In group cases he should repeat this procedure with a few of the roles so as to get a good feeling for the other side of the situation. He may then sit back and imagine the kind of discussion that would occur. After several imagined exchanges he should carefully examine the solution from the viewpoint of the subordinates.

In the light of any differences in opinion, the reader should construct a modified solution, indicating any concessions or changes he would make and the things he hopes to gain by them. When he feels that he has a good revamped solution, he should read any remaining roles and especially the Instructions for Observers, if such a part is included in the section on materials.

The reader is now ready to turn to the exercises concerned with the results and their analyses, devoting time particularly to questions relating to leadership or interviewing skills. These will serve as a guide to indicate to the reader the types of mistakes he is inclined to make and the types of skills he already possesses. He should compare himself with several other supervisors or executives he knows and imagine what each would have done differently. This process of thinking through consequences of alternate procedures that might be used by supervisors should be done leisurely and might consume as much as half an hour or more. A chart or outline will be a useful visual aid.

When the reader is satisfied with his analysis and evaluation, he should carefully study the last section, Comments and Implications. He may find that he is in disagreement with some of the views expressed and this is a healthy sign, since disagreement is the basis for discussion. Any differences in views should be noted because similar issues may arise in later cases. The reader may find inconsistencies in the analysis supplied by the authors and he may find that his own views will change as a result of the case studies.

Once the last section has been carefully digested, the whole case should be reread from start to finish. The purpose of the final reading is to discover minor details that may have been overlooked previously and to appreciate their importance in human relations.

case 1

The New Truck Dilemma

I. Focusing the Problem

Whenever a group of people are involved in a joint activity, the question of fair treatment becomes an important issue and the subject of differing opinions. Every supervisor tries to be fair but he soon realizes that no amount of effort on his part to do the right thing is appreciated by everyone. Rules and company practices are often welcomed by him because they promise to protect him from the charge of playing favorites. These same rules and formalized procedures may be regarded by employees as arbitrary, inconvenient, and a way of disregarding individual differences in needs; yet employees prefer them to favoritism, which they believe will occur if supervisory judgments prevail. Management sees rules and formalized procedures as necessary evils. They interfere with flexibility and personalized practices but they serve as guides and protections from complaints, and they permit the supervisor to let the blame fall on the rule. Thus the rule can be attacked by both parties to a dispute.

What are the issues involved in a dispute over fairness? Are there solutions that can be agreed upon as fair or is disagreement on issues of fairness unavoidable because choices and preferences by their very nature are self-centered? It is apparent that if all members of a group had an equal desire for an object, and regardless of whether all had an equal claim to it, there would be a struggle between them since each would try to get it for himself. An outsider might, however, work out a *just* solution by dividing it equally between members of a group. When an object is such that it can be shared or divided, opportunities for finding fair solutions are not too difficult to find, providing each member respects the claim of others. When, however, needs and claims differ among group members and when an object cannot be shared, the difficulties mount.

Some of the more common fairness issues include the following situations:

Who gets time off for deer hunting?
How can vacation choices be scheduled more fairly?
What is a fair division of overtime?
Who should do a disagreeable job?
Which unit should try out the new chairs?
What group should get more space as a result of a move to new quarters?
How can office space be allocated so that someone is not degraded by getting less space or less elegant furnishings than the others?

Frequently, supervisors are unaware of the many factors that play a part in a dispute about fairness. The above list of problems clearly shows that prestige issues are included, and, when social recognition is attached to the problem of fairness, the emotional involvements become very pronounced.

The incident in this case hinges on the issuing of a new truck to some member of a crew of workers, each of whom uses a truck in his work. The foreman finds himself in a situation in which he must make a wise and fair decision. Since the replacement of trucks has been infrequent in the case in question, the importance of making the right decision is apparent to the supervisor.

The Multiple Role Playing Procedure is used in this case because it is desirable to obtain solutions from a number of groups.

II. Multiple Role Playing Procedure

PREPARATION

1. The audience should divide itself into groups of six persons. A convenient method for quickly forming the groups is for three persons in odd-numbered rows to turn around and join three persons (in even-numbered rows) who are directly behind them. In most instances, some people will have to move in order to make up groups of six. Persons who are left over may join a group and act as observers. (If five persons are left over they may make a group and assume that one of them (George) is home because of illness.)

2. All persons should read the General Instructions on page 26.

3. Each group should decide on who will play the part of the foreman, Walt Marshall.

4. The person in each group who is seated to the foreman's left is to play the part of George. The crew member seated next to George is to be Bill, and the three remaining members are John, Charlie, and Hank in order from left to right of the foreman. (If only five persons are in a group, the role of George should not be assigned. It should be assumed that he is at home sick. The foreman should read his role and assume he gained the information by talking to George on the phone.)

5. The role instructions for Walt Marshall are on page 27. The member of each group playing the part of the foreman should study his role. When he has completed reading it, he should stand up, to indicate to the instructor that he is ready to role play.

6. Crew members should turn to the page indicated: George, page 28; Bill, page 29; John, page 30; Charlie, page 31; Hank, page 32. They should avoid reading any other role or discussing their roles with each other.

7. The observers (if used) should turn to page 33 and read their instructions in preparation for their observations of the role playing scene.

8. Each crew member should write his role name on a slip of paper and attach it to his person so that other members can know who he is. The data on seniority and trucks, given in the General Instructions (page 26), may be consulted freely.

9. The crew members should assume they are in the foreman's office waiting for him.

10. When all participants who are playing the part of the foreman have

indicated by standing that they are ready to begin role playing, the instructor should ask them to sit down. This will be the signal that the foremen have entered their offices to begin their discussions.

PROCESS

1. Groups will need between 25 and 30 minutes for role playing. Those who have not finished at the end of 28 minutes should be given a two-minute warning signal.

2. During the role playing of the scene, the instructor should prepare the easel with appropriate headings for the purpose of recording the solutions and other results from the groups. Sample Table 1 on page 34 illustrates the types of headings and method for recording data that may be used. The first letter of each man's name should be arranged in a column. One column is needed for each group. Arrows may be used to indicate any exchange in trucks. (These should be added later.) An arrow from the left pointing to a name indicates the man who got the new truck, while other arrows (to the right of names) indicate who got his truck, etc. For example, in Group 3, John received the new truck while Charlie got John's truck, and Charlie's truck was discarded. Incidentally, this is not a typical solution.

3. In addition to making arrangements for recording the exchange in trucks, space for other data should be planned. The suggested headings are given below:

a. "Repairs" should be a heading to indicate whose truck, if any, will be fixed up in any way.

b. Heading "Number of exchanges" should serve to record the number of men who benefited by the fact that a new truck was introduced into the crew. In Group 3, shown in the sample table, both John and Charlie received different trucks as a result of the solution.

c. The heading "Foreman satisfied" should be used to indicate whether the foreman is satisfied or not with the solution reached in the discussion.

d. A fourth heading, labelled "Dissatisfied drivers," should be used to record the initials of the men who are not satisfied with the outcome.

COLLECTING GROUP DATA

1. The foreman for each group should report: (*1*) the decision for his group by indicating the name of the man who gets the new truck, the dis-

position that is made of his truck, etc.; (2) whose truck, if any, is to be repaired; and (3) whether or not he is satisfied with the outcome.

2. The instructor should diagram the solution as the foreman reports it, and fill in lines (a), (b), and (c) of the table.

3. The crew should criticize the foreman's report if they see fit, and all those who are dissatisfied should give their reasons.

4. The instructor should fill in the initials of dissatisfied crew members in line (d) of the table.

5. Observers, if used, should briefly report the discussion process they observed, commenting especially on (a) how the foreman presented the problem; (b) how the crew responded in the discussion; and (c) any helpful or interfering things they feel the foreman did.

6. Repeat process until all groups have reported. If more than 12 groups participate it may be necessary to limit complete reports to 10 groups and request the remaining groups to confine their reports to the presentation of the solution.

GENERAL DISCUSSION

1. Discuss ways in which the solutions are alike and ways in which they are different.

2. Which of the several solutions is the best? Determine the percentage of satisfied individuals (all groups combined).

3. Discuss the factors influencing differences in opinion on the question of "best" solution.

4. Could a foreman have made a fair decision on this problem? How many members in a group could he please?

5. What sets of values enter into the question of fairness? The arguments used by various individuals should be listed on the blackboard.

6. Could a company write a rule for the fair way to distribute the new trucks? Discuss the problems briefly.

7. Consider a few solutions that would be unacceptable to management. Were any solutions of this type suggested by groups and if so, could they have been prevented?

8. Can this type of problem (fairness) be settled by a discussion with the crew without the foreman attempting to influence the outcome? Arguments for and against this position should be listed in separate columns.

9. Each person who participated as a crew member should write down (a) what he liked most about the foreman's conduct of the meeting, and (b) what he liked least about the foreman's conduct. The instructor should make a two-column listing of these behaviors. (Key words should be used

to characterize a behavior item and check marks may be made to register duplicate contributions.)   Discuss various interpretations of the two lists.

10. A list of problems that are basically like the new truck problem should be prepared.   In cases of disagreement, differences in opinion should be indicated by means of a modifying phrase.

III. Materials [9]

GENERAL INSTRUCTIONS

You work for the telephone company and one of you will be the foreman while the others will be repairmen. The job of a repairman is to fix phones that are out of order, and requires knowledge and diagnostic skills as well as muscular skills. Repairmen must climb telephone poles, work with small tools, and meet customers. The foreman of a crew is usually an ex-repairman and this happens to be true in this case. He has an office at the garage location but spends a good deal of time making the rounds, visiting the places where the men are working. Each repairman works alone and ordinarily does several jobs in a day. The foreman gives such help and instruction as are needed.

The repairmen drive to the various locations in the city to do repair work. Each of them drives a small truck and takes pride in keeping it looking good. The repairmen have a possessive feeling about their trucks and like to keep them in good running order. Naturally, the men like to have new trucks too, because a new truck gives them a feeling of pride.

Here are some facts about the trucks and the men in the crew that report to Walt Marshall, the supervisor of repairs.

George	17	years	with	the	company,	has	a	2-year-old	Ford		truck.
Bill	11	"	"	"	"	"	"	5	"	"	Dodge	"
John	10	"	"	"	"	"	"	4	"	"	Ford	"
Charlie	5	"	"	"	"	"	"	3	"	"	Ford	"
Hank	3	"	"	"	"	"	"	5	"	"	Chevrolet	"

Most of the men do all of their driving in the city, but John and Charlie cover the jobs in the suburbs.

In acting your part in role playing, accept the facts as given as well as assuming the attitude supplied in your specific role. From this point on let your feelings develop in accordance with the events that transpire in the role playing process. When facts or events arise that are not covered by the roles, make up things which are consistent with the way it might be in a real-life situation.

[9] Role instructions are taken from an article by N. R. F. Maier and L. F. Zerfoss, MRP: A Technique for Training Large Groups of Supervisors and its Potential Use in Social Research, *Human Relations*, 1952, 5, 177–186. Permission to reproduce the roles has been granted by the editors of *Human Relations*.

ROLE FOR WALT MARSHALL, FOREMAN

You are the foreman of a crew of repairmen each of whom drives a small service truck to and from his various jobs. Every so often you get a new truck to exchange for an old one, and you have the problem of deciding to which of your men you should give the new truck. Often there are hard feelings because each man seems to feel he is entitled to the new truck, so you have a tough time being fair. As a matter of fact, it usually turns out that whatever you decide, most of the men consider it wrong. You now have to face the same issue again because a new truck has just been allocated to you for distribution. The new truck is a Chevrolet.

In order to handle this problem, you have decided to put the decision to the men themselves. You will tell them about the new truck and will put the problem in terms of what would be the most fair way to distribute the truck. Don't take a position yourself because you want to do what the men think is most fair.

ROLE FOR GEORGE

When a new Chevrolet truck becomes available, you think you should get it because you have most seniority and don't like your present truck. Your own car is a Chevrolet, and you prefer a Chevrolet truck such as you drove before you got the Ford.

ROLE FOR BILL

You feel you deserve a new truck and it certainly is your turn. Your present truck is old, and since the more senior man has a fairly new truck, you should get the next one. You have taken excellent care of your present Dodge, and have kept it looking like new. A man deserves to be rewarded if he treats a company truck like his own.

ROLE FOR JOHN

You have to do more driving than most of the other men because you work in the suburbs. You have a fairly old truck and you feel you should have the new one because you do so much driving.

ROLE FOR CHARLIE

The heater in your present truck is inadequate. Since Hank backed into the door of your truck it has never been repaired to fit right. The door lets in too much cold air, and you attribute your frequent colds to this. You want to have a warm truck since you have a good deal of driving to do. As long as it has good tires, brakes, and is comfortable you don't care about its make.

ROLE FOR HANK

You have the poorest truck in the crew. It is 5 years old, and before you got it, it had been in a bad wreck. It has never been good, and you've put up with it for three years. It's about time you got a good truck to drive, and it seems only fair that the next one should be yours. You have a good accident record. The only accident you had was when you sprung the door of Charlie's truck when he opened it as you backed out of the garage. You hope the new truck is a Ford since you prefer to drive one.

INSTRUCTIONS FOR OBSERVERS

The following items are furnished as a guide for observing what the leader did and how the crew reacted.

1. How did the leader present the problem?

   a. In presenting the problem, did the leader have the attitude of asking for help?

   b. Did the leader present all the facts?

   c. Was the leader's presentation of the problem brief and to the point?

   d. Did the leader scrupulously avoid suggesting a solution?

2. What things occurred in the discussion?

   a. Did all group members participate?

   b. Was there free exchange of feelings between group members?

   c. Did the group use social pressure to influence any of its members?

   d. On which member of the crew was social pressure used?

   e. Was the leader permissive?

   f. Did the leader avoid taking sides or favoring any person?

   g. What were the points of disagreement in the group?

3. What did the leader do to help problem solving?

   a. Did the leader ask questions to help the group explore ideas?

   b. Were all ideas accepted equally by the leader?

   c. Did the leader avoid hurrying the group to develop a solution?

   d. Did the leader avoid favoring any solution?

   e. Who supplied the final solution?

   f. What did the leader do, if anything, to get unanimous agreement on the final solution?

SAMPLE TABLE 1. RESULTS OF NEW TRUCK PROBLEM

	Group 1	Group 2	Group 3	Group 4	Group 5
Group solution reached	G B J C H	G B J C H	G B J C H	G B J C H	G B J C H
a. Repairs	C	No	C	C,J,H	B
b. Number of exchanges	1	4	2	1	2
c. Foreman satisfied	Yes	Yes	No	No	Yes
d. Dissatisfied drivers	G,B,J	0	G, H,	G	J,C

IV. Comments and Implications

This case usually leads to an experience of success on the part of the participants. Most persons playing the part of the foreman have no preconceived solution in mind; for this reason they do less talking and are quite content to sit back and listen. The importance of this state of mind in the foreman can be dramatically demonstrated by asking a person who is to play the part of the foreman to commit himself ahead of time on a solution that he considers to be fair. Such foremen really have a rough time and are inclined to feel that the crew is unreasonable. When, however, it becomes apparent to the crew that their foreman wants to do what they consider fair, there is a rather free expression of viewpoints. It soon becomes apparent to them that their views are in conflict. The noise level in the room rises to a peak during this stage. Often the foreman is overwhelmed by the arguing and wishes he hadn't consulted the group. However, he usually doesn't know what to do, so by good fortune he doesn't interfere.

After all members have stated their own positions, certain members of the group perceive the conflict as leading nowhere and begin to search for ways to resolve the conflict. Respect for the rights of others becomes more apparent and constructive suggestions are proposed. The sound level now declines considerably. Gradually a solution emerges as differences are ironed out and concessions are made.

It is important for the foreman to refrain from taking sides by agreeing with certain persons, because in so doing he tends only to antagonize others. Rather, he must continue to be patient and regard this conflict as a problem to be solved. Since most groups reach a decision that leaves few or none dissatisfied, it is apparent that the opportunity to express conflicts in opinion can lead to a resolution of that conflict. As a matter of fact, the airing of differences in views in a freely led discussion is an essential process in the reaching of an agreement. No amount of explaining by a foreman can accomplish this satisfactory resolution of conflicts.

When dissatisfactions in the crew remain, they frequently are traceable to something that happened in the discussion. Often, dissatisfied persons are dissatisfied because (a) the foreman took sides against them; (b) other members attacked them while the foreman failed to protect them; or (c) the foreman ignored the ideas they expressed.

Less than completely satisfactory solutions are caused by a tendency (a) to solve the problem before everyone has fully aired his views, and

(b) to settle on the first constructive suggestion that is offered. The foreman can use his office to see that these things do not occur. It is often good for foremen to say, "Before we settle on that plan, let's take a look at some other possibilities." It is perhaps too much to expect that all crew members in all groups be satisfied. Certain problem employees will be found. However, as in real life, they usually number less than 10 per cent.

Since the issue in this case centers on the question of fairness, and since fairness is a personalized matter, it is apparent that the crucial issue is one of employee *acceptance.* The group's decision is perhaps the best way to obtain maximum acceptance, but this does not mean that the foreman should not be concerned with the solution process. He is needed to conduct the discussion and see that every member has a right to express himself. A point of special interest is the fact that George, the senior man, gets the truck about half the time, but he gets it more often when he is considerate of others than when he is demanding of his rights. Seniority, it seems, is respected, but the senior man's conduct can lower the crew's respect for seniority. Each crew member gets the new truck on occasion, so it becomes apparent that the manner in which men conduct themselves in the discussion is a determiner of the outcome. Although the facts as furnished by the role instructions are important, it must not be assumed that they alone should or do determine the solution.

A question of objective *quality* of the solution does play some part in this case, but the results indicate that it is not a serious danger point. A poor solution would be one in which a relatively good truck was discarded. It will perhaps be noted from the results obtained, that even though only sketchy information was supplied, most if not all crews reached the same decision on this point and decided to discard Hank's truck. This solution is in line with the foreman's view and hence is acceptable to management. Even though the foreman may not have suggested this aspect of the solution, it seems that the crews could be depended upon to do the right thing. Thus the fear that a qualitatively poor solution might occur if the men made the decision is an unrealistic hazard.

It is possible also to argue that solutions which give several people a different truck are superior to those in which only one or two get a different truck. However, participants challenge this point and regard it as a matter of preference.

The frequent tendency to repair Charlie's truck, which may have been noted, is of special interest. Usually the foreman agrees early in the discussion to repair Charlie's truck. Sometimes Charlie does not even keep the truck that is to be repaired. The fact that Charlie exaggerates the condition of his truck because he wants the new one tends to be overlooked. The reason why the foreman gives in is that he feels the complaint is a reasonable one and furthermore, the request is an inexpensive one, particularly when he finds that everyone else, at this stage of the discussion, is asking for a new truck. It is a common error to take early complaints too seriously. Of course trucks should be kept in repair, but what constitutes proper repair sometimes is debatable.

How to distribute the new truck is a rather typical example of the problem of fairness. The values and issues raised in this case are similar to those raised whenever it is impossible to treat all persons alike. If a group decides the matter, the issue is resolved in terms of sets of values and needs existing in the group at that time. Fair solutions must be tailormade solutions and no formula can be written that will take all variables into proper consideration. In order to be fair, all persons concerned must be made aware of the needs of others and participants must discover that fairness cannot be arrived at by judging others.

case 2

The Frustrated Supervisor

I. Focusing the Problem

Conflict and misunderstandings between persons frequently arise under a condition of temporary frustration. Disappointments, pressure of work, irritating behavior of other persons, frequent or unwanted interruptions are but a few factors that may give rise to temporary frustration. Most often frustration of this sort is characterized by a sudden or marked change in behavior, which may be triggered off by a seemingly trivial incident. When this occurs, the behavior gives the appearance of being magnified out of proportion to the incident itself. Because the incident by itself does not seem to warrant the behavior displayed, such conditions of temporary frustration often become the cause of serious misunderstandings. Other persons may only be aware of the incident that triggered off the behavior and even the frustrated person himself often regards the incident as the cause of his disturbance, sometimes seeing the incident in its worst light in order to justify his behavior.

However, since the condition is temporary, it can be dealt with most effectively by providing a harmless outlet for the expression of the frustration. An attitude of understanding and permissiveness to facilitate the expression of feelings is the main consideration in furnishing relief. Nevertheless, such treatment of temporarily frustrated persons frequently runs counter to the usual reactions of other persons; in fact, the exaggerated nature and the unreasonableness of such behavior tends instead to produce anger and frustration reactions in others. Therefore, practice in dealing

38

with temporary frustration is highly desirable as a way to develop new approaches, skills, and confidence in their usefulness.

In dealing with a frustrated individual one must get him to feel free to express himself and one must not be misled by confusing an incident that sets off frustrated behavior with the basic cause of the frustration tensions. What he says and feels are the result of these tensions and they do not reveal his true attitudes or his ability to analyze or think clearly.

The present case concerns a first-line supervisor who has trouble with one of his employees. The employee then goes to the division supervisor, by-passing his own boss. The incident creates a situation in which the division supervisor feels called upon to talk to the supervisor. The flareup must be cleared up in order to avoid other incidents. The case gives the person playing the part of the division supervisor a good opportunity to practice his skills in diagnosing a situation, drawing out the feelings of another person, and solving a human relations problem between two other people. The fact that three levels of authority are involved does not make the problem easier.

This case involves a number of policy issues over which there is likely to be considerable difference of opinion. In using the Multiple Role Playing Procedure differences in attitude in the group can be explored. Multiple role playing will also give everyone an opportunity to practice his skills in dealing with a disturbed person. Since the face-to-face aspects of this case are not too advanced, most persons should enjoy a success experience.

II. Multiple Role Playing Procedure

PREPARATION

1. The members of the class should pair up with a person next to themselves, one member of each pair calling himself Jim Wells, the other, Bill Jackson.

2. Persons taking the role of Jim Wells should study the instructions on page 43, while persons taking the role of Bill Jackson should study their instructions on page 44.

3. The members of the pairs are advised not to discuss their roles with each other. They should try to imagine their positions and get in the spirit of the problem.

4. When the Bill Jacksons are ready to begin role playing they should stand up to indicate their readiness to meet with Wells. The instructor will give the Jacksons the signal to begin, which should be taken to mean that all Jacksons have arrived at the offices of their respective Jim Wellses.

PROCESS

1. The instructor signals the Bill Jacksons to approach their Jim Wellses. Each assumes his role and conducts himself as in a real-life situation of this kind. It would be natural for Wells to greet Bill and invite him to sit down.

2. All groups role play simultaneously.

3. Between 15 and 20 minutes usually will allow sufficient time for the interview to be completed. The instructor should terminate the few incompleted interviews after about 20 minutes. A warning of one minute is desirable.

4. During the role playing process the instructor should prepare headings for the tabulations he will make on the blackboard when he supervises the general report from the pairs of role players. The reports from the Wellses require three columns with headings as follows: (a) Jackson's trouble; (b) action to be taken; and (c) assistance offered. The reports from the Bill Jacksons require the form shown in Sample Table 2, page 45.

GENERAL REPORT AND ANALYSIS

1. The Jim Wellses in turn should report (*a*) what they found Bill Jackson's trouble to be; (*b*) what action, if any, they think Jackson should take; and (*c*) the kind of help, if any, they feel they should give Bill. These reports should be listed in three columns on the board. The instructor should tabulate briefly each new item and place a check mark after duplicate suggestions. (When possible the Wells reporting should indicate when his opinion agrees with a report already given by a previous Wells. This will reduce the number of entries.)

2. When all of the Wellses have reported, the instructor should summarize briefly the trend in results.

3. The responses from the Jacksons may be quickly obtained by the leader if the Jacksons indicate, with a show of hands, their reactions to the following questions:

a. How many feel no better toward Blake since talking to Wells?
b. How many feel better toward Blake now?
c. How many want Blake back in their units?
d. How many intend to apologize to their Blakes?
e. How many feel better about their next-door neighbor?
f. How many will apologize to their neighbor?
g. How many felt criticized by Wells?

The instructor should enter the appropriate number in line 1 of the table, arranged as in Sample Table 2.

4. The Bill Jacksons should consider the manner in which Wells dealt with them. He might have scolded or lectured; given considerable fatherly advice; listened but with some advice thrown in; and listened as well as responded to feelings so effectively that Bill found himself telling everything. These four classifications are shown on lines 2, 3, 4, and 5, respectively, of the sample table. The instructor should determine the number of times each type of interview occurred in connection with each of the kinds of feelings listed for Jackson and write the appropriate number in each of the columns.

5. Whether or not a given Wells intended it, he may have caused his Bill Jackson to feel that he was against him, on his side, or neutral. Lines 6, 7, and 8, respectively, allow space to record these feelings of Jackson, under the various column headings.

6. Table 2 should be discussed and conclusions formulated as to the procedure used by Wells that seems to attain the most worthwhile objectives.

DISCUSSION WITHIN PAIRS

1. Each Bill Jackson should tell his Wells what he liked most about how he was treated in the interview.

2. Next the Bill Jacksons should tell their Wellses what they liked least about the treatment they received in the interview and why they reacted as they did.

3. The members of each pair should privately discuss the situational factors (such as rank differences, Blake's bypassing Jackson, work pressure, Jackson's expectation of criticism, etc.) that made for possible misunderstandings between Wells and Jackson.

DISCUSSION ISSUES

1. Is Jackson ready to deal with Joe Blake without embarrassment? Should Wells have covered this problem in the interview? Discuss.

2. A former Wells should play the part of Joe Blake. The Bill Jacksons who believe that Blake is entitled to an apology should be given an opportunity to demonstrate. Blake should indicate what he likes or dislikes in each apology without bothering to respond to the apologizer. The group should discuss and evaluate several kinds of apologies.

3. How does Jackson feel about his neighbor? Is this important? Discuss.

4. How should higher supervisors deal with employees who bypass their immediate supervisors? Discuss.

Note: Class members and role players will raise many questions. These should be discussed and the instructor should avoid supplying answers.

GENERALIZATION OF CASE

1. Develop a list of situations which participants have experienced or observed that are basically like the case presented.

2. Discuss differences in opinion. Revise list as seems indicated by discussion.

III. Materials [10]

ROLE FOR JIM WELLS, DIVISION SUPERVISOR

You are the supervisor of a division employing about 75 men and women and 6 first-line supervisors. You like your job, and the supervisors and employees who work for you, and you feel that they cooperate with you in every way.

This morning you noticed that one of your first-line supervisors, *Bill Jackson,* was rather late in getting to work. Since Bill is very conscientious and was working on a rush job you wondered what had happened. Bill is thoroughly dependable and, when something delays him, he always tries to phone you. For this reason you were somewhat concerned and were about to call his home when one of Bill's men, a young fellow named *Joe Blake,* came in. Joe is a good-natured kid, just out of high school, but this time he was obviously angry, and said that he was not going to work for Bill another minute and was going to quit unless you got him another job. Evidently Bill had come in, started to work, and then lost his temper completely when young Joe didn't do something quite right.

Although Bill occasionally has his bad moods, it is unlike him to lose his temper this way. This latest rush job may have put him under too much pressure but even so, his outburst this morning seems difficult to explain on any reasonable grounds. You feel, therefore, that something must be seriously wrong and if you can get Bill to talk about whatever it is that is bothering him you may get the situation straightened out. In any case you are determined not to get into an argument with Bill or criticize him in any way. Instead you are going to try to get him to talk about his troubles, listen to what he has to say, and indicate that you understand how he feels about things. If Bill seems more angry than Joe's mistake would reasonably justify, you might suppose that there is something more behind all this and Bill would probably feel a lot better if he got it off his chest. If Bill is thoroughly angry with Joe, you may suggest that Joe be fired in order to demonstrate that you have not taken Joe's side in the matter.

You talked with Joe for several minutes and, after he had told his side of the story, he felt better and was ready to go back on the job. You just phoned Bill and asked him to drop around when he had a chance. Bill said he'd come right over and is walking toward your office now.

[10] Role instructions are reprinted from a case in Maier, *Principles of Human Relations,* John Wiley & Sons, New York, 1952, 423–425.

ROLE FOR BILL JACKSON, FIRST-LINE SUPERVISOR

You have just come to work after a series of the most humiliating and irritating experiences you have ever had.   Last night your next-door neighbor, *Sam Jones,* had a wild, drunken party at his house that kept you awake most of the night.   Jones is a blustering, disagreeable man who has no consideration whatever for others, so when you called him at about 3:00 A.M. and told him to be less noisy, he was abusive and insulting.   Things quieted down later on, but when you finally got some rest you overslept.

Since you were in the midst of a rush job at the company, you skipped breakfast to hurry to work and, as you were leaving the house, you noticed that someone had driven a car across one corner of your lawn and had torn out several feet of your new hedge.   You were certain that Jones or one of the drunks at his party had done it so you ran right over to Jones's house, determined to have it out with him.   He not only denied everything, but practically threw you out and threatened to knock your teeth out if you didn't shut up and behave yourself and you know that he is big enough to do it.

When you came to work, more than an hour late, your nerves were so ragged that you were actually shaking.   Everything conceivable had gone wrong, and then the last straw was when you discovered that *Joe Blake,* a young high school recruit, had made a mistake that delayed you several hours on your rush job, or at least it would have if you hadn't caught him in time.   Naturally, you gave him a good going over for his carelessness. Blake said he wouldn't take that kind of abuse from anyone and walked out on you.   You noticed that he went in to see your supervisor, *Jim Wells.* Obviously he is in there accusing you of being rough on him.   Well, you don't like that kind of an attitude in a young squirt either, and if he has gone in there squawking you'll make him wish he'd never been born.   You have had all you can stand and the big boss had better not get tough with you because he'll have one hell of a time getting the job done without you. Jim had that snivelling brat in there and talked to him for quite a while before he phoned you to come in.   Gabbing when there's work to be done —that's certainly a hell of a way to run things.   You are on your way to Jim's office now and have no intention of wasting time on words.

(Try to get into the spirit of this case and feel some of the emotions that would ordinarily be present.)

SAMPLE TABLE 2. BILL JACKSON'S REPORT

(Use Table for Recording Class Data)

	1	2	3	4	5	6	7
	Feel no better toward Blake	Feel better about Blake	Want Blake in unit	Intend to apologize to Blake	Feel better about neighbor	Will apologize to neighbor	Felt criticized by Wells
1. Number of Jacksons							
2. Wells scolded or lectured							
3. Wells gave fatherly advice							
4. Wells listened and advised							
5. Wells listened and got Bill to tell everything							
6. Wells took sides with Blake							
7. Wells took sides with Jackson							
8. Wells remained neutral							
9. Wells brought up problem of how to talk to Blake							

IV. Comments and Implications

A good method of relieving the frustrations of others is to be a good listener. By *listening*, you help the other person to rid himself of his frustration tensions and at the same time you keep yourself from becoming involved. A good listener can avoid setting up defensive reactions, hostile behaviors, and arguments, which only lead to face saving and further frustration.

However, listening is not easily done. Another person often expects you to express your opinions and you must be able to avoid this situation and get the person to talk about his own feelings. In responding to feelings by nodding, asking the other to tell you more, and showing that you understand, you create a *permissive* relationship which is essential for dealing with feelings.

A number of specific aspects of the case raise some problems that often are present in real-life situations involving status, company policy, and face saving. These factors must be dealt with realistically and fit into proper perspective with the counseling type of interview. Some of these problems are examined below, but the suggestions made may not apply to all conditions.

Persons playing the part of Wells may have felt that they had an unusually sensitive person to comfort. This sensitivity is partly due to Jackson feeling somewhat guilty for what he has done but to a greater degree it is due to the fact that he fears Wells may be critical of him. Since he was asked to come up to see Mr. Wells right after Joe Blake had been there it is not surprising that Jackson should have this mental set. In going to see Wells, young Blake went over Jackson's head. This behavior represents an attack on Jackson's status as a supervisor and under such circumstances one should expect to meet a hypersensitive individual.

To cope with this condition it is important that Wells put Jackson at ease on this point as quickly as possible. He must indicate that (*a*) Blake has been in to see him and seemed very upset; (*b*) since Blake was Jackson's employee Jackson should know about this visit; (*c*) what to do about Blake's behavior is Jackson's problem, but that he wants Jackson to know that he is willing to help in any way he can; and (*d*) he is willing to discuss the matter if Jackson so desires.

If Wells, by his manner, makes Jackson feel that he need not defend himself, Jackson will not only feel better toward Blake, but he will be able to face the situation as it was before Wells was brought into the picture.

As long as Jackson has to save face with his superior he cannot cope with the initial problem.

Once Jackson discovers Wells to be uncritical and understanding about his situation, he can tell him about the flareup. He may volunteer to tell more than the incident with Blake, but if he fails to do this, Wells should realize there is more to the story. An office error that was discovered before it caused real damage may be serious, but it does not upset a person to the extent that Jackson's behavior indicated. This is the clue for Wells to realize that there is more to the story than first meets the eye. A question such as "Was there anything else that happened?" may encourage Jackson to tell more.

Responding to feelings of pressure or lateness or no breakfast by saying "I can see that that upset you very much" permits Jackson to feel free to tell still more about his feelings and state of mind. By being sensitive to little hints of other difficulties and by responding with such phrases as "You felt sure that one of the neighbor's guests had damaged your hedge and shown no respect for property rights," Wells can make it easy for Jackson to talk about his feelings and the off-the-job events. Too often people are made to feel that they must justify their conduct and as a result they hide their true feelings and talk about the situation by greatly exaggerating the problem. Respecting feelings makes exaggeration unnecessary.

It is through the expression of true feelings that frustration tensions are released. Once these interfering emotions are reduced through expression, the original problem can be faced in a problem-solving state of mind. Training Blake and getting along with the neighbor are two challenging problems.

The most immediate problem Jackson will face concerns the way he will talk to Joe Blake when he returns to the job. He may want to apologize and yet fear that Blake will think he has won a victory. Thus he is caught in a face-saving situation. Although this fear may be more imagined than real, it must be removed because it will influence Jackson's behavior. Here is where Wells can be of help by seeing to it that this problem is discussed. Together they can work out what Wells should say to Blake in order that Blake will recognize that the problem is back in Jackson's hands and that Wells considers Jackson to be competent to deal with it.

With this fear about Blake removed, Jackson can make a full apology. A partial apology such as "I was wrong, but you must be more careful about your mistakes" usually will not be accepted by Blake and his failure to accept the apology will reinstate the conflict. A full apology such as "I had no business talking to you the way I did. I had a tough night and lost my temper and I'm really sorry about it" usually will stimulate Blake to apologize for his clerical mistake, his sensitivity, his running to Wells, or some combination of these. That generosity shown by one person stimulates it in another is a safe generalization and not only applies in this instance but to many others.

A frequent type of behavior shown by enlightened supervisors when playing the part of Wells is to be sympathetic with Jackson and to indicate that they too have made mistakes. It is comforting to know that others err, but time is better spent if the disturbed person expresses his feelings rather than is comforted by descriptions of someone else's errors. This too is a safe generalization.

case 3

The Truck Seating Order

I. Focusing the Problem

In each company there is a formal organizational structure created by the fact that positions in the company vary in importance and influence. To a great extent this formal structure corresponds with the levels shown on the company's organizational chart. That problems may arise whenever decisions violate or overlook this established hierarchy is fairly well understood by management personnel. Any department head will hesitate to put a superintendent in an office that was previously occupied by a general foreman, even if it is a practical move from the point of view of convenience and accessibility.

It is also known that status accompanies a job grade in that machine operators will ask truckers to go out for sandwiches, but truckers will not expect the operators to take their turn. Now and then a problem occurs because someone rebels and does not accept the social organization, but the basis of a problem of this sort is usually understood and respected by the supervisors concerned.

When status is associated with a series of jobs in which pay rates or job grades are equal, management becomes less understanding. For example, a manager in the telephone company moved a tandem board operator to a long distance operator's position and was surprised when he had a variety of reactions. The tandem operator hesitated, the other long distance operators didn't understand the move, and the information operators talked about a walkout. Overlooked was the fact that there was an informal organization within the telephone operator group that gave differential status in the ascending order as follows: tandem operator, information operator, local operator, and long distance operator.

Informal organizations *within* a homogeneous group sometimes go undetected by outsiders. Occasionally, even the insiders may be quite unaware of them until some problem disturbs the status quo. The tendency for social structuring is so basic that in a very short period of time even a group of animals will develop some sort of hierarchy. In a chicken yard, for example, a pecking order is soon established so that each chicken has a different status position. Thus chick A will peck all other chicks; chick B will peck all others except A; chick C will peck all except A and B, etc., until finally the lowest status chick is pecked by all and pecks none in return. The arrangement may be reached after a certain amount of strife, but in an established group the existence of the pecking order could easily escape attention. Only when a new chick was introduced into the group would evidence of the social structuring come to light.

If social structuring exists in small work groups, it would not be surprising if it escaped attention. Its presence could conceivably interfere with management directives and often lead to misunderstanding. Whether social organization effectively satisfies the needs of its members, protects against the loss of freedom, or violates the democratic right of individuals, are social values regarding which a membership may differ. The fact remains that informal social organization can be created by the mere fact that a group of people have differing preferences. Popularity, seniority, extent of knowledge, ability to relate with people, impartiality, etc., all may be factors that affect interpersonal relations and, as a consequence, have an influence on social organization and social values.

The case of the truck seating order introduces a situation in which behavior is governed by factors not apparent on the surface. The Multiple Role Playing Procedure is used because it is desirable to give participants an appreciation of the fact that outcomes of conferences are influenced by the way this problem is discussed. The solution agreed upon may vary from one crew to another, even though the facts established in the instructions are the same for all groups.

II. Multiple Role Playing Procedure

PREPARATION

1. The class should divide itself into groups of seven persons. Persons left over after groups of seven are formed should serve as observers. (In the event that only one group of role players can be formed, and six persons are left over, a group may be formed by assuming that Jack is home because of illness. His role should be read by the person who plays the part of the foreman and the role information taken as knowledge based upon a phone conversation with Jack. In case only five persons are left over, it is suggested that the instructor play one of the roles.)

2. All persons will want to read the General Instructions on page 55 individually. While the class is doing this, the instructor should place the names of the foreman and the six crew members on the blackboard, supplying the years of service of each man and indicating who serves as the work leader, the truck driver, and the substitute driver. Figure 2 should also be drawn on the board so that the seating arrangement on the truck will be apparent to all.

3. Each group should select a person to serve as the foreman, Bert Jones. He will find his role on page 56. He should take a seat a short distance from the group and remain there until the instructor signals him to join his group.

4. If room facilities permit, the six workers in the crew should seat themselves in a pattern that duplicates the arrangement of the truck seating. For example, they can sit three to a side of a table or arrange three pairs of chairs facing forward. Each person should then indicate the role he will play so as to avoid confusion and duplication of roles. The instructions for role players are as follows: Gus, page 60; George, page 57; Joe, page 59; Bill, page 58; Jack, page 62; and Charlie, page 61. Each person should read his role only.

5. Observers will find two sets of instructions: one concentrating on the behavior of the conference leader; the other on the group process. If two or more persons observe a single group, the observational task should be divided. Half of them should observe the leader's activities and read instructions on page 63; the other half should observe the group's interactions and read the instructions on page 64. Observers should take seats to the right and left of the group they observe, close enough to hear, but as unobtrusive as possible.

6. When all arrangements are completed, the instructor should alert the foremen to be prepared to return to their groups. The crew should assume they are in Jones's office waiting for the scheduled meeting. All role instructions, except those used by the observers, should be put aside and remain out of reach during role playing.

ROLE PLAYING PROCESS

1. At the instructor's signal, the foremen should join the groups taking seats to face Gus and George.

2. When the foreman joins his group this will mean that he has entered his office. All participants should be in character.

3. All groups should role play simultaneously.

4. Approximately 20 minutes is adequate for most groups to reach a solution.

5. All groups should be given a chance to finish, but if some seem to be having a particularly difficult time, the instructor should tell the foreman to do the best he can in the next two minutes.

6. The blackboard should be prepared for recording the results while the groups are engaged in role playing. Sample Table 3, on page 65, shows the column headings that should be used.

TABULATING RESULTS

1. The column with the heading "Solution" (see Sample Table 3) should be used by the instructor to enter a brief description of the solution reached by each of the groups. If the group reporting had an observer for the conference leader, he should report the solution. If no observer was present for a group, the foreman should report the solution. The instructor should ask the men if the report accurately describes their understanding of the solution. In case the group was unable to reach a solution in the time allowed, the phrase "no solution" should be entered in the column for that particular group.

2. The column with the heading "Dissatisfied men" should be used to indicate the names of any dissatisfied crew members. The observers of the group interaction, with the assistance of the foreman, should report their opinions of who appears unhappy with the outcome. This report should be checked to see if it corresponds with the role players' feelings of "dissatisfaction." In cases of discrepancies, the differences in opinions should be entered in the table by underlining the name of the man whose feelings

were not understood. A little time should be spent in determining why the observer or foreman obtained an inaccurate impression of a man's feelings.

3. The column with the heading "Quality" should be used to evaluate each group's solution. The role of Bert Jones contains a statement to the effect that his boss, Mr. Stevens, requested that the tailgate be operated by one of the men in the cab. The question is whether Mr. Stevens will be satisfied with the solution. Observers, foremen, and workers should indicate their opinion by indicating "yes," "no," or "questionable." The instructor should record the results in the left side of the column. He should then poll the opinions of other members of the class who participated in other groups and in this manner obtain the opinions of "outsiders." These results should be placed in the right half of the column.

4. Observers of the leader should report briefly on the conference leadership functions that seemed to influence the success of the discussion. The instructor should briefly note items in the column with the heading "Leader behavior." In the event no observers were used, the members of the group should comment on the leader's behavior.

5. Observers of the group interaction should report briefly the types of conflict and alliances they observed, especially as related to George. The instructor should make brief notes in the last column with the heading "Group process."

6. If the number of groups is two or less, the observers and/or the foremen of the groups should suggest some alternate solutions, so that a total of four or five solutions may be discussed. These solutions should be tallied and the workers of the group concerned should indicate whether they would be satisfied. The solutions should also be evaluated from the point of view of quality.

DISCUSSION OF RESULTS

1. The table of data should be examined to determine why the solutions differed or why they came out the same way. Differences in leader behavior or group processes should be carefully examined. Participants may wish to copy the results in Sample Table 3 of their books.

2. Persons reporting dissatisfactions should describe the nature of their dissatisfactions.

3. Quality evaluations by "insiders" and "outsiders" should be compared. If differences occurred, a little time should be spent to discuss the reasons.

4. Quality and dissatisfaction should be related. It is often found that questionable quality and dissatisfaction go together.

5. If foremen or observers supplied solutions, why were these less acceptable?

GENERAL DISCUSSION

1. The request of Mr. Jones undoubtedly created both favorable and unfavorable reactions. A discussion should be used to develop a list of the disturbing issues raised by the request.

2. When the final solution was reached it was probably found that most or all of the participants were satisfied with the solution of their group. Each member of each of the groups should describe the specific nature of the satisfaction he obtained from the discussion or the solution. This satisfaction may be as minor as having helped someone save face or as great as having sold the accepted plan to the group. Each person should carefully introspect to see if he can find a specific satisfaction that is the cause of his general satisfaction with the outcome.

3. Some time should be spent discussing the extent to which management should inconvenience itself in order to respect an informal social organization. Agreement on this matter should not be sought, rather the purpose should be to discuss the extent of difference in the thinking of group members.

4. The group should explore their own experiences for examples of status problems they have encountered. A few of these should be discussed and related to the present case.

III. Materials

GENERAL INSTRUCTIONS

You seven men all work for a utility. Six of you make up one of several crews whose job it is to maintain power lines. The seventh man is your foreman, *Bert Jones.* Jones is in charge of three crews such as yours so that when you are out on a job you work under the supervision of your senior man who acts as work leader. The six of you and your years of service are as follows:

George, with 17 years service, work leader.
Bill, with 12 years service.
Joe, with 10 years service.
Gus, with 9 years service, driver of truck.
Charlie, with 5 years service.
Jack, with 3 years service, substitute driver.

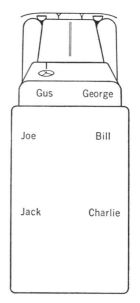

Figure 2.   Truck seating arrangement.

You meet in the garage in the morning to catch the truck you use to ride to and from job locations, which change from day to day. The senior man sits in front with the driver while the rest of you sit on benches behind the cab of the truck. The seating arrangement is shown in Figure 2. Since the driver is responsible for the truck and the safety of the crew while riding to and from work, he and his substitute are selected on the basis of special tests. For greater safety and also to keep tools from sliding out and getting lost, each truck is equipped with a tailgate which is hinged on the bottom edge and held shut with chain fasteners. In order to keep the chains out of the way and also for greater safety and simplicity of construction, the fasteners are on the outside of the truck, out of reach from the inside.

It has always been customary for the man with the least seniority to have the duty of closing and fastening the heavy tailgate after everyone else is seated and then climbing over it into the back of the truck just before starting. When the destination is reached he then jumps out to unfasten and lower the tailgate so the other men can get out more easily.

You are all in Bert Jones's office this morning for a meeting before you go out on the job. He has these meetings regularly and you are waiting for him to show up.

ROLE FOR BERT JONES, FOREMAN

Since you are foreman of three crews you seldom go out on the job except in emergencies or on inspection trips. However, you meet your crews in the garage in the morning to give out the job assignments to the work leaders. You have noticed that when the trucks leave the garage each man takes a particular seat. In Crew A, for example, *George*, the work leader with 17 years service, sits in the cab with *Gus* who is the regular driver, and who qualified for the job on a driving test. Gus has 9 years service. The other four men on the crew sit in back. *Bill* tried out for the driver's test but failed to pass it. However, *Jack* has qualified on the driver's test and, as substitute driver, takes over when Gus is away. As low seniority man, Jack always operates the tailgate, even when he drives.

There have never been any complaints from your crew that this arrangement is in any way unsatisfactory. As a matter of fact, you had never given the seating order any particular thought until the other day when your boss, *Mr. Stevens,* called you in and asked you to have one of the men who sits in the front seat open the tailgate in the future. Apparently there have been some recent cases of sprained ankles and other injuries to men in other crews when they jumped out to unfasten the chain. There have never been any injuries of that nature in your crews but the idea makes good sense to you so you have decided to meet with each of your crews to discuss the problem. This morning you are meeting with Crew A and are about to enter your office where the meeting is to be held.

ROLE FOR GEORGE

As work leader and senior man in your group you always ride in front with the driver. You like to direct the driver to the particular job location for the day and you have to be comfortable to plan things. You rode in the back on the benches for years before you became top man in seniority and you have earned your right to the front seat. All over the company the senior man has first choice in the seating arrangement. This is one of the few remaining recognitions a man gets for his length of service. A few years back some young college recruit tried to grab the front seat and you and the driver had to throw him out. You got him transferred the next week for picking a fight. *Jack*, who has the least seniority, has younger legs than you and he has always kept his place.

ROLE FOR BILL

With 12 years of service you are next to George in seniority. You have always ridden in back of the truck except when *George* was sick or on vacation. Your regular seat is the one just behind the cab on the right side. It is smoother riding there because you don't sit over the rear wheels. When George gets promoted or transferred you will inherit the front seat privilege. You tried out on the driving test but didn't get a high enough score so the only way you can get the right to the front seat is to wait it out. As things are, the man with least seniority should sit in the back so he's handy for opening and closing the tailgate.

ROLE FOR JOE

You joined the company 10 years ago and that was when the present type of truck was first bought so you had your turn handling the tailgate for a year until Gus was hired and took over the job. In those days the trucks were even higher so it was much more difficult to get in and farther to jump when you got out of the truck. You hurt your feet and ankles a few times but never complained about it. You think the present arrangement is fair and being behind the cab on the left, you are out of the wind. *George* shouldn't be quite so fussy about always insisting on having the front seat. Even when one of the men isn't feeling well George won't offer to let him sit in front. After all, the whole crew works together and that ought to call for a little give and take. This rigid seating arrangement strikes you as childish.

ROLE FOR GUS

You had the job of handling the tailgate for four years before *Charlie* was hired and you got sick of it. You feel there is a lot to be said for having the man who sits in front handle the tailgate but since you are the driver it is only fair that someone else should do it. After all, you passed the driver's test and are the official driver. Being the driver, you are working while the others just sit so you are entitled to some consideration.

ROLE FOR CHARLIE

You had the job of opening and closing the tailgate for two years before *Jack* was hired and the fairest way to handle the matter is for the man who sits in the front seat to open and close the tailgate. You never complained when you had the job because each man ought to take his turn like everyone else, but it doesn't seem fair that the newest man should do it all of the time. There ought to be some way of balancing out the menial work and the privileges so that the newest man isn't always a marked man.

ROLE FOR JACK

You have been low seniority man on the crew since you joined the company 3 years ago. You didn't mind the job of opening and closing the tailgate at first but you are tired of being treated as a flunky. You passed the driving test a year ago and now are the substitute driver and take over when Gus isn't on the job. When you do this you still have to operate the tailgate. Some of the older men have more right to the front seat than you do and you wouldn't care particularly for the seat anyway if it meant that you had to handle the tailgate, but just the same one of the men who sits in the front seat should be willing to operate the tailgate. You have never injured yourself climbing into the truck or jumping out, but you have hurt your feet and ankles a few times when you accidentally came down hard on your heels. There is danger, too, when the man in back jumps out of the truck since he is not always sure that the driver may not start up again. When a fellow wants to play safe and wait until he is sure the driver has really stopped, George yells to him to "snap out of it."

INSTRUCTIONS FOR OBSERVERS OF CONFERENCE LEADER

One aspect of a conference is the conduct of the discussion leader, who in this instance is the foreman, *Bert Jones*. Jot down notes on the things he does that serve the constructive functions given below:

1. Clarifying the problem.
2. Assisting in resolving conflicts.
3. Getting all men to participate equally.
4. Preventing hurt feelings or protecting a member who was attacked by others.

If the foreman takes sides with any of the men or shows a preference for a particular solution, he is likely to be a source of friction. Note whether he arouses unfavorable reactions and determine the cause.

The observer should carefully note the solution agreed upon since he may be asked to report it to the class.

INSTRUCTIONS FOR OBSERVERS OF GROUP INTERACTION

The second aspect of a conference is the reaction and interaction of the membership. Take notes in order to be prepared to supply answers to the questions stated below:

1. After the leader presented the problem, which crew member resisted the change most strongly and which one was most in favor of the change? Can you see a status factor that accounts for this difference of opinion?

2. To what extent were the arguments based on feelings and emotions as compared to logical reasoning?

3. What were the choices open to George, the work leader? Which one did he settle for, and why? How would you characterize George's problem?

4. Was social pressure used to influence certain members one way or the other? If so, where did it come from and toward whom was it directed? What effect did it have?

5. Did the crew divide into subgroupings? If so, how did they line up?

6. Were there any changes in who favored whom during the discussion? Note down some examples.

7. Who, if any, of the members are dissatisfied with the solution?

SAMPLE TABLE 3.   RESULTS FROM DISCUSSION ON SEATING CHANGE

(Use Table for Recording Class Data)

Group	Solution	Dissatisfied men	Quality		Leader behavior	Group process
			Insiders	Outsiders		
A	Jack in front seat with George and Gus.	George Gus Bill	5 yes 1 no	6 yes 2 question-able 8 no	Didn't under-stand. Impatient. Gave good reasons for change.	George was stubborn and disliked Jack. Bill wouldn't talk at the end.

IV. Comments and Implications

The present case is based on an actual instance and the complications it caused were a source of surprise to management because the existence of a seating order was unknown to them. Nevertheless, every one of the trucks had a seating order and the new ruling disrupted relationships on each one until a new order was established.

A change in status symbols disrupts the best established persons the most. This is true in community relations as well as in offices and work crews. George happens to be that person in the case under consideration. He has the preferred seat but the suggestion that Mr. Stevens has passed along by way of Bert Jones requests that he either perform the most menial task in the group or give up his status position in the truck. Almost anyone in the group would be willing to perform the menial task if the status seat went with it, so George's resistance may not be understood by everyone.

Jack, the low status man, stands to gain the most by the order. This, too, may be hard to take and consequently requires the intermediate status members to make a choice between supporting the person with status above themselves, or the person with status below theirs.

These conflicting loyalties are usually ironed out in group discussion, being influenced not only by the issues in the situation but by the conduct of the individuals involved. If Jack shows a grasping type of behavior, he may find himself without support.

In some instances George gives up his seat and one of the other members of the crew may perform the menial task and gain the front seat. In other cases George accepts the menial task, and he does this with satisfaction if it so happens that closing the tailgate is built into a prestige duty. For example, group discussion may make it a safety precaution and the duty of the work leader. Sometimes George will agree to a trial period only. This probationary period may serve to test the group's reaction. If Jack tells him to hurry or if someone makes a wisecrack, the problem may be reopened.

Other solutions put Gus on the spot. If George's status is respected, group members may suggest that Gus perform the menial task. If he resists, Jack the substitute driver may indicate his willingness to both drive and take care of the tailgate. Usually someone will rescue Gus, but this, too, will depend on the respect that Gus as a personality can command.

The fact that groups in general successfully solve this problem suggests the value of group discussion and group decision as a procedure a foreman may use to solve complex problems of this sort. Since so many of the factors that influence the social structure of a group can never be known by a supervisor, he could not succeed even if he were a superman. However, the group approach quite simply resolves a pattern of conflicting forces that would escape scientific measurement and evaluation.

Actually, a good deal of the success in the problem solving of the group depends upon the foreman's failure to have a ready solution. He is caught somewhat unaware and lets the group talk it out. If he took sides or showed a preference for a particular solution, there would have been less satisfaction.

Status problems are often found where we least expect them. In some offices one learns of the room temperature problem. Windows are opened by some and closed by others. Why can't people shift positions in a room so that temperature variations in a room will correspond with temperature preferences in individuals? Often it is because the preferred temperature spots are not at preferred locations, and these locations have acquired status values. The suggestion that people dress according to the temperature they enjoy may also be made. This too may raise a controversy since those who adapt to the room conditions feel they are accepting a lower status in the group.

Status problems are often involved in the following types of circumstances: when employees are asked to work outside their job classification; if there are variations in conditions of work or in types of desks and chairs occupied by members of a single work unit; if a change is made in who should be consulted for information when a new employee is in need of assistance; when the foreman makes the choice of who introduces a new employee into a unit; and if a new group member takes it upon himself to transmit complaints to the boss. Whenever a whole group is disturbed by a ruling or by what on the surface seems to be an improvement, it is worthwhile to examine the social organization.

It should not be supposed that status resulting from informal organization is undesirable. It was undoubtedly found that most persons who role played a member of the crew in the seating problem obtained certain satisfactions, and in many instances these must have been of a social nature. Group organization makes for security and a feeling of belonging. One gains this feeling most effectively when he fits a particular niche in a group. Persons who enter a new work group remain insecure and anxious until they find their places. Often they quit because they do not feel accepted. The question is not whether to encourage or discourage informal organization in work groups, but rather how to respect and deal with it so as to maximize the potential satisfactions.

case 4

A Problem
with "Old Girls"

I. Focusing the Problem

When individuals disagree they frequently present facts to support their respective arguments with the expectation that when the other person has learned the facts of the situation he will be won over to the desired point of view. In some instances this approach may be effective, as when one party to the disagreement lacks certain essential information. Much more often, however, disagreements are based not merely on differing factual information but on attitude differences. In this event, the presentation of facts by means of argument is inefficient at best and may actually cause the attitude of the other person to become more rigid than before.

Most of the techniques used in persuasion are intellectual approaches in that they appeal to facts and logic. Each party to a dispute presents his side and attempts to find fault with the other's position. When people argue, each gives his position and attempts to prevent the other from speaking. Discussions are more polite in that there is respectful listening, but the emphasis still is on getting one's own position clarified. Frequently the "yes-but" approach is used: one person accepts the point made by the opposition but counters with a better point of his own. What is called "selling" falls into the same category: the seller is busy giving his side while the other looks for weaknesses and hence is concerned with opposite interests.

The failure of factual argument to resolve disagreement based on attitude differences becomes more understandable when it is realized that one of the important ways attitudes influence behavior is to cause individuals to use only facts that are consistent with their attitudes. Facts inconsistent with the attitudes are either ignored, or reinterpreted in ways that are consistent with the particular point of view. Thus, regardless of the facts of the situation, persons who differ in attitude are very prone to misunderstand each other and the facts of the case become irrelevant. When this occurs communication becomes faulty.

The following role playing case is specifically designed to demonstrate how attitude differences tend to lead to conflict and reduced communication. The case is based on a situation in industry and concerns attitudes regarding the relative desirability of employing "old" and "young" girls in an office. Two persons are involved in the actual interview. One is a personnel director who sees the problem of "old" girls from his position and personal experience and the other is an office manager who is production oriented and sees the problem from a different side. When they discuss the issue of employing and placing "old girls," they are therefore likely to disagree. The manner in which the facts of the case influence the behavior of the participants, the kinds of human relations skills practiced by each, and the satisfactions created in various pairs of role players will furnish interesting comparisons.

The Multiple Role Playing procedure is described for this case because it allows for a comparison of results and the collection of relevant data. If the case is used with a highly trained group of persons, Single Group Role Playing may be used to test the more advanced skills.

II. Multiple Role Playing Procedure

PREPARATION

1. The class should divide into groups of three. When a class is not divisible by 3, either two or four persons may be used to form one or two pairs of role players.

2. One person in each group accepts the role of Mr. Jones, a second, the role of Mr. Smith, and the third member becomes the observer.

3. After all participants have been assigned roles, the Background Material on page 73 should be read by everyone. It is desirable to have the instructor read this material aloud slowly so that participants can become thoroughly familiar with the situation.

4. When the situation is clarified the individual roles should be studied. Those playing the part of Mr. Jones will turn to page 74 and study their roles; and those playing the part of Mr. Smith should leave the room and study their roles, which they will find on page 75. Observers should remain in the room with the Joneses, and read their instructions, which are on pages 76 f. (Participants are requested to read their roles only, and they should not communicate with each other concerning their plans prior to the playing of the scene.)

5. When observers and Joneses have finished studying their parts and the observers have obtained the strategy their Joneses plan to follow, they should stand up to indicate that they are ready.

6. When the observers have indicated by standing that they are ready, the instructor should ask the Smiths to return. At his signal they should join their groups and assume they have entered Mr. Jones's office to keep the scheduled appointment.

PROCESS

1. It is not intended that this case will be carried to the point of completion. It is a difficult interview and should be terminated when no new factors or approaches are introduced into the discussion.

2. Usually a period of 15 to 20 minutes is sufficient to clarify the type of approach that the interviewer is using. After 15 minutes have elapsed the instructor should check with several observers and obtain their estimates of progress made.

3. The instructor should prepare table headings on the blackboard as shown in Sample Table 4, page 78, while groups are actively role playing.

4. The instructor should give the signal terminating all groups simultaneously, regardless of the differences in stages they may have reached.

OBSERVER'S REPORTS

1. The degree of progress made by Jones in converting Smith should be evaluated by the observer. (If no observer was present the report should be made by Smith.) Letter grades A, B, C, D, and E may be used to indicate a range of progress from "excellent" to "failure." The instructor should write the letter grade in the proper place he has prepared on the blackboard (see Sample Table 4 on page 78).

2. The type of approach planned and actually followed by Jones should be described. If possible the following categories should be used to classify the approach: angry argument, logical argument, the "yes-but" discussion, selling method, friendly discussion, and cooperative solving of a problem of mutual interest. Both the planned approach and the one followed predominantly should be indicated in the table. (If no observer was present, Jones should supply this information.)

3. The observer should give his opinion of whether future relations will be better, worse, or about the same as a result of the interview. (If no observer was present, Jones and Smith should give their observations.)

DISCUSSION OF OBSERVERS' REPORTS

1. The Smiths should discuss the ways in which they agree or disagree with their observers' reports. They should then assign a grade of A, B, C, D, or E to indicate their observers' abilities to judge their feelings and methods. These letter grades should be entered in the table. (Omit if no observer was present.)

2. The Joneses should discuss the observers' reports from their viewpoints and likewise assign them letter grades. (Omit if no observer was present.)

3. Table 4 should be discussed to determine if the degree of progress was related to the method used. It is possible that all interviews erred in the same direction—that of each participant telling his side.

DETERMINING WHETHER ATTITUDES SELECT FACTS

1. The facts as classified in the observers' instructions should be listed on the blackboard as in Sample Table 5. The instructor should poll the

observers to determine for each fact whether it was first mentioned by Jones or Smith. He should write the numbers of Joneses mentioning a given fact in the second column and the number of Smiths in the third column.

2. When the polling is completed, the totals should be filled in. The totals of the Smiths for unfavorable vs. favorable facts indicate the degree to which they selected facts to support their attitudes, and the totals of the Joneses for favorable vs. unfavorable facts indicate whether they also selected facts to support their positions. These totals for Smith and Jones may be expressed as ratios.

3. The degree to which each participant selected facts favorable to his position indicates the extent to which he was selling or arguing. If the Joneses showed a lesser discrepancy between their totals of favorable and unfavorable facts we can credit them with being less defensive and good listeners. Listening is what the interviewer should do.

4. The grand total gives the combined number of facts mentioned by the Joneses and Smiths. It is desirable that this total be less for the Joneses than for the Smiths because the interviewer is supposed to get the interviewee to talk. Generally speaking the grand total reflects the amount that each talked.

5. Time should be allowed to discuss the tabulated data, to introduce additional observations, and to exchange different opinions as to the best way to conduct this interview.

III. Materials [11]

BACKGROUND MATERIAL

In a commercial office employing a large number of women there was a period when business was slack and very few new employees were hired. Following this period, business improved and there was a good deal of expansion. Thus during the past five years many new girls have been hired. As a consequence of this development there are 90 girls who have worked for the company 10 or more years; 15 who have been with the company from 5 to 9 years and who were hired during the slack period; and 450 girls who have less than 5 years of service. This hiring pattern has created a unique situation in the office. There is a fair-sized group of oldtimers and a large group of newcomers, with an age difference of about 5 years between them. These two groups do not get on too well with each other. The younger group often refers to the oldtimers as old biddies, old maids, sour pusses, etc., whereas the old group refers to the younger group as jazz kids, dumb bunnies, man-crazy loons, and young hussies. The office force has recognized the problem and it is common for them to divide the women into "old girls" and "young girls."

Mr. Jones is in charge of the personnel office and for the past 15 years has done all the hiring and placing of employees. All transfers, changes in pay rates, etc., must be cleared through him. He is in a staff position and his office was set up as a service to the line organization.

Mr. Smith is the manager of one of the large offices. There are four supervisors who report to him and his position in the organization is comparable in rank to that of Mr. Jones. Since Smith and Jones report to different vice-presidents neither has authority over the other.

Mr. Jones has asked Smith to see him to discuss a problem in connection with the "old girls." Smith is about to enter Jones's office.

[11] Role instructions are taken from a case in Maier, *Principles of Human Relations,* John Wiley & Sons, New York, 1952, 103–104.

ROLE FOR MR. JONES OF THE PERSONNEL OFFICE

You have a persistent problem with *Mr. Smith*, the manager of a large office group in the company. He objects to older employees and refuses to accept transfers. He also gives poor ratings to older girls and tries to get you to find other places for them. As far as you can tell he is prejudiced. You believe that the older girls make good, stable employees. You find them more conscientious, more dependable, more businesslike and generally more capable. You can't understand Smith's position and therefore have decided to talk to him to see if you can't convince him tó take his share of old girls and to give them a better deal. It is just about time for Smith to arrive.

Here are some things you know about the behavior of old girls as compared to young girls. Naturally you keep certain records and keep in touch with what goes on around the place.

Adapt slowly to new jobs
Know company set-up
Know how to do a greater variety of jobs in company
Object more to changes in methods
Less sociable
Same production
Less willing to do unpleasant jobs
Less tardiness
More time in restrooms
Absenteeism lower

Do not try to memorize these points. Just consider them to be background information such as you would be familiar with in a real-life situation.

When you have finished studying your role tell your observer what you have as your objective in this interview and how you plan to conduct the interview. If you have no observer, jot these points on a slip of paper.

ROLE FOR MR. SMITH, MANAGER OF OFFICE FORCE

You have had considerable trouble with *Mr. Jones* in the personnel office. He isn't cooperative with you regarding the kind of employees you want and doesn't help you in obtaining new jobs for those you want to get rid of. Mostly, the issue centers on problems concerning older girls. You refuse to accept girls over 30 years of age and you try to transfer your old girls whenever you can. You like a young force. You have had dealings with all types of employees and you and the four supervisors who report to you all agree that old girls are no good. You don't like to deal with them and see no reason why the company should put up with them. However, if the company wants to keep them let those who like them take them into their units. As far as you are concerned, they aren't worth the pay they get. They are inefficient, undependable, and slow. (Before attempting to play this role try to feel dislike for old girls. Just remember you've had some headaches with them.)

You have an appointment with Mr. Jones of the personnel office. He has asked to see you to discuss your views concerning older employees. You are a busy person and get kind of tired discussing problems the personnel staff dreams up. As you see it, the personnel department is supposed to assist the line organization but they seem to talk more than assist.

Here are some things you know about the behavior of old girls when compared to young girls:

Absenteeism lower
More time in restrooms
Less tardiness
Less willing to do unpleasant jobs
Same production
Less sociable
Object more to changes in methods
Know how to do a greater variety of jobs in company
Know company set-up
Adapt slowly to new jobs

Do not try to memorize these points. Just consider them to be background information such as you would be familiar with in a real-life situation.

INSTRUCTIONS FOR OBSERVERS

In their roles, Smith and Jones are given the same facts concerning "old girls." However, the men disagree with each other as soon as they begin their discussion because they have been given different attitudes toward "old girls." Smith's role is designed to induce an unfavorable attitude toward "old girls" and the role for Jones is designed to create a favorable attitude. You should observe the extent to which the participants use primarily the facts concerning "old girls" that are consistent with their own attitudes and how they deal with those facts that are inconsistent with their attitudes. Since the purpose of this case is to illustrate how persons with different attitudes may disagree even when they both have the same facts, the role playing may be terminated when it has become apparent that the two men treat facts differently. The instructor may check with you to determine whether or not your pair of role players has ceased introducing additional factual material.

The facts supplied the role players are given below. For your convenience they are divided into three groups: (a) those favorable to "old girls"; (b) those unfavorable to "old girls"; and (c) those which are neutral or which may be interpreted either way. While observing the role playing, place the initial S or J before a fact to indicate whether Smith or Jones was the first to bring it into the conversation.

FACTS ABOUT "OLD GIRLS"

Favorable

_____ Absenteeism lower

_____ Less tardiness

_____ Know how to do a greater variety of jobs

_____ Know company set-up

Unfavorable

_____ More time in restrooms

_____ Less willing to do unpleasant jobs

_____ Object more to changes in methods

_____ Adapt slowly to new jobs

Neutral

_____ Same production

_____ Less sociable

Mr. Jones has been instructed to tell you what he plans to accomplish by his interview with Smith. Make a note of his objective and ask him also to indicate the approach he plans to use. Make a note of this plan too, but do not give him any assistance.

SAMPLE TABLE 4.   SUMMARY OF PROGRESS IN INTERVIEW CONCERNING
"OLD GIRLS"

(Use Table for Recording Class Data)

Group number	Observer's rating of progress	Observer's description of approach Jones		Observer's estimation of future relations of Jones and Smith	Smith's judgment of observer's report. (Letter grade)	Jones's judgment of observer's report (Letter grade)
		Planned	Actually used			

SAMPLE TABLE 5. HOW ATTITUDES SELECT FACTS

(Use Table for Recording Class Data)

	No. of Jones	No. of Smiths
Facts favorable to "Old girls"		
1. Absenteeism lower	———	———
2. Less tardiness	———	———
3. Know greater variety of jobs	———	———
4. Know company set−up	———	———
Total		
Facts unfavorable to " Old girls "		
1. More time in rest rooms	———	———
2. Less willing to do unpleasant jobs	———	———
3. Object more to changes in methods	———	———
4. Adapt slowly to new job	———	———
Total		
Neutral facts		
1. Same production	———	———
2. Less sociable	———	———
Total		
Grand total		

IV. Comments and Implications

Arguing, "yes-but" discussions, and selling approaches differ in the degree of courtesy shown by two participants in an interview but they are alike insofar as the person using them is presenting *his* views to the other person. When one presents his views to another, he is trying to get the other person to see and accept his way of looking at a subject as the correct one. Instead of accomplishing this, however, he often finds that the other person defends his own viewpoint more vigorously. Thus in our case we saw that attempts on the part of Jones to make "old girls" more acceptable to Smith often were met with increased hostility.

If these approaches are ineffective, let us look in a different direction for an effective procedure. Instead of Jones trying to get Smith to see his side of the problem, suppose that Jones would try to see and understand Smith's position. This means that he would have to take an approach almost opposite to the one usually taken, and try to understand rather than explain. To accomplish this he must create a discussion climate that is conducive to making Smith feel free to tell Jones how he feels about "old girls." In order for Jones to learn Smith's viewpoint he must listen, and this means he must get Smith to talk freely. In order to get the real facts, he must not challenge any statements, since critical behavior will force Smith to resort to presenting reasons or facts that he considers acceptable to Jones. These are not the causes of Smith's viewpoint.

In order to create a free discussion climate, Jones might express an interest in Smith's views because Smith's office has first-hand experience with the work of various groups of employees. He can indicate that "old girls" are a problem for the company and sincerely desire to have Smith evaluate their behavior. After a few preliminary reactions, he can proceed to make a list of the undesirable behaviors. This gives Smith an opportunity to tell all the bad things he knows about "old girls" without being challenged. Jones should accept all points and patiently wait while Smith thinks up as many items as he can.

When this list is completed, Jones may ask Smith whether the "old girls" have any good points. If Smith indicates there are a few, Jones should list them also. Ordinarily Smith will be glad to give good points because the opportunity to talk about their bad points will have made him more generous. If both the bad and the good points have been contributed by Smith, it is obvious that he accepts these as relevant, and once this is accomplished problem solving behavior can begin. The problem for discussion may be expressed in terms of the best use the company can make of "old girls." This leads to a consideration of abilities of "old girls," the types of jobs available in a department, the number of "old girls" in the company, the best way to mix girls with differing lengths of service, and many other issues that may be of interest and concern both to Jones and Smith.

We call the above approach to an interview the "Two-Column Method" because it is designed to permit one party to express the two sides of an issue, one after the other. The side favored by the interviewee should be expressed first. This method is useful whenever there is a disagreement over facts that are in the nature of common knowledge. Whenever a situation or controversy is fluid and the actual problem is difficult to locate, the Two-Column Method is useful for clearing the ground and pointing up the problem-issue for discussion.

Attitudes not only organize facts and thereby determine their meaning, but they select facts as well. This means that discussions about facts are irrelevant to the opinions held. The Two-Column approach to a problem eliminates the dispute over facts and meanings by having all of them come from one source. When this occurs there is at least some basis for co-operative problem solving. The method is not a cure-all, but it can be useful in separating facts from a controversy and facing more squarely the real problem—the difference in attitude. Once some respect and understanding of an attitude is expressed by an interviewer, the interviewee feels less in need of protecting his attitude. An attitude that is not defended can undergo a change.

case 5

The Change of Work Procedure

I. Focusing the Problem

It is frequently necessary for industry to adapt its operations to new market demands and engineering advances in production methods. The changes involved usually entail the solving of a variety of problems. Thus new patterns of consumer needs must be anticipated, decisions must be made involving the utilization of new or existing equipment and procedures, job grades and pay rates may be altered, and employees must be trained in new skills and methods. Despite the rapidity and magnitude of the changes, satisfactory and even ingenious solutions to the technical and engineering problems are often found.

However, changes in operations and methods are seldom confined to the technical aspects of production; they may also require alterations in the work of the employees. When this is true, the new methods not only must be of high quality in that they are workable and efficient from an objective standpoint, but they must also be *acceptable* to the employees concerned.

This added factor of acceptance makes the problem of introducing changes different in certain important ways from purely technical problems of evaluating new equipment or procedures. For one thing, the *quality* of a solution and its *acceptability* are different characteristics and do not necessarily go together. A second complicating aspect stems from the fact that while management can control solution quality by reserving decision making to itself, acceptance is inherently voluntary with the employees and is not subject to the will of management. At the same time, failure to obtain employee acceptance of changes that affect them aggravates many of the problems of management. In some instances resistance is expressed directly in the form of grievances about rates and earnings, quits, work stoppages and open hostility toward management. In other instances, the resistance may be shown in such indirect ways as restriction of output, waste, low-quality workmanship, slow learning of the new methods, excessive absenteeism, and the like.

Management's concern with these negative reactions to change is of comparatively recent origin and has led to the development of various ways for dealing with the problem. One of the most widely used methods is that of "selling" the employees on the advantages of the change. Facts and arguments are presented, the expectation being that when the employees have the same facts and information as management they will take a similarly favorable view toward change. To the extent that resistance to new methods is based on a lack of correct information, this procedure has merit. However, this deficiency is seldom the case. Instead, resistance nearly always involves feelings of insecurity, distrust of management's motives, and anxiety for the future. Facts and arguments provide small comfort when skills are made obsolete and they have little or no effect on unfavorable attitudes.

The limited success of the "selling" approach has led to the search for other methods. One of these is a procedure by which supervisors consult with the employees concerning proposed changes as well as other problems. The mechanics of what is known as consultative management vary in detail from one company to another. However, the essential feature is that an attempt is made to learn the ideas and feelings of the employees, with management reserving the right to accept or reject the employee contributions as it sees fit.

Insofar as ways for obtaining acceptance are concerned, the two methods are very different in that the "selling" approach emphasizes the presentation of the management point of view whereas the consultative approach is designed to obtain an expression of employee opinions. In this sense the latter method is a further step in the direction of consideration for the welfare of employees. The two methods are alike in that both reserve the decision making function for management, the intent being to protect the quality of the decision.

The insistence of management on protecting solution quality by retaining the power to decide raises several questions regarding the relative importance of solution quality versus acceptance. Is solution quality always the prime consideration, or may there be circumstances in which a high quality solution that fails to gain acceptance is less efficient than a solution of lesser quality that has the support of the employees concerned?

Do management solutions insure high quality, or are there other procedures by which certain problems can be solved more effectively? Is a sacrifice of one or the other characteristic of an effective solution necessary, or can both quality and acceptance be achieved with a single procedure?

There is no single formula that will be effective for all instances of resistance to change. The suggestion of changes in a work situation sets in motion a series of reactions and unless one knows what they are, the handling of the matter is likely to be inappropriate. Persons involved in a new plan wonder what effect it will have on their incomes, their futures, and their group status. They know how they are doing under present conditions, but a change means new and consequently strange conditions. How will a change affect a man's work? Will it be easier, more pleasant, and more steady? Will it require the learning of new and difficult skills? When changes are suggested, someone initiates the program. If he is on the side of the persons who must adopt the change, it means one thing; but if he is on the side of someone else, it has a different meaning. The reaction to change cannot be separated from the reaction to the person or group that initiates the change.

It is apparent that resistance to change is not mere inertia. Rather, a change carries with it a threat. If changes could be made without threatening someone they could be discussed in an intellectual manner and facts would be welcomed, but as long as the threat is present, facts serve to increase the threat.

In order to deal with problems of change, the first step is to learn the nature of the resistance. In the present case there are a variety of forces operating. Some of these are in the direction of change, some opposed. The supervisor in charge will want to use the constructive forces to improve conditions as much as possible. The kind of discussion he stimulates may introduce new negative or new positive forces so that the outcome may, in part, be determined by the discussion he initiates.

The case is set up for Multiple Role Playing so that the maximum number of persons can participate as leaders in a lively discussion. The persons playing the part of workers will have a profitable time getting on the inside of the meaning of change.

II. *Multiple Role Playing Procedure*

PREPARATION

1. The audience should divide themselves into groups of four. Those left over after groups have been formed may join separate groups to participate as observers. Their instructions are on page 94.

2. All groups are to select one of their members to act as the foreman, Gus Thompson. After the foremen have been chosen they should raise their hands to indicate that the group has a conference leader.

3. The other three individuals in each group will be crew members. Beginning with the foreman and going in clockwise order, their names will be Jack, Steve, and Walt.

4. When all members have received their roles, the instructor should read aloud the section entitled General Information found on page 89.

5. The role players should then study their individual roles in preparation for the small group discussions. The role for Gus Thompson is on page 90; that for Jack is on page 91; Steve's role is on page 92; and Walt's is on page 93. Participants should read only their own roles.

6. The Gus Thompsons should stand up beside their groups when they have finished studying their roles, thus giving the instructor a signal that they are ready to begin.

PROCESS

1. When all foremen are standing, the instructor may help to set the stage for the role playing by commenting that the foreman has asked the crew members to meet with him in his office to discuss a problem before starting work. He should explain that when the foreman is asked to sit down this will be the signal that Gus has entered his office. He hopes that the men will speak to him as he enters.

2. When everyone understands his function, the instructor should ask the foremen to sit down. All groups should role play simultaneously.

3. During the role playing the instructor should prepare a blackboard with the headings shown in Sample Table 6, page 95. This table is to be used for recording the results of the various group discussions.

4. Approximately 25 minutes are needed by the average group to reach a decision. At the end of this period the instructor should observe the

progress of the various groups. If most of them have finished he should give the remaining few groups a two-minute warning signal.

COLLECTING RESULTS

1. The foreman of each group should report the solution agreed upon. The instructor should enter the solution, in abbreviated form, in the proper column of the table he has prepared (see Sample Table 6). Care should be taken to include any special or unique features such as rest pauses, partial rotation procedures, arrangements for helping one another, etc.

2. The foreman should indicate the degree of his satisfaction with the solution so that the instructor can enter his response in Column 2.

3. The members in each crew should indicate whether they are satisfied or dissatisfied with the results. The instructor should indicate the number satisfied in Column 3. Occasionally a member will be mildly inclined in one direction or the other, in which case a question mark should be entered to indicate his feelings.

4. Each foreman is asked whether any crew members were unusually stubborn, hostile or troublesome and, if so, who these were. Then the initials of the members should be written in Column 4 of the table.

5. The crew members should report whether they think production will go up, down, or remain the same as the result of the discussion. When they think there will be a change, they should agree on a per cent increase or decrease, and the instructor should enter this figure in Column 5 of the table.

6. The observers (or crew members) should report what they feel is the main thing the leader did to help the group reach their decision. The members should agree on this point so that the instructor can summarize their consensus on the blackboard under Column 6.

7. The observers (or crew members) should report what the leader did to hinder the discussion the most. This point should be summarized on the blackboard under Column 7.

CLASSIFICATION OF SOLUTIONS

1. After the results from all groups have been tabulated, the solutions should be reviewed briefly in a general group discussion to determine which solutions represent rejection of changes in work method. These can be indicated by the letter R in the margin.

2. Solutions that indicate acceptance of the management solution with minor or no modifications should be selected by the group and labeled with the letter A in the margin.

3. The remaining solutions should be examined for new features and various compromises, such as rest pauses, partial rotation, more time in best position, ways for the crew to help one another, trial periods, and so on. These solutions should be indicated in the margin by the letter C. They represent compromises and the development of new ideas. A short time may be taken to discuss the contributions of the various types of provisions to the satisfaction of the crew members.

4. The solutions should be examined to determine the number which are provisional or for a limited trial period. Some time should be spent to discuss why foremen made these concessions.

EVALUATION OF METHODS USED

1. The attitudes of the leaders should be discussed in relation to the types of solutions developed. General conclusions should be drawn as to what constitutes a helpful leader attitude versus an obstructive attitude.

2. Discussion should be used to determine the ways in which the airing of feelings and hostilities in the crew influenced the final outcome.

3. On the basis of the tabulated results and the role playing experience, the group should attempt to determine the foreman's part in influencing the outcome of the discussion. Both satisfaction and productivity should be considered in relation to the type of solution reached and to the foreman's conduct, as described in Columns 6 and 7.

4. Column 4 should be examined to determine whether certain crew members caused most of the trouble. If different men were trouble makers in the various groups, this suggests that certain events in the discussion, rather than the role instructions, were the cause of their troublesome behavior. In any case, the problem employees should report why they acted as they did.

ANALYSIS OF RESISTANCE FORCES

1. From the group as a whole, the instructor should obtain the various objections to change expressed by the different crew members and list these on the blackboard. This list usually will include such factors as aversion to boredom, dislike of the time study man, fear of rate cuts, fear of speed-up, fear of running out of work, and the like.

2. Next to the objections the instructor should develop a list of the possible gains or advantages to the crew by changing to the new method. Usually the item of more pay will be mentioned. Other factors, such as time for rest pauses, satisfaction with being in one's best position, etc., may be offered. However, only those aspects actually mentioned in the role playing discussion should be accepted.

3. The two sets of items listed as (a) objections to changing work methods and (b) advantages of change can now be considered as forces against change and forces toward change, respectively.

4. The list of resistances to the new work method can now be examined in discussion to determine the ones that indicate fear and hostility and those that have a more intellectual basis.

5. Ways for reducing fears and negative feelings should be discussed. Results from the previous role playing cases may be considered, if they seem relevant.

6. Methods for dealing with realistic objections to change, for example the boredom problem, should be discussed.

7. Evaluation of employee participation methods for obtaining acceptance of change should be discussed in relation to methods which do not involve participation of employees in making changes. Emphasis should be given to a comparison of the motivational effects of participation vs. non-participation.

8. The relative importance of solution quality vs. acceptance should be discussed. Is the most efficient solution without acceptance preferable to a less efficient solution having acceptance?

III. Materials [12]

GENERAL INFORMATION

In a company manufacturing subassemblies for the automobile industry, the assembly work is done by small groups of employees. Several of these groups are under the supervision of a foreman, *Gus Thompson*. In one of these groups, *Jack, Steve,* and *Walt* work together assembling fuel pumps.

This operation is divided into three jobs or positions, called Position 1, Position 2, and Position 3. Supplies for each position are located next to the bench where the man works. The men work side by side and can help each other out if they wish. Since all the jobs are simple and fairly similar these three employees exchange positions on the line every now and then. This trading of positions was developed by the men themselves. It creates no financial problem because the crew is paid by a group piece rate. In this way the three members share the production pay equally.

[12] Role instructions are taken from a case in Maier, *Principles of Human Relations*, John Wiley & Sons, New York, 1952, 154–156.

ROLE FOR GUS THOMPSON, FOREMAN

You are the foreman in a shop and supervise the work of about 20 men. Most of the jobs are piece rate jobs and some of the men work in teams and are paid on a team piece rate basis. In one of the teams, *Jack, Walt,* and *Steve* work together. Each one of them does one of the operations for an hour and then they exchange, so that all men perform each of the operations at different times. The men themselves decided to operate that way and you have never given the plan any thought.

Lately, *Jim Clark,* the methods man, has been around and studied conditions in your shop. He timed Jack, Walt, and Steve on each of the operations and came up with the following facts.

TIME PER OPERATION (IN MINUTES)

	Position 1	Position 2	Position 3	Total
Jack	3	4	$4\frac{1}{2}$	$11\frac{1}{2}$
Walt	$3\frac{1}{2}$	$3\frac{1}{2}$	3	10
Steve	5	$3\frac{1}{2}$	$4\frac{1}{2}$	13
				$34\frac{1}{2}$

He observed that with the men rotating, the average time for all three operations would be $\frac{1}{3}$ of the total time or $11\frac{1}{2}$ minutes per complete unit. If, however, Jack worked in the number 1 spot, Steve in the number 2 spot, and Walt in the number 3 spot, the time would be $9\frac{1}{2}$ minutes, a reduction of over 17%. Such a reduction in time would amount to a saving of more than 80 minutes. In other words the lost production is about the same as that which would occur if the men loafed for 80 minutes in an 8-hour day. If the time were used for productive effort, production would be increased more than 20%.

This made pretty good sense to you so you have decided to take up the problem with the men. You feel that they should go along with any change in operation that is made.

ROLE FOR JACK

You are one of three men on an assembly operation. *Walt* and *Steve* are your teammates and you enjoy working with them. You get paid on a team basis and you are making wages that are entirely satisfactory. Steve isn't quite as fast as Walt and you, but when you feel he is holding things up too much each of you can help out.

The work is very monotonous. The saving thing about it is that every hour you all change positions. In this way you get to do all three operations. You are best on the number 1 position so when you get in that spot you turn out some extra work and so make the job easier for Steve who follows you in that position.

You have been on this job for two years and have never run out of work. Apparently your group can make pretty good pay without running yourselves out of a job. Lately, however, the company has had some of its experts hanging around. It looks like the company is trying to work out some speed-up methods. If they make these jobs any more simple you won't be able to stand the monotony. Gus Thompson, your foreman, is a decent guy and has never criticized your team's work.

ROLE FOR STEVE

You work with *Jack* and *Walt* on an assembly job and get paid on a team piece rate basis. The three of you work very well together and make a pretty good wage. Jack and Walt like to make a little more than you think is necessary but you go along with them and work as hard as you can so as to keep the production up where they want it. They are good fellows and often help you out if you fall behind, so you feel it is only fair to try and go along with the pace they set.

The three of you exchange positions every hour. In this way you get to work all positions. You like the number 2 position the best because it is easiest. When you get in the number 3 position you can't keep up and then you feel Gus Thompson, the foreman, watching you. Sometimes Walt and Jack slow down when you are on the number 3 spot and then the foreman seems satisfied.

Lately the methods man has been hanging around watching the job. You wonder what he is up to. Can't they leave guys alone who are doing all right?

ROLE FOR WALT

You work with *Jack* and *Steve* on a job that requires three separate operations. Each of you works on each of the three operations by rotating position once every hour. This makes the work more interesting and you can always help out the other fellow by running the job ahead in case one of you doesn't feel so good. It's all right to help out because you get paid on a team piece rate basis. You could actually earn more if Steve were a faster worker, but he is a swell guy and you would rather have him in the group than someone else who might do a little bit more.

You find all three positions about equally desirable. They are all simple and purely routine. The monotony doesn't bother you much because you can talk, daydream, and change your pace. By working slow for a while and then fast you can sort of set your pace to music you hum to yourself. Jack and Steve like the idea of changing jobs and even though Steve is slow on some positions, the changing around has its good points. You feel you get to a stopping place every time you change positions and this kind of takes the place of a rest pause.

Lately some kind of efficiency expert has been hanging around. He stands some distance away with a stopwatch in his hand. The company could get more for its money if it put some of those guys to work. You say to yourself, "I'd like to see one of these guys try and tell me how to do this job. I'd sure give him an earful."

If Gus Thompson, your foreman, doesn't get him out of the shop pretty soon you're going to tell him what you think of his dragging in company spies.

INSTRUCTIONS FOR OBSERVERS

1. Observe the leader's attitude toward change during the discussion.

   a. Was he partial to the new method?

   b. Did he seem mainly interested in more production or in improving the job for the crew?

   c. To what extent was he considerate of the objections raised by the crew? How did he react to their opposition?

   d. Did he defend the new method or argue for its acceptance? What effect did this have on progress in the discussion?

2. Make notes on characteristic aspects of the discussion.

   a. Did arguments develop?

   b. Was any crew member unusually stubborn?

   c. Did the crew members have their say?

   d. Did the leader really listen?

   e. What were the main points of differences?

3. Observe evidences of problem solving behavior.

   a. What was agreed upon, if anything?

   b. In what respects was there a willingness to compromise?

   c. What did the leader do to help or hinder a mutually acceptable work method?

SAMPLE TABLE 6. GROUP RESULTS ON PROPOSED CHANGE

(Use Table for Recording Class Data)

Group No.	1 Solution	2 Foreman satisfied	3 Number satisfied in crew	4 Problem employees	5 Future production	6 Leader actions that helped	7 Leader actions that hindered

IV. Comments and Implications

The solutions obtained by various groups usually fall into two categories: those in which the old rotation method will be continued, sometimes with the group's promise that they will try to increase production if allowed to continue the old method; and those in which the men accept the plan suggested by the time study man, usually with the understanding that they can return to the old method if they wish. The foreman ordinarily goes along with either decision, indicating that he either convinces the group that they should change or the group convinces him that they should not change. Most foremen recognize the importance of gaining acceptance and invariably they make the concession of allowing the change to be on a trial basis. The men know they can make or break a solution with this provision. Thus, regardless of the outcome, a discussion tends to bring about a meeting of minds.

Now and then the conflict will not be resolved and then there is dissatisfaction. Often the men threaten a walkout if the foreman goes ahead with the change or threatens to discharge individuals who refuse to make the change.

The reason why solutions tend to fall into two categories is partially due to the way the problem is posed. When the foreman suggests a plan, the men can either accept it or reject it. Thus the problem becomes a choice between the new and the old way.

However, if the foreman does not suggest a new method but presents the facts obtained by the time study man and indicates that the men can use the facts in any way they see fit, no one solution is favored by the foreman. As a result, a variety of solutions is possible, each of which not only takes the time study facts into account but also makes use of the feelings of the men toward their jobs. Examples of such solutions are (a) Jack and Walt exchange jobs, but Steve works permanently at his best position; (b) each man alternates between his two best positions; and (c) the old rotation plan is continued, but each man works a longer stretch on his best position.

An experimental study made with this case [13] demonstrated that the selling approach resulted in none of the above three types of solutions, whereas the problem solving approach yielded 37.5 per cent of such solutions.

[13] N. R. F. Maier, An Experimental Test of the Effect of Training on Discussion Leadership, *Human Relations*, 1953, *6*, 161–173.

These solutions replaced nearly all of the resistance-to-change type solutions that the selling approach yielded in 50 per cent of the groups.

When groups participate in change, resistance is greatly reduced [14] because people do not have to fear decisions they make themselves. This means that consultative management does not go far enough toward participation, since involvement that merely allows the voicing of objections falls short of involvement in the solution. However, the consultative approach is better than the selling method because too skillful a selling technique may actually increase fear. Of course, the direct approach of enforcing a change because it is management's prerogative engenders the most fear and hostility.

In handling a discussion in a problem of this sort it is desirable to differentiate between various forms of resistance. In this particular case it is probable that the following types of response were supplied as reasons for not changing:

a. Hostility toward the time study man.
b. Claims of boredom from working on one position.
c. Fear of pay rate cuts.
d. Distrust of management's motives.

These four types of response may be divided into two categories: emotional, and factual or situational. All except the statements about boredom involve attitudes and emotion. To a great extent these may be imagined or unfounded, but regardless of how unreal they may be, they are a source of feeling. This means that they are not subject to change through reason and logical refutation.

Responses having an emotional loading must be expressed by the group and accepted by the leader. He can use such phrases as, "I can see that the time study man bothered you"; "Do the rest of you feel the same way?"; "I am sorry if I didn't explain his function to you." The leader can give the group confidence and assurance by such statements as "You understand we don't have to use the time study man's data" or "An expert's job is to supply information, but we will decide what to do with it." The release of emotional expression, acceptance of feelings, and assurance of status reduce emotional responses, while arguments and facts increase them because they threaten. The discussion leader's attitude, understanding, and tolerance will also aid him in being patient and willing to listen, even to unreasonable statements.

When various hostilities and fears have been expressed, the group will

[14] L. Coch and J. R. P. French, Jr., Overcoming Resistance to Change, *Human Relations*, 1948, *1*, 512–532.

become interested in facts. They will ask questions and may supply facts of their own. This is the beginning of problem solving.

The objection of boredom may now be seriously considered by the leader. The men may have mentioned it in connection with the other emotional responses, but now it remains as a true obstacle. They see a change as boring and in a sense they are in a rut, since for them change is synonymous with each man working his best position. When thinking seems to be curtailed by a lack of variety, the leader can do a lot to break up this stereotypy in thought. He can ask, "Are there any ways of relieving boredom other than by our present method of rotating?" This question tends to separate the old method as a way of doing the job from its merits for dealing with monotony. Once working the old way is no longer associated with absence of boredom, and a change as leading to boredom, it becomes possible to search for a new method that is not boring. Thus the above question causes the men to think of rest pauses, music, partial rotation, and modified rotation as aspects of new methods.

The use of exploratory questions is an excellent leadership approach for dealing with sterility in thinking because a group often finds itself in a rut as far as ideas are concerned. It is a device for improving the quality of group thinking, once emotional resistance has been reduced. However, it is not recommended when the group is angry or defensive, since the leader must not influence the direction of thinking on such occasions. Exploratory questions do not direct a group toward certain ideas, but they cause the group to look elsewhere; and as long as variability is stimulated, progress in ideas can be made.

case 6

The Safety Belt Rule

I. Focusing the Problem

The enforcement of safety practices in industry is a frequent source of misunderstanding and conflict. There are several reasons for this but probably the most important one is that safety as such has little or no positive goal character. Instead of being a source of satisfaction, safety is missed only when an accident has occurred. Moreover, there frequently exist negative motivations that act against safety. Among these are pressure of work, safety procedures that interfere with the work, safety devices that can be circumvented, and hostility toward management or safety programs. Whether safe work methods will be followed is often a matter of how the various motivational forces are resolved. When a particular situation contains more forces against safety than forces toward safety, the tendency will be to follow methods that are unsafe.

Once safe methods have been developed and employees have been trained in them, the problem becomes one of motivation. There are two general motivational approaches to the problem of safety in work. One is the use of punitive methods to induce fear of following unsafe work methods. This is perhaps the most frequently used system in industry and involves various safety rules with a set of penalties for their violation. However, fear-motivation has a number of serious shortcomings. For one thing it places the supervisor in a position of a spy to detect violations. In addition, fear-motivation does not necessarily produce the desired behavior but rather tends to highlight the undesired methods and hence can cause learning of incorrect or unsafe methods. Since punitive methods depend on a supervisor's authority and assume he has power to enforce rules, fear-motivation tends to weaken or break down when authority is inadequate. Further, punishment is often frustrating and as a result the unsafe behavior may be strengthened rather than corrected. At best, fear can cause men to avoid the unsafe methods they know, but this avoidance does not necessarily lead to a knowledge of the safe method.

Positive methods of motivation, on the other hand, involve the establishment of desirable, need-satisfying, and attainable goals that give an employee a rewarding experience. Such motivation is always constructive in nature in that it encourages safe behavior rather than discourages unsafe behavior. Since positive motivations are rewarding they do not depend in any way on outside authority or force for their effectiveness. Thus the supervisor is no longer placed in the role of a policeman or spy in which he must detect violations and punish offenders. Instead his role becomes a training one, in which his duty is to find ways to make safety a satisfying experience. Obtaining the help of subordinates in solving safety problems is one of the best ways to stimulate awareness of hazards and to create acceptable goals.

In the safety belt case, there are many avenues open to the supervisor for dealing with a situation that has arisen. Whether he adopts methods that lead to hostile or defensive behavior or whether he handles the contact with the employee in a way that leads to a satisfactory solution to a mutual problem will depend on (a) the extent to which he adopts a constructive attitude, and (b) his skill in motivating the employee toward positive safety measures.

In order that skill practice will be optimum the Multiple Role Playing Procedure is used.

II. Multiple Role Playing Procedure

PREPARATION

1. Participants should form subgroups of three members each. (In order that no persons will be left over one or two subgroups of two persons may be arranged.)

2. One member in each group is to be the foreman, one is to be the employee, and the third (if present) will act as an observer.

3. Role assignments should be settled by each subgroup. (When the same subgroup participates in several cases, role assignments should be distributed so that everyone has the opportunity of being a supervisor at one time or another.)

4. All persons turn to the General Instructions on page 104 while the leader reads them aloud.

5. The person playing the role of Jim Welch should read his role on page 105; the person playing the role of Bill Smith should read his role on page 106; and the observers should read the instructions on page 107. Roles should not be exchanged since this reduces the value of the discussion.

6. All participants who are in the role of Jim Welch, the foreman, should leave the room to study their roles and they should remain outside until requested to return by the instructor. When they return they should join their respective employees, ignoring the observers, and proceed to conduct themselves as in a real-life situation.

7. When those who are to play the roles of the employees have finished reading their parts they should stand on a chair to simulate being up a pole. When the foreman returns they should watch him out .of the corners of their eyes.

8. Observers should be prepared to take notes. They should not enter into the discussion in any way.

PROCESS

1. The instructor should give the signal for the Jim Welches to enter the room and for each to walk toward the telephone pole where his Bill Smith is working.

2. About 15 minutes will be needed to play the roles. When more than half of the role players have reached some kind of decision the instructor

should give a two-minute warning signal and ask the remaining pairs to come to a stopping place in this time. (The instructor may check progress with the observers.)

3. During the role playing period, the instructor should prepare a table like Sample Table 7 on page 108.

COLLECTING RESULTS

1. Each observer (or foreman) should describe in a few words the outcome of the interview. As each subgroup reports, the instructor should indicate the solution reached by certain key words and write these in Column 1 of the table he has prepared. (See Sample Table 7.) The report may indicate that sufficient time was not allowed and in this case "no solution" may be recorded. Other solutions might be classed as "forgiven," "warned," "scolded," "reduced lay-off," and "full lay-off."

2. The observers should report how the foreman handled the violation. It may have been ignored, admitted, denied or hinted about, but never established. This should be entered in Column 2. A little time should be taken to determine whether the foreman believes a violation occurred in cases where it is denied.

3. Each observer (or the two role players) should briefly describe the type of interaction that occurred. The foreman may have done most of the talking and lectured, scolded, or pleaded; the two may have discussed an equal amount and argued, discussed differences, or tried to solve a problem; or the foreman may have gotten the employee to do most of the talking by listening, asking questions, and trying to understand the employee. The instructor should briefly indicate the report on this point in Column 3.

4. Each observer as well as the role players should report the kinds of motivations that were used. The instructor can indicate these as plus and minus signs to indicate positive (praise, participation, recognition, etc.) or negative (threat, danger of falling, family responsibility, etc.) incentives, respectively, when filling in Column 4.

5. Each foreman should report how he feels about his employee. The instructor should indicate in Column 5 whether the employee went up, down, or remained the same in the foreman's estimation.

6. Each employee should report how he feels about his foreman. The instructor should summarize by indicating in Column 6 whether the foreman went up, down, or remained the same in the employee's estimation.

7. Each employee should report how he feels about his future safety

and the instructor should summarize the response in Column 7 with the words "more," "same," or "less."

8. Each employee should report how he feels about his future productivity and the instructor should summarize in Column 8 with the words "better," "same," or "worse."

DISCUSSION OF RESULTS

1. The class as a whole should attempt to determine the types of approaches that yielded the best results from the point of view of

   a. Employee morale.
   b. Safety.
   c. Production.

2. Observers should pool their views regarding what they consider to be the good and the poor practices that they observed. The instructor should prepare two columns on the blackboard, one for "good" and one for "poor" practices, and list the points raised. When the same point is listed in both columns, some time should be devoted to discussion of the reasons for the differences. If no agreement results after a brief exchange of views, the item should be either left in both columns or removed from both.

3. The group should prepare an outline of the way they think the interview should be handled. The following steps should be covered.

   a. Type of greeting.
   b. What discussion topic or problem should be raised.
   c. How the employee's attitude should be explored.
   d. The kinds of motivation that should be used.

If time permits, various kinds of statements may be tried out on persons who played the part of employees.

4. Discuss the following practical considerations.

   a. If the foreman discovers that a violation has occurred, must he invoke the penalty? What are the consequences of failure to invoke the penalty?

   b. If the foreman lays the man off, might a grievance result? Would the company support the foreman if a walkout occurred as a reaction of the crew to the lay-off?

   c. Suppose the foreman is caught in the middle in that he takes a risk when he fails to invoke the penalty as well as when he invokes the penalty. What is the best way to escape this trap?

III. Materials [15]

GENERAL INSTRUCTIONS

Jim Welch has been foreman of a repair crew in a telephone company for the past two years. There are 12 men in his crew and they usually work alone or in pairs. The work involves maintenance of telephone lines, replacing worn or damaged equipment, and the like. It is Welch's responsibility to visit his men at their work locations to see how the work is progressing, and give such supervision and assistance as is needed. As supervisor, Welch is also responsible for the safety of his men. This is an important function since the men do most of their work atop high utility poles. This requires them to use climbers and a safety belt. By setting his climbers securely into the pole and looping his safety belt around the pole or over a crossbar, the repairman's hands are free to do the work. In order to make the repairs the men not only have to work fairly rapidly but frequently must shift around on the pole and often have to work in an awkward position. In addition to the danger of falling, there are other hazards such as high voltage wires from nearby power lines, wet or slippery poles, and adverse weather conditions which add to the danger. Thus the company has very strict safety rules and as part of the safety program has instituted such penalties as a three-week lay-off for anyone caught violating safety practices.

[15] Role instructions are based on a case in Maier, *Principles of Human Relations,* John Wiley & Sons, New York, 1952, 106–107.

ROLE FOR JIM WELCH, FOREMAN

You are the foreman of a repair crew of a telephone company. You have 12 men who go on jobs and the men usually work alone or in pairs. As foreman you spend your time visiting the work locations of your men, checking on progress and giving such help, training, and instruction as is needed. You are also responsible for the safety of your men and the company judges you partly on the safety record of your crew. At the present time there is a company safety drive. The slogan is, "No job is so important that it cannot be done safely." The company has passed a ruling that anyone found violating a safety practice will be laid off for three weeks.

You have just driven up to the place where *Bill Smith* is working. You stop your car some distance away (you cannot drive directly to the work location) and see Bill working on top of the pole. As you stop the car you have a distinct impression that Smith snapped his safety belt. Apparently he was working without using his belt and this is a safety practice violation.

Smith is an employee with 20 years of service. He has four children ranging in age from 5 to 12. He is a good workman, but is quite independent in his thinking. You wish to do what you can to correct this man and give him a better attitude toward safety. You have been supervisor of this crew for two years and don't know too much about Bill's past record. You have 10 years service with the company.

ROLE FOR BILL SMITH, REPAIRMAN

You are a member of *Jim Welch's* repair crew in a telephone company. You have been in the company for 20 years and for the past two years Jim has been your supervisor. You feel you know the job and consider your technical knowledge perhaps somewhat greater than Welch's who has worked in the company a total of 10 years. You believe Jim has done a fair job as foreman, but feel that he supervises too closely.

You usually work alone on repair jobs except for several visits a week from your supervisor. You are now working on top of a pole and haven't bothered to snap your safety belt. You are a careful worker and use it when it is necessary, but you find it uncomfortable and in the way, so frequently you don't bother to snap it. You have learned little tricks that give you a rest from the safety belt. One of these is looping your leg over the cross-bar and then hooking your foot behind the pole. You have strong legs and find it easy to support your weight in this manner.

Welch has just driven up so you hasten to snap your belt. There is an annual safety drive on and the company has threatened to lay men off for safety violations. You can't afford having time off. You have four children and living expenses use up all your earnings. You are quite sure Jim didn't see you snap your safety belt. He is walking toward your pole now.

OBSERVER'S INSTRUCTIONS

1. Observe how the foreman opens the discussion. Does he put the employee on the defensive or does he try to put him at ease?

2. The method of the foreman might be to find fault or to try and see the employee's side. His approach will determine whether (a) an argument ensues and both talk a lot; (b) he does most of the talking; (c) he listens to the employee and tries to draw suggestions from him; or (d) they try to solve a problem of mutual interest to both.

3. Take notes on how the violation is raised, if at all. It might be ignored, the foreman might accuse, the foreman may try to draw the answer from the employee, or the employee may admit it despite what the foreman does.

4. Does the foreman discover the employee's attitude? Take notes on what he discovers about the employee's attitude. Does he try to change it or try to understand it?

5. Take notes on the various ways the foreman tries to influence the employee's behavior. Note whether he tends to use negative motivation by threatening punishment, talking about injury, making emotional appeals about his family, etc., or whether he tends to use positive motivation by getting employee participation in the program, obtaining suggestions about safety, asking for help in promoting safety among other employees, etc.

6. Make a list of good and bad things the foreman did in the interview.

7. Be prepared to describe briefly the decision reached by the foreman. Pay special attention to the manner in which the safety rule was interpreted and applied.

SAMPLE TABLE 7. TABULATION OF RESULTS OF INTERVIEW

(Use Table for Recording Class Data)

Group reporting	1 Solution or decision	2 Approach to violation	3 Type of interaction	4 Motivation used	5 Foreman's estimate of employee	6 Employee's estimate of foreman	7 Future safety	8 Future production

IV. Comments and Implications

There are several unsuccessful approaches which the foreman may take in the interview. One is to accuse the employee of violating the safety rule. This will frequently bring a denial. On the other hand, if the employee admits the violation, the foreman must decide whether to invoke the penalty. If he does this he leaves himself open to a charge of being too strict and harsh and creates bad feelings with the rest of the crew as well as with this employee. If he does not invoke the penalty he is open to disciplinary action by his own superiors or the union may involve him in a case of discriminatory practice. In the role playing, as is frequently true in actual practice, the foreman usually does not invoke the penalty, but instead brings up the matter of safety violations and gives the employee a lecture on safety. In doing this he overlooks the fact that the employee has been on the job for 20 years and is well aware of the rules. To give a safety lecture to one who knows the job and the rules is to talk down to him. This is likely to be resented and even when safety may be improved temporarily, there will be reduced motivation.

Basically, there are three general reasons why approaches such as this will fail to improve safety and instead contribute to misunderstanding. One reason is that attention is focused on violations and the unfairness of the penalty, and this is not only nonconstructive but often leads to argument as to whether the penalty is too severe or a difference in opinion as to whether a violation actually occurred. This kind of discussion puts both participants on the defensive and new problems are created instead of old problems being solved. The second reason for the failure of such methods is that they do not lead to finding out the real reasons for safety violations, but actually tend to prevent this discovery. The third reason for failure is that the methods are not ways for providing positive motivation for safety, but are punitive and rely on fear motivation.

Since the foreman merely suspects that a violation occurred, the best approach is not to bring up the matter of safety violation at all. All he can learn from his observation is that some men do not always use their safety belts. This is an important discovery and it makes it a problem in his crew rather than an individual matter. If safety is a group problem, it can best be handled by calling a meeting of the whole crew and asking them for their ideas and suggestions on how to improve safety. The current safety campaign will provide ample justification for such a meeting so that no one will feel accused of a safety violation. Further, this puts the problem to the entire group in constructive terms and hence will elicit cooperative problem solving behavior with everyone allowed to participate. Social pressure becomes a force working in the direction of safety if the group can plan their way to promote safety and assist in making the campaign a success.

An alternative approach that often is fruitful is to hear the employee's side, request his suggestions, recognize his superior knowledge of the job, ask his help in setting an example for younger men, and inquire if he is willing to help train new men in safety. In view of the employee's long service, such a request can be made in complete sincerity.

In using this case with many supervisory groups it is found that the majority (93 per cent) do not invoke the penalty if the man admits the violation. It is obviously much more difficult to carry out a penalty than it is to make the rule. This is because the application of the rule brings one face to face with a particular person and then the full impact of the rule and how the penalty creates hardship must be experienced. As a consequence foremen are reluctant to enforce rules. Many give the person another chance and this leads to nonuniformity of practice; others just fail to "see" the violation and this leads to disrespect for rules. The experimental findings showed that when the foreman and the employee had a pleasant visit, the employee indicated he would be more safe in 82 per cent of the cases, and this occurred whether or not the violation was discussed; but when the visit was unpleasant, only 30 per cent said they would be more safe. The whole problem of safety must be reexamined from the point of view of the foreman. Rules made by safety departments and higher management may create as many new problems as they solve. New ways in discipline require the involvement of the foreman, and he in turn can involve his crew. Positive methods of motivation require more imagination and involve more people but they also are more satisfying and more effective.

case 7

The Proper Use of Office Phones

I. Focusing the Problem

Generally speaking, decisions receive better acceptance when employees have a voice in their formulation. In order to obtain employee participation in problem solving and decision making, it is necessary for the supervisor to present the problem to them for discussion. The manner in which the problem is presented becomes an important skill for supervisors who wish to use employee resources in solving some of the day-to-day problems that frequently plague management.

To clearly and successfully pose a problem, a particular difficulty or obstacle must be located. Most situations present a variety of alternate routes to an objective or goal but a problem exists because all the more obvious paths are blocked. A solution would be obtained if any route were opened up, a route without an obstacle were found, or a new or better goal that was not obstructed could be discovered. Thus clarification must occur before problem solving can begin. One way of locating an obstacle or finding a new objective is for the supervisor to ask himself why he feels he has a problem. An obstacle may be located in the group, in the job situation, or even in the supervisor's attitude. When there are several routes or approaches to the solution of a difficult problem, each blocked by a different obstacle, the removal or circumvention of any one of the obstructions is all that is needed. However, some obstacles cannot be overcome, others are circumvented with difficulty, and a few are easily eliminated or circumvented. Successful group problem solving is aided when the leader presents a problem in terms of an obstacle that can be success-fully surmounted. If these approaches fail, it is desirable to explore alterna-tive objectives.

In order to assist the supervisor in formulating a problem for the group, the general principles described below may be found useful. However, it will take considerable practice to make these principles a useful guide so that, if at first sight they do not appear practical to the reader, he should not be discouraged. One may have to violate a principle several times before one appreciates its full worth.

Principle One. A single objective should be located. Only one objective should be presented for discussion. If the supervisor talks about poor quality, poor production, and high accidents as current problems or con-ditions to be remedied, the group may wonder where to begin. Which is the real problem? If the supervisor mentions many deficiencies, group members are likely to feel that things aren't that bad and consequently are likely to let the boss worry about them. When a discussion leader talks about many things that he wishes to achieve it usually means that he has a particular solution in mind. This solution may produce several benefits, but a different solution may yield even more and better ones while also attaining what might have been called the major objective.

Principle Two. The problem or difficulty should be presented in *situational* rather than *behavioral* terms. If a foreman presents a problem by saying, "You fellows are having too many accidents, and the difficulty is that you don't abide by safety rules, and I'd like to discuss what you want to do about it," he will cause the group to immediately become defensive. They will deny the charge, or make the countercharge that the rules are no good, but show no inclination to attack the safety problem in a con-structive manner. A situational approach to a problem in this area might be, "What are the hazards on the job that are causing us to have accidents?"

Principle Three. The statement of the problem should not imply a solu-tion. If a supervisor states his problem to be "the excessive amount of tardiness," he not only is putting a problem in terms of behavior, but he is closing the door to the discovery of a solution. His statement of the problem implies the solution to be "reduced tardiness." The group now can accept or reject the suggestion: they cannot discover a remedy.

A similar but lesser difficulty is created when the supervisor presents his group with a choice. For example, a problem in a power plant may be stated as, "Do you want to clean furnaces the old way or the new way?" Such a statement gives the group little opportunity to come to grips with the problem. Rather the problem solving has been done for the group before the actual meeting and the supervisor is likely to find that his crew makes the choice he considers wrong. In most instances there are more than two possibilities and even when only two exist, much is gained from their discovery by the crew who must do the job.

Principle Four. The problem should be expressed in terms of a mutual interest. Employees may not be interested in discussing methods for increasing company profits or in ways to get the foreman a promotion, but they might be interested in developing their job skills, improving their job placement, increasing the quality of a product, improving service, decreasing accidents, and finding improved work methods. Employees do not expect the company to solve problems that are of interest to employees only, and they might distrust the motives of a supervisor who was trying to do favors for his employees; rather they want a fair give-and-take relationship, without either them or the company taking advantage of the other. What is perceived as fair, however, may differ and this is the cause of misunderstandings and defensive behavior.

The present case will not be carried to the point of solution since the main purpose is to discover the effects that different presentations have on the outcome of a discussion. A combination of Multiple and Single Group Role Playing will be used in order to provide a variety of reactions to different presentations of the problem and a final opportunity to analyze one presentation in detail.

II. Multiple Role Playing Procedure

PREPARATION FOR MULTIPLE ROLE PLAYING

1. All group members should familiarize themselves with the background of the case by reading the General Instructions on page 118. It is often helpful if the instructor reads this section aloud and all others read silently at the same time. At the proper time the instructor should write on the easel the name, age, length of service, and marital status of the office girls as indicated in the General Instructions. In this way the information will be readily available to the participants if desired during the role playing.

2. The members should form into the role playing groups with six persons in each group. As many as five members may be left over and they should be assigned to role playing groups to serve as observers.

3. After the role playing groups have been formed, the instructor should designate one person in each group as the supervisor, Jim Telfer. (This imposed assignment will help avoid face-saving problems if discussions seem to fail to yield results.) When all groups have a leader, the roles for the office girls may be adopted by the remaining members in the group in a clockwise order. The participant nearest the leader will be Betty Northrup; the next on her right will be Mary Olsen; then Irene Wilson; then Mabel Zimmer; and finally, Stella Browning.

4. The supervisors for each group should turn to page 119 and study the role for Jim Telfer. When they are ready to begin the role playing, they should rise and remain standing until given the signal to sit down. The act of sitting down should be taken to mean that they are entering their offices.

5. Participants who are the girls in the office should study the roles for their individual parts. The roles and page numbers on which they will be found are: Betty Northrup, page 120; Mary Olsen, page 121; Irene Wilson, page 122; Mabel Zimmer, page 123; Stella Browning, page 124. All participants should avoid reading any role but their own.

6. All observers should turn to page 125 and familiarize themselves with the section entitled Instructions for Observers.

7. The girls should assume that they are sitting in Mr. Telfer's office for a meeting he has called. He is out of the office at the moment, but when he sits down this will mean that he has entered the office.

8. Role playing will *not* be permitted to continue to the point of com-

pletion. In many instances the discussion may have just gotten nicely underway when the interruption occurs.

PROCESS

1. When all Jim Telfers are standing and have indicated their readiness to begin, the instructor should give them the signal to sit down and begin the role playing. The role playing should be interrupted after five minutes. (This may be a bit difficult because the groups will tend to resist the interruption.)

2. During the role playing the instructor should write the headings for tabulating results on the easel. These are shown on page 126, Sample Table 8. Space should be provided for recording data from all role playing groups separately.

RESULTS OF MULTIPLE ROLE PLAYING

1. The observers of the first group, or role players if no observer is present, should briefly summarize the way the leader stated the problem. The instructor should enter a key word or phrase which characterizes the statement in Column 1. (See Sample Table 8.) Such expressions as "fairness," "abuses," "improving efficiency" are examples.

2. The observer should then report whether he thinks the office girls understand the problem and the instructor should register a "yes," "no," or "somewhat" in Column 2. The girls should then indicate how they feel about the supervisor's communication of the problem. The number of girls who agree with the observer's report should be added to Column 2 and may be regarded as the rating of the observer's sensitivity. If no observers were used, the number of girls indicating "yes," "no," and "somewhat" should be tabulated.

3. The observer or employees should remark on the directness of the approach used by Telfer. Such descriptive words as "circled the problem," "came to the point early," "lots of preliminaries," etc., should be entered into Column 3 by the instructor.

4. The observer and supervisor should present their views on the girls' reaction to Telfer's problem. The instructor should enter in Column 4 the descriptive term that best summarizes the discussion on this point. Such terms as "helpful," "defensive," "hostile," "disinterested," etc., may apply.

5. The observer, or the employees, should characterize Telfer's method, once the problem was stated. Such terms as "permissive," "defensive," "argumentative," "good listener," or a combination of them, may be relevant. The appropriate entry should be made in Column 5.

6. The observer should give his opinion as to (*a*) whether relations between Telfer and the girls became better, worse, or remained the same; (*b*) whether or not he predicts that an acceptable and reasonable solution would have been reached had no interruption occurred; and (*c*) whether the group is divided, unified against him, or unified with him. The instructor should enter items as (*a*), (*b*), and (*c*) in Column 6. Employees should remark on the observer's sensitivity. If the group had no observer the group opinion should be entered in the table.

7. Each group should quickly make a similar report. If more than five groups were used, the remaining groups should turn in their reports and the instructor may complete the tabulating during the break.

REPETITION OF ROLE PLAYING

1. All groups should repeat the role playing episode from the beginning, with the same Telfer attempting to state the problem to his group again. Role players should reread their roles for a refresher, while the Jim Telfers stand waiting for the instructor's cue to begin.

2. The instructor gives the cue for role playing to begin.

3. After four minutes the instructor should interrupt the role playing.

4. Each group reports in turn, whether things went "better," "worse," or "the same."

PREPARATION FOR SINGLE GROUP ROLE PLAYING

1. The instructor should make up a new group of women employees, as far as possible using observers and persons who previously played the part of Jim Telfer.

2. All remaining members in the class should assume that they will take the part of Jim Telfer.

3. After each of the five roles has been assigned, the group should be asked to leave the room, but to refrain from exchanging information about their parts while outside.

4. Five chairs should be arranged in an arc in front of the room. These are for the employees to occupy when they return.

5. Jim Telfer's role should be read by all persons left in the room. Par-

ticipants should also quickly review the principles for stating a problem for group discussion.

6. After arrangements are completed, the girls should be asked to return and take the prepared seats in the order of Betty, Mary, Irene, Mabel, and Stella.

MODIFIED GROUP ROLE PLAYING PROCESS

1. The instructor should ask a Jim Telfer to state the problem to the group, keeping preliminaries to a bare minimum.

2. After a little interaction, the instructor should ask the girls what they like or don't like about the approach.

3. Another Jim Telfer should try his hand under similar conditions.

4. This procedure should be continued for half an hour, with as many Jim Telfers testing their skills as possible.

DISCUSSION OF SINGLE GROUP ROLE PLAYING

1. The most successful statements of the problem should be listed. Three examples would be adequate.

2. The statements should be analyzed from the point of view of the four principles discussed on pages 112–113.

III. Materials

GENERAL INSTRUCTIONS

Jim Telfer is the manager for one office unit in a large insurance organization. His unit serves to make available various kinds of information kept there in large files. Other units in the company call his office for information and data and the office clerks must refer to their records in order to answer these requests. This means that the office has a good many phone contacts with several other units of the company. There are five women clerks who report to Telfer. Each girl is in charge of a particular class of information. All clerks have phones on their desks, but all of the phones are on one line. This means that only one person can use the phone at any one time. There is a buzzer system that is used to call any of the clerks in the group when the call is for them. Usually the person who answers the phone first is the girl with least service. At the present time it happens to be Stella.

The girls in the unit are as follows:
Betty Northrup—28 years old, 5 years with company, unmarried.
Mary Olsen—23 years old, 5 years with company, married, has one-year-old son.
Irene Wilson—20 years old, 3 years with company, unmarried.
Mabel Zimmer—19 years old, 1 year with company, unmarried.
Stella Browning—18 years old, 6 months with company, unmarried.

The peak work load is between 9:00 and 11:00 in the morning and between 2:00 and 4:00 in the afternoon. All girls are allowed a 15-minute relief period both morning and afternoon. However, these are not scheduled since the group is small and the demands of the work change from day to day.

ROLE FOR JIM TELFER

You are the supervisor in a general office of an insurance company. The group you supervise is made up of five girls who work at desks. A good deal of the work involves telephone contacts with company people who require information which various girls have in their files. Since all of the phones are on one line the person who answers uses a buzzer signal and in this way the person requested or who has the needed information can take over the call. You yourself never answer the phone unless one of the girls informs you by buzzer that the call is for you. Ordinarily the girl with the least service answers the phone and then buzzes the girl who can handle the call.

A relief period of 15 minutes both morning and afternoon is given to the girls and this is regarded as adequate for the usual personal needs. You've asked them to take their relief one at a time so as to keep coverage of the office. When the work is heavy, the girls frequently skip their relief.

Your boss complained that you are hard to reach by phone because the line is always busy. He says that he can reach other units which do the same type of work as your unit and he thinks that your group is making too many personal calls. You know that the girls do call out freely and that they receive quite a number of personal calls because, on several occasions, you have picked up your phone and found that the conversation had nothing to do with business. For example, twice during the past week you found *Irene Wilson* talking with her boy friend. You told your boss you would do something about it, and have decided to talk it over with the group first.

Since the load is light from 8:00 to 9:00 A.M.; 11:30 to 1:30 P.M.; and 4:00 to 5:00 P.M. you have used these times for discussions, conferences, and interviews with the girls. Because you want them all in today you set a meeting for 4:00 P.M. It is now time for the meeting and the girls are arriving in the office. You plan to take any remaining calls in your office.

The girls' general performance ratings are as follows:

1. Betty Northrup—Rated slow, but very conscientious.
2. Mary Olsen—Rated very superior.
3. Irene Wilson—Rated very productive, but breaks rules.
4. Mabel Zimmer—Rated as average.
5. Stella Browning—Rated as progressing very rapidly.

ROLE FOR BETTY NORTHRUP

You are very conscientious and seldom go out for coffee during the relief period to which you are entitled. Instead you stay at your desk and work or make personal telephone calls. Some of the girls, especially *Mary*, receive and make calls on company time, but you do not feel that this is right. Lately *Irene* has been getting a lot of calls from a new boy friend.

ROLE FOR MARY OLSEN

You consider yourself as very efficient and perhaps do more work than the others. You have a one-year-old boy whom you leave with your mother while you are at work. She lives just a block from where you live. You frequently call your mother during office hours to check on things and sometimes she calls you. Now and then you talk to your little boy. You enjoy your work and stay with the company even though you could make more money elsewhere. You have to have a job where you can be easily reached by phone.

ROLE FOR IRENE WILSON

You like your present job because the hours are good and your boss is not too strict about things when you are late. You go out nights quite a bit and sometimes oversleep, but you make up for this by skipping your relief period and working faster. You seldom use the phone for personal business as others do, especially *Mary*. Lately one of your boy friends has been pestering you with phone calls. You don't know how he got your number. This has been kind of embarrassing because your boss noticed you talking with him and he obviously didn't approve. This worries you, but what can you do when someone calls you up?

ROLE FOR MABEL ZIMMER

You take your relief periods and go out for coffee in the middle of the morning, and again in the afternoon. You stay away for 20 minutes or so and no one has ever criticized you. You enjoy your phone contacts with people in other departments and often extend your calls while doing business with them. However, you never make purely personal calls and rarely receive one. The phones are for company business and you believe that people should realize this.

ROLE FOR STELLA BROWNING

You are new in the company and like your job. You like to deal with other people and especially enjoy working with the phone. You hope that soon your work will be more interesting. At present you do routine filing, answer the phone just to buzz for one of the girls, and help out when others are on relief or busy. The other girls seem to have a good deal of fun visiting with girls and men in other units. You are gradually getting acquainted so that now you can kid with some of the people who call before buzzing one of the other girls when a call comes to the unit. You never make personal calls, however. You have a relief period mornings and afternoons and make all of your personal calls from the lounge.

INSTRUCTIONS FOR OBSERVERS

1. Make brief notes on the way in which the leader stated the problem. Ways to state the problem are in terms of improving service during rush periods; reducing the number of personal calls; finding a fair way to handle calls; determining what constitutes a justified personal call, etc.

2. Did the office group understand Telfer's statement of the problem?

3. Was the leader's approach direct, or did he hesitate in coming to the point?

4. Keep a list of the types of reaction to the way the problem was put to the group.

5. Observe the conference methods used:

a. Was the leader permissive and receptive to various ideas and feelings?

b. Did all the members have their say?

c. Did Telfer show any defensive reactions?

d. Were there any disagreements between the leader and the group members?

6. Evaluate the approach:

a. Did relations between the leader and the group improve or get worse?

b. Will the group eventually reach a solution?

c. Is the group divided or united against the supervisor?

SAMPLE TABLE 8.   RESULTS OF GROUP ROLE PLAYING

(Use Table for Recording Class Data)

Group	1 Statement of problem	2 Clarity of problem	3 Directness of approach	4 Type of reaction	5 Method used	6 Evaluation of success

IV. Comments and Implications

The problem used in this case is a difficult one because employees are doing something undesirable from the point of view of management and this raises the question of discipline. If the supervisor takes an authoritarian approach he may be met with unified hostility or he may cause his group to divide and as a result lose out on morale. Usually supervisors are aware of the difficulties resulting when they "lay down the law" and frequently postpone facing the problem.

In this situation the supervisor is asked to face the problem, and to confront the group as a whole. Since role players speak somewhat more freely than real-life employees, he is assured of a group of sensitive individuals. They may actually find his remarks to be critical of their behavior even when he had no such intent. A major factor making the employees hypersensitive is the fact that they are guilty of taking advantage of a rather free situation. People who are highly sensitive to criticism or who counterattack vigorously and repeatedly are doing so because of their own feelings of guilt, and the more guilty they are the more righteous indignation they will express. Thus, the timid remarks of a supervisor explaining the issue of the personal use of telephones is likely to be met with silence, hurt feelings, demands that he name people and times, denials, and questions that tend to put him on the defensive.

It is possible that if he permits the group to talk and refrains from accusing them or becoming defensive himself, he may bring them around to the point of discussing a better way to budget their personal calls. This will presume that his own attitude is an understanding one and that he is disinclined to use an authoritarian approach.

Let us examine some of the locations of Telfer's problem. Examination of his role suggests the following possibilities:

1. Some girls use the phone freely for personal use.
2. Telfer's boss thinks the girls make too many personal calls.
3. Telfer finds that girls use phones for talking with boy friends.
4. Telfer has his own ideas of what is fair in the way of the use of company phones.
5. The girls are busier at certain hours than at others.
6. There may be a shortage of phones.
7. Service might be analyzed to determine ways to improve it.

It is apparent that if all these points were made to the girls, a specific solution would be implied: stop personal phone calls. This solution is more extreme than Telfer would impose, but the reaction would be to assume that this is what he wanted. This approach is critical of behavior, it states too many problems, it implies a solution and there is no mutual interest. The immediate counter-solution would be "get more phones."

Let us next take the problems one at a time. The first one tends to accuse some girls of taking advantage of the company. This is critical of behavior and produces defensive responses. If some girls agree with Telfer, the group is split into factions. Some girls might have a mutual interest with the boss, but not as members of a group.

The second problem tends to "pass the buck" to Telfer's boss. Telfer must then either side with the girls or with his boss. A side issue then becomes "Where does Telfer stand?" If he sides with the boss, the problem becomes like number one above; if he sides with the girls, the solution may tend to be in the direction of ways to cover up for Telfer, some of which may be good, others bad from the point of view of efficiency and service.

The third approach to the problem is almost certain to point the finger at particular members of the group. These persons may be no more guilty than others since observed abuses may be no worse than those which go undetected. This way of locating the obstacle in the problem has the following deficiencies: (a) it raises the issue of fair treatment for all employees; (b) it tends to divide the group because of differences in their needs and interests (no mutual interest); and (c) it puts the problem in terms of behavior rather than the situation.

The issue stated in problem four locates the problem in the supervisor's attitude. Even though his attitude may be justified, it is likely the girls will view his remarks in terms of their own attitudes. If, however, Telfer made his attitude a problem for discussion it might be possible to capture a mutual interest as well as put the problem in situational terms. For example, Telfer might say, "I have an attitude that is out of line with yours and even though I try to change it, I find myself unable to do so. We all have an attitude about the use of company phones for personal reasons and I am frequently critical of you when you use them for your own needs, especially during the busy periods. Can we talk about this problem and see if you can help me get a perspective that will make us all more comfortable?"

Problem five states a fact about the situation and this almost directly raises the issue of how to even out the work load and the use of phones. This problem is located in the situation, mutual interests are apparent, and the goal is somewhat different than in the previous problems, but perhaps more inclusive and more worthwhile. The discussion might raise the issue of making personal calls during slack periods, reducing the length of business contacts, and even suggest changes in procedures that will improve efficiency and increase service quality.

Problem six states a goal that might be in the employee's interests but not in the interest of the company. Increasing the number of phones might actually increase the abuses rather than improve the service. It is possible, however, that if Telfer raised the question of whether or not more phones were needed, employees might, after full discussion, indicate that enough lines were now available if they were used efficiently. This could lead to a correction of the abuses, and the reason for the success of this approach would be the fact that the problem is presented in situational terms.

The last problem is stated in terms of a general goal and permits the employees the opportunity of locating the difficulties themselves. If abuses are flagrant, they would be one kind of obstacle in the path to the goal that could be removed. However, the employees might see other obstacles as well, and as a consequence a series of other problems, perhaps unknown to the supervisor, might be solved. This byproduct would be more likely to be attained in a real-life situation than in a role playing case because the former would include richer situational backgrounds to draw from. The merits of this more inclusive goal are that it permits mutual interests to be explored and discussed, it is a situational problem, and no solutions are implied.

It is apparent that problems stated in situational terms are the most likely to prevent defensive reactions and the most likely to contain a mutual interest. However, interest in problem solving might cause some employees to become critical of others. It is at such times that the leader must take the position of protecting the individual attacked. He can point out that we want to solve the problem in a manner suitable to all, that there are bound to be differences in values and viewpoints and that the purpose of the discussion is to understand and resolve the differences. It may be appropriate for him to say, "No one really wants to hurt someone else, so let's just lay our gripes on the table and treat them as kinds of misunderstandings or reasonable differences in opinion." At all times the leader's job is to keep the discussion situation-oriented and to respect differences in needs, values, and attitudes.

case 8

Painters and Inspectors

I. Focusing the Problem

Much of the work of industry requires that men work in teams in the sense that the work of each is in some way dependent upon the work of others. This type of relationship between crew members introduces some problems that are absent in a group in which the work of each person is largely independent of the work of others. The sociological problems of all types of group work include morale, congeniality, attitudes regarding a good day's work, and fair treatment from the supervisor, and these indirectly influence productivity. However, when men work as a team, one employee can directly alter the work accomplished by his coworkers. At one extreme, a team of workers can perform in a coordinated and supportive manner and at the other extreme there can be disorganization and interference.

Whether or not jobs should be organized and structured so that teams rather than independent workers are to be utilized depends on the kind of group structure that can be developed. The team requirement can be a significant asset if supervisors know how to build teams. In one instance the daily productivity of six girls, working independently in that each did $\frac{1}{6}$ of the work that passed on a conveyer, was 25,000 units with 4116 rejects. The job was then modified so that they worked as a team. The first two girls (working on opposite sides and facing each other) did what they wished, the next two did some of the work that the first two left undone, while the last two did the remaining jobs. With the new arrangement it was found that production rose to 30,000, but most important, rejects dropped to 26. No attempt was made to equalize the work in the group. The girls varied their productivity and the last two usually had little to do. They served more as inspectors and a source of relief. From time to time all girls exchanged positions and this was done in an informal manner. One day one of the girls was late and the supervisor put in a substitute, partly to punish the girl for being late. The production and rejects were so bad during the first hour that the original team had to be reinstated. Of interest is the fact that the poor work was not intentional. The whole team went to pieces with the new girl in the group because there were so many things to explain and so many informal arrangements which she didn't like or understand that good coordinated effort was impossible.

The present case deals with a situation in a furniture company in which painters and inspectors work together to produce a finished product. The relationship between them leaves much to be desired and it is the problem of the foreman to see if he can transform them into a cooperative team. To accomplish this it is necessary for him to get at the root of the difficulty and this may require him to use considerable skill to solve a group problem.

The Multiple Role Playing method is recommended since it is desirable to obtain a variety of solutions.

II. Multiple Role Playing Procedure

PREPARATION

1. The General Instructions on page 135 and the layout of the job situation in Figure 3, page 135, should be available to all members of the class. The instructor may wish to read the General Instructions aloud while the class members follow the text. This will insure adequate familiarity with details for all.

2. The case requires seven participants. When possible two or more groups of seven persons should be formed. The remaining persons should serve as consultants. If one, two, or three persons are left over they should act as representatives from one firm, but if four, five or six persons remain, two groups of consultants should be formed, each to give its own report.

3. Role players should decide on roles by having the person nearest the aisle become the foreman, Joe Evans. His instructions are on page 137. From Joe Evans as a starting point, role assignments should be made in a clockwise direction, the sequence being Mike, Ed, Bill, Jack, Hank, and Charlie. Each person should read his own role, shown on one of the pages between 138 and 144.

4. After the foreman has read his part he should stand up and walk a short distance from his group, in readiness to rejoin them. The painters and inspectors should make small signs out of folded sheets of paper and write their names on them, as well as indicate whether they are painters or inspectors. The signs should be placed in the breast pocket, with the writing in plain view. In this manner participants and the foreman will be able to refer to persons by their proper role names.

5. Consultants should read their instructions on page 144.

6. Each group of role players should assume they are in their foreman's office waiting for him to arrive and conduct the meeting he has called. When he rejoins the group this indicates that he has entered his office and the meeting should proceed.

PROCESS

1. When everyone is ready the instructor should give the signal to begin. Each foreman then joins his group and conducts his meeting while consultants study their data and prepare to make a report to the company.

2. Approximately 25 minutes is needed to complete this case. Nearly all groups should obtain a solution. If a few groups are somewhat slower in settling differences than the others the instructor should request them to hurry a bit. Ordinarily the groups require very much the same amount of time so that there is little waiting on the part of fast working groups.

3. While the groups are busy role playing, the instructor should prepare the blackboard for tabulating results. The headings shown in Sample Table 9 (page 145) have been found effective.

COLLECTING RESULTS

1. The consultants should be asked to give their reports first. They should indicate what they consider to be the major cause of the difficulty in the crew and describe what they recommend should be done about it. The instructor should briefly summarize the difficulty and the solution reported and enter the key words in Columns 1 and 2, respectively. (See Sample Table 9.)

2. The consultants should be asked to report on the reception they feel higher management will give their proposal. Such degrees of acceptance as "likely," "probable," "questionable," and "poor" should be entered in Column 3. (Differences of opinion volunteered by other members of the class should be entertained but general discussion of the question should be postponed for the discussion period.)

3. If more than one consultant was present in the group reporting, the number of persons with minority reports should be indicated in Column 4.

4. After the consultant groups (if used) have reported, the role playing groups should in turn present their analyses of the difficulty, the solution reached, the probable acceptance of higher management, and the names of the men (including the foreman) who are not satisfied. The instructor should fill in Columns 1, 2, 3, and 4 as the foremen, with the aid of group members, give their reports.

5. Group members should decide whether the foreman was helpful or a source of interference. If neither word fits, the instructor should enter a question mark in Column 5, otherwise he should enter the appropriate word.

6. A vote should be taken to indicate the number of persons in the group (including the foreman) who think team spirit will (a) go up, (b) remain the same, and (c) go down. These data should be entered in Column 6.

7. A vote should be taken to indicate the number of persons in the group who think production will (a) go up, (b) remain the same, and (c) go down. These data should be entered in Column 7.

DISCUSSION ISSUES

1. The reason for the foreman's effective handling of the problem should be discussed. In most instances the groups will have a success experience and the foreman will conduct a good discussion. Since this degree of skill is not displayed in all role playing cases, there must be a basic reason for the successes in this case. Such factors as previous experience, cooperative persons happening to be playing the roles, absence of conflict in the case, whether or not the foreman had a solution in mind at the outset, whether or not he was inclined to take sides, etc., should be considered and evaluated.

2. The solutions should be examined from the point of view of: (a) cost to company to introduce; (b) organizational changes in status or wages of either painters or inspectors; (c) change in layout of work or situation; (d) change in attitude as a result of discussion.

3. Was there something that all groups agreed to change in the same manner? If so, why was there such agreement on one specific aspect of the problem?

4. What was the main cause of conflict in the group? Persons who played the parts of foremen, painters, inspectors, and consultants should give their respective versions of the real source of trouble.

5. Which of the four kinds of changes listed in the second discussion question could not be achieved by consultants? If consultants were used, what difference in approach is in evidence?

6. Discuss why group members might reject solutions offered by consultants. Will one group of role players accept solutions reached by other groups?

7. A solution of high quality might not be reached by the group. What can a leader do to cause his group not to overlook good ideas? Consider such leader activities as (a) suggesting good ideas, (b) pointing out weaknesses of suggestions considered by the group, (c) asking questions of the group, (d) getting the group to examine several different ideas before settling on any one of them, (e) getting each person to feel free to tell what bothers him, (f) preventing members from speaking their minds, etc.

III. Materials

GENERAL INSTRUCTIONS

You seven men are all employees of the Home Furniture Company. Four of you, *Mike, Ed, Bill,* and *Jack,* are painters; *Hank* and *Charlie* are

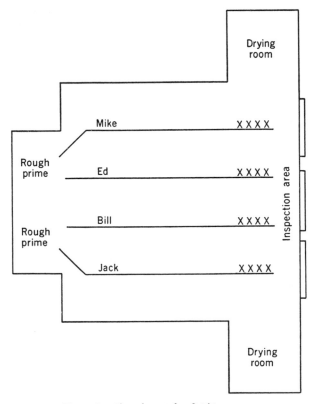

Figure 3. Plant layout for finishing room.

inspectors; *Joe Evans* is the foreman. The painters and inspectors are all union members.

The painters and inspectors are on piece rates which are based on time study units, so that each job gives a specified number of credit points. The inspectors, however, are graded lower than the painters and earn about 15 per cent less per week than the painters.

The appearance of the finished product is naturally quite important.

Inasmuch as the paint dries quickly, the pieces must be inspected and the blemishes and bare spots must be touched up before the finish coat dries. As the job is laid out now, the inspectors spend most of their time applying the rough priming coat. Every half hour they take turns making a tour of inspection, which takes between 15 and 20 minutes. When the inspector finds a flaw, he calls the painter who applied the finish coat. The painter leaves the job he is working on and corrects the defect. This happens very frequently. As a result, there is bad feeling between the painters and inspectors regarding the work. The painters have as little to do with the inspectors as possible. Frequently there are heated arguments over what constitutes a defect and this situation has gradually become worse.

Figure 3 shows the layout of the Paint Room. The X's at the end of each line represent pieces of furniture awaiting inspection. The inspectors walk from the rough-paint area at the left to the right side of the room whenever they take a tour of inspection.

The foreman, Joe Evans, has called a meeting of the crew in his office this morning.

ROLE FOR JOE EVANS, FOREMAN OF FINISHING CREW

You have been foreman of this crew for three years now and it has always been a tough job because of the endless bickering between the painters and inspectors. They wrangle constantly and when a blow-up comes and you try to put a stop to it each party accuses you of taking sides and being unfair. During the past few months things have become worse. Scarcely a day goes by without a flare-up of some kind and some of your best men have threatened to quit. Individually all of them seem to be nice fellows but they just don't get along as a team.

You have called this meeting because you think something must be done about the situation. The painters and inspectors are waiting for you in your office.

ROLE FOR MIKE SULLIVAN, PAINTER

You work toward the rear of the room where the lighting isn't very good. Unless you turn each side of every piece up to the light it isn't easy to tell whether you have covered the whole area or not. Near the windows where the inspectors work there's more daylight and that makes it a lot easier to see. If you had light like that, you could do better work with less eyestrain. Besides, when one of the inspectors yells for you, you have to run over and touch up whatever he wants you to fix and that means dropping what you are working on at the time. This constant interruption makes you sore as hell. There must be some way of doing the job that doesn't require constant interruptions. It's the inspector's job to catch the oversights so it's reasonable that they should have the best light, but how can you make any money on the job when you spend so much time leaving your job at the beck and call of the inspector?

ROLE FOR ED JONES, PAINTER

You are sick and tired of all this bickering with the inspectors and you are going to give Joe Evans an earful about it the next chance you get. Why doesn't he take your side once in a while instead of always sticking up for the inspectors? Something has to be done to put the inspectors in their place. All they do is find fault and make a big fuss about a minor defect. You are sick of being criticized and ordered about by them. If they were painters, they would make more mistakes than you do. As you see it, most of the oversights and poor jobs are caused by the inspectors themselves. They call you over to fix a part you missed and that interruption causes you to overlook something on the job you're working on at the time of the interruption.

ROLE FOR BILL BAKER, PAINTER

You don't like this bickering and quarreling between the painters and the inspectors. The foreman, *Joe Evans,* is a nice enough fellow and tries to do his best, but when painters and inspectors can't get along, there isn't much he can do about it. You have been keeping out of things as much as possible but it is easy to see that something has to be done. The inspectors are really nice guys but they are on the spot. You find that if you are agreeable with them, they are very helpful. The trouble with the rest of the painters is that they give the inspectors a rough time so the inspectors fight back. Every time an inspector calls, one of the painters has to drop what he is doing and go over and correct his mistake and that seems to be the real source of the trouble. If the inspector could just wait until a painter came to a stopping place, things would be better, but you can't expect the inspector to stand around and wait. However, there ought to be some way to eliminate the interruptions. You have observed that there seems to be enough touch-up work to keep a man busy. Maybe if someone were to do nothing but correct defects it would eliminate all of the irritating interruptions and the waste of time in the painters' running back and forth.

ROLE FOR JACK ANDERSON, PAINTER

This bickering between painters and inspectors is getting you down. You don't even feel like talking in a civil way to your own friends on the job and lately you have been grouchy with your wife and the kids when you come home. No job is worth that and unless things get straightened out here you are going to quit. Why should you drop what you are doing and go over and touch up a bare spot just because some damn inspector yells at you? Whenever you tell him you'll fix it up later, the inspector says, "O.K., but I'll have to report it to the boss." These inspectors act as if they had more rank than you do and it's time they were put in their places. They act as if a little oversight is a crime and talk about mistakes and poor workmanship.

ROLE FOR HANK PORTER, INSPECTOR

You and *Charlie Smith* are inspectors and you are both sick of the job. Every time you call a painter over to correct a mistake, he gets belligerent and takes it as a personal insult. Why don't those guys do things right in the first place if they can't take criticisms? You have tried pointing out defects in a nice way but, except for Bill Baker, the painters pull their rank and you have to stand around and wait until they feel good and ready to come over to fix up the defect. You've got your job to cover and if you spend too much time standing around, you are likely to get into trouble. So naturally you start getting touchy with them too. Charlie seems to think there's something about the way the job is set up that is causing all this trouble, but you are satisfied that the whole trouble is with the painters who are stubborn, childish and abusive, and that the foreman ought to lay down the law.

ROLE FOR CHARLIE SMITH, INSPECTOR

You and *Hank Porter* are inspectors. You agree with Hank that it is a poor place to work with the painters on your neck all day long trying to treat you as flunkies. In some ways, though, you can appreciate how the painters feel when you or Hank interrupt them in the middle of a job. You do a lot of painting around your house and often feel resentful and picked on when your wife interrupts your work to have you run errands or won't let you finish a job because your supper is getting cold. As you see it, the painters are nice enough fellows, but it's the job set-up that's wrong. They have their work to do just as you have yours, and yet every time you call one of them over, he has to drop whatever he is doing and touch up the spot he missed. That's the way the job is laid out and it isn't a good way to handle touch-up work at all. Sometimes you actually borrow a brush and touch up some minor spots just to keep out of trouble. It saves time too. You'd like the job of just touching up the bad spots and there certainly ought to be a way to handle that, even on a piece rate basis.

INSTRUCTIONS FOR CONSULTANTS

The Home Furniture Company has hired you to help them solve a problem in one of the finishing crews. Cooperation between painters and inspectors is very poor. There seems to be no particular trouble maker and it has been difficult for the company to place the blame. They feel that you as an expert on team organization and morale may be able to study the matter and come up with some practical recommendations.

In approaching this problem you have made yourself familiar with the job lay-out and the job procedure. You also had an assistant interview each man to find out how he feels about the job. When the instructor gives the signal for others to role play you will work alone or as a member of a team (depending on the number of consultants present in the group) and study the case. Examine the roles of *Mike, Ed, Bill, Jack, Hank,* and *Charlie* on pages 138–144 and assume they are the summaries of the interviewer's reports. Also feel free to refer to the plant layout on page 135 and the General Instructions on page 135 in analyzing the problem and evaluating ideas.

The company wants a practical solution. Try and come up with a recommendation that the company will accept and that you feel will improve relationships between the men as well as increase their productivity.

SAMPLE TABLE 9.   ANALYSIS OF SOLUTIONS TO PAINTER-INSPECTOR CASE
(Use Table for Recording Class Data)

Group	1 Major source of difficulty	2 Solution characteristics	3 Probable acceptance by higher management	4 Names of workers not completely satisfied	5 Did foreman help or interfere	6 Team spirit	7 Production

IV. Comments and Implications

One of the first things usually agreed upon in discussing this case is to improve the lighting. A painter in the group complains about the light and since no one has an opposed view, the idea to increase the lighting is accepted. However, it must be recognized that this is a minor factor and the painter may have made the complaint to justify or defend himself because he feels criticized or guilty. The general dissatisfaction with conditions is the more basic difficulty and specific complaints must not be allowed to cloud the issue. Instead, reactions and complaints should be accepted and respected but, generally speaking, action on them should be postponed until the problem has been more thoroughly explored. Job dissatisfaction in this case seems to originate from a conflict or split in the group.

One of the important sources of conflict in this case is that of status. Painters are superior to inspectors, as evidenced by their pay and by the fact that inspectors aspire to become painters, yet they are placed in a position in which they must appear to take orders from inspectors. This condition makes them hypersensitive, hence they are inclined to perceive the inspector's report as an attack on their prestige. They defend themselves by verbally abusing inspectors, making excuses (poor light), denying errors, etc., and these responses only cause inspectors to be less diplomatic and perhaps more critical of errors. When the inspectors feel they are misunderstood they lose their respect for painters and this in turn degrades the painters more.

Inspection jobs frequently are of this nature and in this sense the case is a typical problem created by low-status persons appearing to give orders to high-status persons. Waiters in restaurants may have similar problems with cooks if they take customer complaints to the cook. Messengers may likewise become the center of a misunderstanding between persons of like or unlike rank and the solution may be as simple as substituting direct communication for the messenger service. In the present case the inspector has to record the error but the job may be changed so that he does not have to communicate the touch-up order to the painter verbally. Some of the solutions reported undoubtedly arranged for a painter to accompany the inspector and make all corrections. It is also possible that a change in attitudes could cause the inspector's comments to be seen as constructive and helpful by the painters. Group discussion in some instances may have supplied acceptable ways by which the inspectors should report errors and oversights.

A second source of disturbance in this case has to do with the fact that the job is laid out in such a manner that painters will have to be interrupted in their work. Interruptions are sources of frustration that frequently are overlooked. Once a person begins work on a task there is set up in him a strong tendency to carry it to completion. Perhaps everyone has been frustrated by interruptions and has reacted with hostility toward the interrupter. The present· arrangement of the job makes it necessary for inspectors to interrupt painters each time they find an error and thereby become the innocent victims of the abuses caused by interruptions. Can the job be arranged so as to reduce or eliminate interrupting painters without the quality of workmanship being reduced? If this can be accomplished the bad feeling between painters and inspectors may be completely corrected and it is also possible that a more efficient method of correcting deficiencies might be invented. Any solution that accomplished even a part of these objectives would be a distinct improvement.

It is important to examine every work situation from the point of view of interruptions. Reducing and preventing them may require reorganizing a job. The desire to carry a task to completion makes an interruption a frustrating experience, but this same desire also introduces a natural kind of job motivation that should be utilized rather than destroyed. Many interruptions are needless and are due to a failure to appreciate the degree to which they disturb people. An awareness of the problem and its importance to the other fellow should reduce these types of interruptions. Frequently the failure to immediately respond to an interruption is taken as a sign of disrespect, whereas in reality it is merely the normal desire to continue a task.

It is the opinion of the authors that this case is likely to lead to a successful solution, not because it is simple, but because the foreman has no preferred remedy. He goes into the conference without having made up his mind and as a consequence he is open minded, receptive to ideas, and a good listener. It becomes apparent, therefore, that a leader can upgrade his conference leadership by simply refraining from thinking through a problem to a solution before he conducts a meeting. His planning should be confined to such functions as (a) finding a way to present the problem without criticizing anyone, (b) determining from his superior the degree of freedom of action he possesses in the matter, and (c) assuming that there are at least two sides to the problem and being of the conviction that the purpose of the meeting is to locate the sources of misunderstandings that exist.

case 9

Unscheduled Coffee Breaks

I. Focusing the Problem

The coffee break is becoming the source of a variety of problems for management. Within the span of a few years the relief period, initially meant as a privilege for women employees only, has expanded into a coffee drinking custom that all employees regard as a right. Not only have non-supervisory employees acquired the need for coffee breaks but supervisors and even higher management personnel are to be found in the company cafeteria in increasing numbers.

Some companies have faced the problem and have scheduled the time and the facilities for coffee breaks. Bell signals sometimes are used to control the time, and various units take their breaks on slightly different schedules in order to reduce congestion in elevators and coffee shops. However, most companies have complicating problems. Some of the questions raised are as follows:

1. Should all types of work receive the same consideration with regard to the frequency and length of the break?

2. Should the same consideration be given to men and women?

3. Should the coffee break represent a rest period and therefore fall near the middle of a work period?

4. If a break interrupts work activity, can employees be permitted to choose the time?

5. Should the company open its restaurants for coffee?

6. How far should the company go in furnishing facilities when there are no restaurants nearby?

7. How can one prevent abuses of the coffee privilege?

Some companies have been reluctant to state a policy on the matter. They fear that an announced policy will sanction coffee and thereby cause persons who previously refrained from going out for coffee to do so regularly. In the absence of an announced policy a good many employees sneak out for coffee, often without coats, and consequently catch colds. Perhaps the biggest complicating factor is that management itself is not agreed on the coffee issue. There are nearly as many attitudes toward coffee privileges as there are company top officials. It is difficult for supervisors and employees to know just how to conduct themselves when the issue remains vague and explosive, and it is difficult for higher management to settle a policy matter when their attitudes are conflicting and unsettled. Since the issue is not one that must be settled by a given time there is a tendency to postpone action whenever sharp disagreements arise. In some instances there may have to be strike threats for coffee breaks in order to bring the matter into the open for a clear-cut decision.

One of the consequences of delaying a decision is its effect on delegation. The coffee problem is discussed as an over-all company matter not only at the top management level but perhaps at every management level below. As a result there is a failure to break down the problem into separate sections or parts in order to determine the issues that should be solved at each level.

If rank and file employees are the worst offenders, how much freedom should first-line supervisors have in setting up a plan that is acceptable to themselves and to the employees? As long as supervisors lack freedom to decide on what constitutes a violation, they tend to be arbitrary and inconsistent. Periodically, higher levels feel that things are getting out of hand, so for a spell they disturb morale by threatening to take certain actions if things do not improve. Like other human beings, top management personnel are fair-minded men and agree that they want to do the reasonable thing. However, if the discussion is pressed further they do not agree on what is reasonable. This then becomes a real source of confusion and leads to non-uniform practices within units or departments of the same company.

The present case deals with some aspects of the coffee problem and should reveal a variety of values. Whether or not this is an issue on which a mutual interest between employees and management can be found remains to be seen.

The procedure is set up for Single Group Role Playing not only because the number of participants is too large for simultaneous group discussions but also because a more detailed analysis is possible when all observers discuss the same incident.

II. Single Group Role Playing Procedure

PREPARATION

1. Thirteen persons can participate in the role playing. (If the class has less than 13 persons, some participants may take the individual instructions for two persons and make them a part for one person.)

2. The instructor should select a class member to play the part of Mr. Johnson, the supervisor.

3. The twelve persons seated nearest the center of the room will become the crew members. They should count off from 1 to 12 and remember their numbers, but each should retain his own name in the role playing scene. (In the event that less than 12 persons are available to play the parts of crew members, the counting should proceed, with each person taking a second number until the twelve numbers are used up.)

4. Persons in excess of the actual role.players should arrange themselves on the two sides of the crew in order to be able to observe the over-all actions. The person assuming the role of Mr. Johnson should remain on the sidelines until the action begins.

5. When the room arrangements are completed, everyone should turn to page 153 and read the section entitled General Instructions.

6. The specific roles or instructions should then be studied by the various participants:

    a. The person given the part of Mr. Johnson will find his role on page 154.

    b. Crew members should turn to page 155 and read the Role for the Crew. They should then decide among themselves who are especially good friends and frequent places together. These subgroups of 3 to 5 persons may assume that their territories lie close together. Finally, crew members should turn to page 156 and read the instructions opposite the number they received when they counted from 1 to 12 during the preliminaries (see step 3 above). Crew members should adopt the suggested attitude, but not feel obligated to reveal it to the supervisor unless they consider it relevant and appropriate to the discussion. They should also feel free to reveal any opinions or attitudes of their own which develop in the discussion.

    c. Observers will find their instructions on page 157. They should feel free to take notes but should not converse with role players.

    d. The instructor should make sure that everyone reads the proper roles or instructions and is prepared for the action. He should observe whether the crew members formed subgroups and read their personal attitudes as well as the roles for the crew. He should also be sure that there is a chair in front of the crew for Mr. Johnson and that Mr. Johnson has access to a blackboard in case he wishes to use it.

e. When the instructor asks Mr. Johnson to join his crew everyone should be in character.

PROCESS

1. The instructor should signal for Mr. Johnson to approach his crew and take the seat provided for him.

2. Role·playing should be allowed to proceed to a solution if progress is being made. In case the supervisor finds himself in serious difficulty, the instructor should rescue him by interrupting the role playing. The observers (or role players if there are no observers) should indicate the reasons for the difficulties and suggest a new approach. After a brief discussion, role playing should be resumed. It is permissible to begin over or to resume from any point that is desired.

3. Role playing, including interruptions, should be limited to 45 minutes or less, unless interesting new developments occur and the group wishes to continue.

ANALYSIS

1. The class as a whole should develop, through discussion, a list of all of the attitudes or arguments mentioned by the repairmen during the role playing. (The instructor should briefly record the items on the blackboard.)

2. This list should be checked with the twelve attitudes planted in the repairmen (page 156). (The instructor should take each item, one at a time, and determine from the group whether or not it is in the list.)

3. Observers (or the group as a whole) should discuss why the list developed contains items not given in the roles or why items supplied in the roles were not brought out in discussion. (Observers should reach a conclusion based upon observation, and the role players concerned with the item should comment on the accuracy of the observer's analysis.)

4. The observers (or the group as a whole) should evaluate the way the supervisor handled each contribution. Descriptive terms such as "accepted," "rejected," "agreed with," "disagreed with," "supplied reasons against," "was sarcastic," "belittled," "ignored," etc., may be written beside

each item on the board. These terms should be checked with the way the repairmen felt.

5. The discussion should be evaluated in terms of whether the crew's feeling toward the company and foreman became worse or better as the discussion progressed.

6. The supervisor, Mr. Johnson, should predict whether his men will be more careful or less careful about coffee breaks as a result of the discussion. Each observer should then voice his opinion. (If there are many observers, this can be done by a show of hands.) Finally, each man in the crew should describe in what manner he will behave differently.

7. In order to demonstrate the difficulties under which Johnson worked, he should read his role to the group.

8. Since this is a difficult problem to handle satisfactorily, a plan for the initial stages of the best approach to the problem should be outlined. This discussion should include (*a*) locating the problem, (*b*) deciding on an objective, and (*c*) methods for confronting the group without producing defensive behavior. (Reference to Case 7 should be made if it has been used by the group.)

9. If time permits, a few of the presentations may be tested by having one person, acting as Mr. Johnson, state the problem to the repairmen and then letting them report how they like it. (A half dozen trials should serve the purpose.)

III. Materials [16]

GENERAL INSTRUCTIONS

Mr. *Harold Johnson* is the supervisor of one of the repair crews in the American Telephone Company. Repairmen are highly skilled craftsmen and take pride in their ability to diagnose difficulties and do high quality work. The men are well paid and most of them regard telephone work as a career.

Mr. Johnson's office is located in a large garage, which is in a central location for the western half of the city. Three other repair crews work out of this garage besides Mr. Johnson's crew. The building not only houses the repair trucks, but serves as a storage place for the supplies used in making repairs. There are also several tool shops in the building as well as offices and conference rooms.

Each repairman reports to his supervisor's office in the morning in order to pick up his individual assignment. When Mr. Johnson has a general problem to discuss with his men he schedules a meeting first thing in the morning before the men get out on their calls. These are held in the conference room adjacent to his office. One of these meetings is arranged for this morning and the repairmen are gathered in the conference room awaiting the arrival of Mr. Johnson.

[16] Based upon case material in Maier, *Principles of Human Relations,* John Wiley & Sons, New York, 1952, 127–129.

ROLE FOR MR. JOHNSON, SUPERVISOR

You are a supervisor in a large utility, the American Telephone Company, and are in charge of a crew of 12 repairmen who leave the garage and go to work in different sections of the city. Your supervisor has reported to you that there has been too much time wasted with men stopping their trucks at restaurants to get coffee in the morning. It seems that groups of them meet at certain places directly after leaving the garage and have a good morning visit over coffee. This condition seems to apply to all groups who work out of garages so that your group has not been selected as a bad example. However, your boss points out that it has gone too far and the abuse must be stopped. The company is very sensitive about public opinion and wonders what people will think if several company trucks are parked in front of a restaurant.

Employees who work in offices are given 15 minutes relief both morning and afternoon. No such arrangement has been made for drivers and outside workers, but it is common for them to take pauses as their work permits. You know men stop for coffee and you did it yourself when you were a repairman. Some supervisors are strict and say that outside workers do not need rest pauses. Thus, the issue of rest pauses has not been clearly defined for workers who work outside the office building. This, you believe, is the main difficulty. Your boss told you that he didn't object to a cup of coffee now and then, but he did object to the organized stops and the long visits with company trucks parked outside.

You have called your group together for a meeting and want to go over the issue with them before they go out on their calls. You feel that if an authorized rest pause were allowed in the middle of the morning, you would be able to improve the situation. You feel it may be necessary to define rest pauses for your group. The production of your crew is slightly but consistently above average. You feel that your men should be given the same consideration as the office workers. The men are waiting for you now. You have meetings of this kind whenever a general problem has to be discussed and clarified.

ROLE FOR THE CREW

You are members of a crew who work for the telephone company. You do repair work on phones that are out of order and make as many as 5 to 8 repairs per day. All of you leave the garage in the morning and return at night. It is your practice to drive off in groups of 3 or 4 and stop your trucks at favored spots for a cup of coffee. When the load isn't too heavy you may spend as much as a half hour having a nice chat. Although the company has never stated a company policy on the matter, you assume it is all right. Office workers get 15-minute relief periods both morning and afternoon, and they can visit in the company restaurants. Your boss has never raised a question of coffee stops and you are not sure that he knows about them. Some supervisors don't permit the men to stop for coffee, but the men do it anyway. The boss has asked you to wait in the garage this morning to discuss a problem. He has these meetings about twice a month.

ATTITUDES OF DIFFERENT MEMBERS OF THE CREW

No. 1. You find that if you go directly to your job, you frequently cannot go to work because customers are not ready and you have to wait. By arriving a bit later you find people more likely to be up and ready for you.

No. 2. You find coffee makes you feel better and you can be more friendly.

No. 3. You like the coffee at the particular restaurant and do not want to get coffee elsewhere.

No. 4. You find that a visit with the crew keeps your interest in the job.

No. 5. You stop for coffee because everybody else does.

No. 6. You often meet your friends who work for another utility at the restaurant and you like to kid with them.

No. 7. You need a cup of coffee in the morning. Your wife is an invalid and you get the kids off to school in the morning. Then you like to relax with the boys over a cup of coffee.

No. 8. You have stomach ulcers and drink a glass of milk rather than coffee. You carry some milk with you but by stopping for milk in the morning your thermos bottle supply holds out.

No. 9. Your girl friend works in the restaurant where you stop and you insist on going to this place a half mile from the garage.

No. 10. You like the group you stop with and join them at these stops.

No. 11. You believe you can work much better if you stop for coffee. It starts the day out right.

No. 12. It is your understanding that coffee privileges are company practice. Office workers have them. Why shouldn't you get your coffee when you want it? You prefer having it early, particularly on cold mornings.

INSTRUCTIONS FOR OBSERVERS

This problem is difficult because it is not easy to state without producing an unfavorable reaction in the crew. It will be difficult for the supervisor to prevent either becoming defensive or siding with them. Observe especially the following points:

1. How is the problem stated? (Consider the principles of mutual interest, use of situational terms, avoidance of implying or suggesting a solution, and presentation of a single objective—see Case 7, pages 112–113.)

2. What caused the crew members to be suspicious or uncooperative? (Take notes on any cause-and-effect relationships.)

3. If the supervisor becomes defensive, what is the first evidence of it?

4. Make a list of the various opinions or attitudes expressed by the crew members, and note how the supervisor deals with each.

5. Make a list of cooperative statements expressed regardless of whether the supervisor observes them or not.

IV. Comments and Implications

This problem is a troublesome one because the objectives are vague and it is difficult to determine Mr. Johnson's responsibility. His boss initiated a problem by asking Johnson to do something about the repairmen spending too much time in coffee spots. He also reacted unfavorably to seeing several company trucks parked in front of a restaurant because of the unfavorable impression this would make on the public. Three quite different lines of action are open to Mr. Johnson. Should he assume that his boss is merely reacting to an incident that he observed and soon will forget when he cools off? Should he take the hint and try to do something without damaging morale? Or should he tell the men of his boss's criticism but take their side and thus protect himself and morale by "passing the buck"? There is no policy on coffee breaks that covers the men, but it is known that repairmen make coffee stops; and since there is no rule covering the number of company trucks that can be parked together, the supervisor has reason to be confused. He has little basis for assuming that men have been abusing certain freedoms that he has previously granted them.

In many ways this is a problem in which the cooperation of the men is desired and not one in which a disciplinary matter should be raised. It is Mr. Johnson's boss who gives the behavior of the repairmen an unfavorable appearance. Of course, it is quite possible that the men have been taking excessive time for coffee, but Mr. Johnson lacks information on this point.

Vague and elusive problems often can be clarified by group discussion, providing clarification rather than correction is the stated purpose of the discussion. A discussion method, which the authors of this volume choose to call *Two-Column Method,* seems to be especially suited to clarifying problems of this sort. Using this method in the present case, the supervisor, after the usual preliminaries and niceties, would state that the coffee issue for repairmen was a confused matter and neither the men nor the company know what is right and proper. This being the case the supervisor could then proceed to ask the group if they would like to clarify the matter in their unit, at least, and then try to come up with some plan that would be satisfactory for the crew as a whole.

Statements of this kind should lead to the establishment of a *mutual interest.* Once the men favored clarification, the discussion should turn to a listing of the benefits of coffee breaks. The supervisor's role would be one of accepting, clarifying, and writing all contributions on the blackboard. He should make sure, too, that the list is complete.

The next step would be one of listing any disadvantages of coffee stops to the company as well as to themselves. This list should also be complete and the supervisor's role should be the same as above. In a utility where revenue rates are controlled, potential public criticism would undoubtedly appear in this list.

With both lists complete, the problem could be stated as follows: How can we set up a coffee plan for ourselves that will retain as many of the benefits and exclude as many of the disadvantages as possible? This statement is in *situational terms* and it does not imply a particular company answer. Thus it satisfies the criteria for good statements of problems discussed in connection with Case 7.

The Two-Column Method is especially useful when a group is inclined to be defensive. It is important to give persons who may feel attacked ample opportunities to get their viewpoints out in the open and have these accepted as soon as possible. If this is not done, their attitudes will appear as criticisms, objections, and distractions throughout the discussion. The first listing should always be the one dealing with the items that concern the group. Once the group feels they have been understood, they can examine alternative viewpoints objectively and then proceed to engage in constructive problem solving. The Two-Column procedure has the additional advantage of creating a situation which makes it rather easy for the supervisor to listen and accept the attitudes of the men. While engaged in listing the items, he is forced to listen and made to try to understand each item so that he can post it. As a result he has less time and interest in making evaluative judgments.

There are many vague problems that arise from time to time which could be prevented if first-line supervisors had more freedom and if the problems of delegation were clarified. Improper delegation makes supervisors rigid and too concerned with consequences to listen and respect contributions.

The process of delegation is a downward kind of communication. Beginning with the highest level involved, each supervisory level should solve only such aspects as directly concern them, and pass as much of the problem down the line as possible.

For example, in dealing with any large or general question, policy and financial aspects of the problem should be decided at a top level. Thus the decision to permit a reasonable coffee break and whether to furnish a place to drink coffee may be made at this level. The next level might then implement the meaning of "reasonable" by setting up general practices for various types of work, making allowances for different distances from the restaurant, conditions in various company buildings, etc. At the same time a staff committee might work with the restaurant manager to arrange for personnel, extra equipment, etc.

Problems involving uniform practices, employee attitudes, job coverage, and control of time should be delegated to levels that are most concerned. The important thing is that each level that delegates a function will be willing to accept the decisions on the problem issues they have delegated. It is this willingness to accept decisions of subordinates that determines the extent and degree of delegation an executive is able to make. It is important that enough of the problem remains so that first-line supervisors will have freedom for problem solving beyond that of policing. It should also be added that in passing different aspects of the problem down the line, there is an opportunity for group decisions to be made at each level by the group involved.

Management today is overworked and one of the skills that must be learned, if this pressure is to be relieved, is that of delegation. Delegating duties and routines is not enough. Only when freedom for certain decisions is delegated will responsibility be stimulated and developed. If superiors and executives fail to accept the decisions of subordinates, this needed responsibility will not be developed. Instead, subordinates will try to anticipate the wishes of their superiors in order to prevent criticism or rejection of their recommendations. Thus, instead of solving problems, subordinates try to please their bosses. To get the full worth of a subordinate's talents, the executive must discover the abilities of his men and then delegate accordingly. On some matters a subordinate may not decide as his superior would have hoped. On these occasions the decisions sometimes may be better and sometimes worse than would have been the case had the superior been in charge. However, the process of executive development requires that a superior be willing to balance the good with the bad on such occasions because the screening of ideas does not promote responsible problem solving and growth.

This stage of full delegation is a gradual process. At first, duties only are delegated. As a man's knowledge grows, he should be encouraged to participate in an increasing number of matters. Finally, full delegation is given in specified areas and he is held responsible for the *results,* not for making decisions that his superior approves.

The areas in which a supervisor has freedom for decision making and problem solving should be made clear to him. Without this understanding he is inclined to be unimaginative and routine in his management techniques.

case 10

The Storm Window Assignment

I. Focusing the Problem

Ordinarily, job assignments can be made in a fairly matter of fact manner. Job descriptions and good employee training methods have clarified the duties and requirements of a given job both for the supervisor and for the individual worker. However, the lack of controversy does not mean that an assignment is accepted wholeheartedly. The job performance of a given individual may vary considerably depending upon whether the employee accepts his duties with enthusiasm or with resentment. Some jobs are assigned in such a way that they give a man a feeling of pride, whereas others give him a degrading feeling. Are there ways of asking a man to do a job that influence the manner in which he will react?

Many factors contribute to the status of a given job or duty and some of these may be beyond the supervisor's control. Pay, conditions of work, amount of judgment required, degree of confinement, and the relative job status of neighboring groups affect the way an employee feels about his job, but the supervisor can influence these aspects only indirectly. However, a supervisor can control his discussion of job progress and his manner of giving a particular job assignment to a man, and these acts have direct effects on an employee's job pride and job execution.

The problem of job assignments becomes even further complicated when the men in a crew perform diverse duties and execute different functions from time to time. The foreman must now be fair in his assignments and neither expect too much from certain individuals nor underestimate the

161

capacity of others. He must not only be sensitive to the abilities of the men and the complexities of various job assignments, but also be aware of the prevailing social values of the group and the individual attitudes of the workers. This seems like a big order but sometimes the effort is rewarded not only by increased employee satisfaction but by the prevention of work stoppages, grievances, and hard feelings.

The present case is purposely set up to be difficult and will challenge the wits of the best supervisors. The background conditions are set up by means of a skit which poses a problem situation. Role playing begins where the skit leaves off. We have called the procedure the Skit-Completion Role Playing Method. The Single Group Role Playing Procedure is prescribed because this case is a fairly complex one and emphasis is placed upon observing the skills needed for discovering attitudes and feelings in other people. Getting the other fellow to talk about the real reasons for his actions rather than giving excuses demands a high level of skill.

II. Single Group Role Playing Procedure

PREPARATION AND READING OF SCRIPT

1. Six persons are needed to play the parts in this case. The background for actual role playing is created by the reading of a prepared skit.

2. A table and four chairs should be placed in the front of the room to form the setting for the scene during which the script will be read. The chairs may be arranged around the three sides of the table so that the audience can observe the action.

3. Four participants will be the crew members, Jack, Steve, Dave, and Bill. As soon as they are selected they should seat themselves around the table in a clockwise direction. A fifth person should be selected to read the part of Mr. Brown, who plays the role of the foreman in the prepared script. He should remain away from the table until such time as the script calls for his entrance.

4. After the crew members are seated around the table, presumably having their noonday lunch, the instructor should select the individual who will be the foreman during the role playing scene. In order that he may know the names of his crew, each person at the table should write his name on a piece of paper and display it in front of him. When these details are finished this role player should leave the room and study the section entitled Instructions for George Brown, on page 167. He is to remain outside the room during the reading of the script.

5. All members of the class not assigned a part will act as observers and critics.

6. When the stage is set, the instructor will read aloud the description of the scene on page 168.

7. While the instructor reads the descriptive scene, the four crew members should open their books to page 168 and be prepared to read their lines from the script. They should go through the business of reading the newspaper and finishing up lunch.

8. When the instructor has finished his introduction, the reading of the script should proceed and continue through Parts I and II to the end.

9. After the script has been played through, the foreman should return to his former place in the group. However, the crew members should resume their places at the table in preparation for the role playing episode.

PREPARATION FOR ROLE PLAYING

1. To introduce the scene, the crew members will reread the lines through Part I only. This is to the point of the foreman's entrance. This time, the person who has been out of the room will play the part of Mr. Brown, the foreman.

2. Steve, Dave, and Bill should go through the business of returning to their work by going to their seats in class. They should remain there until they are called back by the foreman for one reason or another. The foreman may wish to talk with any one of them alone or all of them together.

3. During the rereading of the script, Part I, the instructor should check with the role player (the new Mr. Brown who is still outside the room) to determine whether he understands his role. Mr. Brown should be reminded that he is to walk up to Jack, who is still seated at the table, and take up the matter he has in mind. How he introduces the job assignment will be left to his discretion.

4. Mr. Brown, the role player, should stand in readiness for the instructor's signal to enter the room. He should be out of earshot, however, while the preparations for role playing are in progress.

5. Observers should pay special attention to the crucial skills of the foreman. Knowing the case, they can be sensitive to oversights as well as to the successful and unsuccessful actions he takes or the expressions he uses.

ROLE PLAYING PROCESS

1. As Jack reads the last line of the script in Part I, the instructor should signal Mr. Brown to enter the room as required in the script. Brown should approach Jack who is seated at the table.

2. All actions and lines spoken should be without script.

3. Role playing should continue until some decision is reached. If this decision involves a next step, such as discussing the matter with other persons, this next step should be role played, too. It is desirable to role play all the steps that would be taken in a real-life situation in order to settle the matter one way or another.

4. Occasionally the foreman will look for an out by postponing the decision for a week or so. In such instances he should either try again (assuming the time has passed) or a different George Brown should attempt to solve the problem. If an observer is used to take the role of Mr. Brown, it should be understood that he has the advantage of knowing the background of the problem. This knowledge makes the task easier, but many obstacles still remain.

5. If the interview with Jack has been fairly successful, the foreman usually decides he must take up the storm window problem with the crew as a whole. In case this does not occur, the instructor should intervene. He can have the role playing continued by requesting Mr. Brown to take his problem with Jack to the crew. It is suggested that he call the men back to the table in front of the room for a discussion. Whether or not he includes Jack in the meeting should be left for him to decide. Perhaps he and Jack should talk it over to determine whether it is best for Jack to be present or absent.

ANALYSIS OF ROLE PLAYING BETWEEN MR. BROWN AND JACK

1. How soon did the foreman recognize that he was dealing with a problem that involved the other employees? Indicate the ways in which this recognition was reflected in his behavior. The foreman should comment on the accuracy of these observations.

2. What significant things did Jack say or do that the foreman failed to respond to or follow up? List the items. Jack should supplement the list but confine himself to points he actually expressed in the role playing. (Role instructions should remain private unless they are brought out in the role playing.)

3. The foreman should express his opinions on the following questions:

   a. Is Jack more stubborn than most people would be under the same circumstances?

   b. Is Jack a desirable employee?

   c. What are Jack's real reasons for trying to avoid the assignment?

   d. Would Jack put up the storm windows if he were told that failure to do so meant discharge?

(If several foremen role played parts of the case, each should answer these questions.)

4. The discussion method should be used to develop a list of skills that the foreman used in arriving at the correct answers. A list of the skills he might have used to obtain more valuable information should be prepared and discussed.

ANALYSIS OF ROLE PLAYING WITH MR. BROWN AND CREW MEMBERS

1. Why is it better to exclude Jack from a meeting of this kind? Discuss the difference between Brown's role as a referee and a discussion leader.

2. Did Mr. Brown put the crew members (Steve, Dave, and Bill) on the defensive? How?

3. What did the foreman learn from the group that he did not learn from Jack? List the items.

4. What were the outstanding skills demonstrated by the foreman in conducting the group meeting? Discuss and indicate points of agreement and disagreement.

5. If the group failed to cooperate, what were the basic causes of this failure? Observers only should participate in developing this list.

6. Crew members should voice their opinions of the observers' analyses and make corrections and additions.

7. Did the foreman take Jack's side and thereby assume a stand against the crew members? The foreman, observers, and crew members should give their answers in turn.

8. What would the foreman have to do to remain impartial? Participants and observers should discuss together.

9. What caused Jack to be in a face-saving situation? Discuss, using Jack as a sounding board to test the accuracy of the observers' analyses.

10. Under what conditions can the foreman find himself in a face-saving situation in this case?

11. What determines whether or not the crew members find themselves in a face-saving situation? Crew members should indicate the way they felt in this regard.

III. Materials

INSTRUCTIONS FOR GEORGE BROWN

You are a foreman in the Plant Department in the Telephone Company and have your headquarters in a small town. The department is located in a two-story frame building, which contains the operation equipment. Your crew is required to maintain the central office equipment, repair lines, install phones, etc. A total of four men report to you and this number is entirely adequate. There is no handyman or janitor in the group because there are practically no upkeep problems. When a door lock needs repairing, someone fixes it when he has a spare moment. Often you fix little things if the men are busy. However, now and then certain jobs have to be assigned. The accepted practice you have followed is to give these assignments to the man with least seniority. This procedure is followed quite generally in the company, and no one has even questioned it as far as you know. You put in your share of dirty work when you were new. One of these special jobs that comes up periodically is the washing and putting up of storm windows in the fall and taking them down in the spring. There are 12 windows on the first floor and 12 windows on the second. The windows are stored in the basement. There is a new aluminum ladder there that you just got. That ought to make the job easier.

The time is late October. It's getting chilly, but today is a nice day. It is a good day to put up the storm windows. *Jack, Steve, Dave,* and *Bill* are in the other room having lunch. They bring their lunch and have coffee in thermos bottles. You got them this table, and they seem to like eating together. It's time for everybody to get back to work so it's a good time to assign the job. Steve, Dave, and Bill have just left for work so Jack is now available.

Jack has the least seniority so you are going to ask him to do the job. Since you have had no replacements for some time, Jack has done this job several years and knows the ropes. He is a good fellow and cooperates nicely.

SCENE

Telephone crew men work out from a small building which contains central office equipment serving the community.

Although *Jack* has been on his job five years, he has the least seniority of anyone in his group. Many of the unpleasant jobs around the place fall to him because he is the newest man. One of these is washing and putting up the storm windows each year. There are 12 windows on the first floor and 12 on the second. Jack has made no complaint about this assignment.

However, after lunch one day when he is sitting around with other members of the group, the conversation takes an interesting turn. Let's listen in:

SCRIPT: PART I [17]

JACK: Boy, that hot coffee really tastes good.

STEVE: Yeah, it's getting chilly outside. Almost had a frost last night.

DAVE: Yeah! Time to finish my fall plowing in the south forty.

BILL (*reading from paper*): Here's a special on storm windows that looks good. It's time to start thinking of them. By the way, Jack, seems to me we ought to be getting them put up here, too, shouldn't we?

STEVE: Sure, Jack, get out the Glasswax and shine 'em up.

JACK: Aw, quiet—you guys are always riding somebody.

DAVE: What's the matter, don't you like the job?

BILL: Takes all your brains to do it, doesn't it, Jack?

STEVE: That's a real stiff job! You have to figure which one to wash first and which end is up.

JACK: Why don't you dry up?

DAVE: What's the matter, Jack? Don't you like the job?

BILL: Aw, it can't be that! He's been doing it for years. He must like it.

JACK: You know well enough I don't like it.

STEVE: Well, you keep doing it, don't you?

JACK: I'm going to get out of it, though.

DAVE: This I must see!

BILL: What are you gonna do—jump the seniority list?

JACK: I don't know, but I think it's time somebody else did it.

STEVE: Not me!

DAVE: You don't hook me on it either. I had my turn.

JACK: For how long? One time, that's all you ever did it.

BILL: And that was enough, too, wasn't it, Dave?

STEVE: What's the matter, Jack, can't you take it?

JACK: Sure I can take it. I have for five years.

DAVE: Looks like you're gonna make it six years, too.

[17] Dialogue taken from Maier, *Principles of Human Relations,* John Wiley & Sons, New York, 1952, 114–116.

JACK: Not me—I'm through doing all the dirty work around here.
BILL: What do you mean dirty? You get your hands clean, don't you?
STEVE: Who do you think's gonna put 'em up—Brownie himself?
JACK: I don't care who does it but not me any more.
DAVE: Aw, you talk big but you can't make it stick.
BILL: Yeah, Jackie, you're just asking for trouble.

SCRIPT: PART II

Mr. Brown, foreman, enters.

BROWN: Hello, fellows (*Greetings from the group*). Say, Jack, could I see you a minute? I don't want to break up the lunch session. (*Looks at some papers in his hand.*)
DAVE: Oh no—it's time we were getting back on the job, anyway.
JACK: Yes, sure, Mr. Brown. (*Picks up paper bag and waxed paper and throws in basket.*) Anything wrong?
BROWN: No, Jack, not at all. I just wanted to remind you about the storm windows. (*Laugh from group at the table.*)
JACK: What about 'em?
BROWN: It's starting to turn cold, Jack. I think we ought to get 'em up. Don't you think so?
DAVE: This is where we came in, fellows, let's go. (*All but Jack leave.*)
JACK: Yeah, I guess *somebody* ought to put 'em up.
BROWN: Will you take care of that, Jack—anytime this week you can manage it.
JACK: I wanted to talk to you about that, Mr. Brown. I'd rather not do it this year.
BROWN: Do what—put up the storm windows?
JACK: Yes, Mr. Brown, I'd rather not do it.
BROWN: Well, Jack, it won't take you any time at all. I'll get you some help to get 'em out when you're ready.
JACK: It isn't that—I just don't want to do it again. I've had it for five years. It's not fair!
BROWN: Well, now—I know how you feel, Jack. I know it's a chore but somebody has to do it.
JACK: If you don't mind—count me out this time.
BROWN: But I do mind, Jack. We've got to do what's part of our job. And you're the newest man here. Be a good fellow.
JACK: I've been the goat around here for five years. Let somebody else do it for a change.
BROWN: Now, Jack, the others had their turn.
JACK: For how long? Dave did it once and so did Bill. I don't think Steve ever had to put 'em up. Why pick on me?
BROWN: Nobody's picking on you. We just have to do our jobs, that's all.
JACK: Well, it's not part of my job—it's not in my job description.
BROWN: It *is* part of your job, and I think we have a right to expect you to do it.
JACK: **Count me out.**

BROWN: Now, be yourself, Jack. I don't want to be unreasonable about this thing, but after all—

JACK: Well, I think I've done my share.

BROWN: We can try to work something out on this next year, but suppose you take care of it this time.

JACK: No, Mr. Brown, I just don't feel I ought to do it.

BROWN: Jack, I think I'll have to say you've got to do it.

JACK: I'm sorry, but I'm not going to do it this time.

BROWN: It's an order.

JACK: Not to me it's not.

BROWN: You'll take an order, Jack, or get out.

JACK: You're not firing me. I quit and you can give your dirty job to some of those other guys. I'm through.

END

IV. Comments and Implications

According to the script, the attempted job assignment ends in a case of insubordination. Most observers regard this outcome as unfortunate because they understand Jack's reason for not wanting to put up the storm windows. Unless one knows the reason for Jack's resistance, he appears as a stubborn and uncooperative person. As a consequence, the foreman who role plays the case must be sensitive to the feelings behind Jack's evasive behavior if he is to solve the problem.

The first evidence of Jack's deepseated problem is the determined stand he takes. He is unresponsive to coaxing and flattery, and he makes his decision quite clear at the outset. Ordinarily a person leaves himself more opportunity to back down or to alter his views. This determined stand should be the foreman's cue not to move too quickly, otherwise he may place himself in a face-saving situation such as the script related.

When the foreman asks Jack for reasons, he is likely to get excuses, and much time can be wasted in evaluating the merits of the excuses offered. Usually Jack says he has done the job more often than the other men. This makes the assignment unfair and may put Mr. Brown on the defensive. To discuss this point leads nowhere because it is not Jack's reason for refusing the assignment. That this is an excuse may be detected from the fact that Jack repeats himself many times without making it clear to the foreman why he cannot put up the storm windows just once more.

Jack may also talk about the job as if it were beneath him, and again no progress is made if the foreman points out that everyone does some work he doesn't like or that is below his level of ability. This excuse, like the one above, fails to convince the foreman that Jack should not do the job. If the foreman learns no more than this about Jack's resistance he will be inclined to believe that Jack is stubborn and adopt the opinion that he will put up the storm windows if he is ordered to do so.

If Jack tells about the kidding he received, the foreman may recognize that he has a group problem. This information adds to the foreman's understanding of Jack, because he will see that Jack's status in the group is threatened by the assignment and that he will be kidded even more if he puts up the storm windows now. However, he will find Jack unresponsive to his show of understanding or any remarks about everyone learning how to take a little kidding. Most men will not throw away a good job because of such kidding, and although this comes closer to Jack's true reason, it lacks the essential ingredient.

Jack cannot put up the storm windows because he told the group he wasn't going to put them up this year. The others in the crew also have committed themselves—they want to see Jack get away with it before they believe it. Here we have an emotionally loaded situation. The problem is how to save face for Jack and, to a lesser degree, for the crew members. If the foreman has gone too far in committing himself, he too may be in a face-saving situation.

In order to get Jack to talk about his problem and his feelings, Mr. Brown must try to understand Jack's position. This means he would have to refrain from judging Jack and instead use such skills as are needed to make Jack feel free to talk. Jack has done a silly thing in maneuvering himself into this face-saving position and he will not talk about it too readily. Listening skills and the ability to respond to and reflect Jack's feelings would be essential to the foreman's success.

When the foreman recognizes that he has a group problem, either because he learned about the kidding or the face saving, he will change his approach. He realizes that he must call the group in for a discussion and his first decision will have to do with whether or not Jack should be present. It is the writers' belief that Jack should not be present at the meeting. He is one faction in the controversy and has already had his say. It is now the foreman's task to discuss the matter with the other faction.

The psychological reason for not wanting Jack to attend such a meeting is that his presence would tend to cause the foreman to become a referee in the dispute. Each faction would try to win him over and the gap between them would gradually be widened. It would require a very gifted person to conduct a meeting with all men present and not give any one the impression that he was partial. If he took sides, or merely appeared to, the problem of face saving would be aggravated. Usually the foreman is sympathetic with Jack by the time he takes the problem to the group and this very understanding of Jack becomes the cause of trouble with the group. If the foreman is seen by the others to be partial to Jack, they will take a defensive position; instead of confiding their contribution to Jack's stubbornness they will show hostility toward Jack.

In order to hold a meeting without Jack in attendance, the foreman will want to obtain Jack's permission. To do this he would have to guard Jack's confidence and not make a squealer of him. Jack usually gives his permission fairly readily.

An effective way to introduce the group problem to Steve, Dave, and Bill is for Mr. Brown to state that he has a problem with Jack. He can point out that when he asked Jack to put up the storm windows Jack became very resistant, so much so that it appears that he would quit before he would put them up. The foreman can point out that he doesn't feel he should press the matter further until he talks things over with them.

This type of introduction causes the men to ask questions in order to determine whether Jack has squealed. When they are satisfied that this is not the case and realize how seriously Jack has been hurt, they soon supply information regarding the incident that occurred during lunch. If the foreman shows understanding and the discussion focuses on how to save face all around, a cooperative solution usually emerges. The group must make some concession to Jack for this particular year, and it should involve Jack's helping with the job in order to prevent him from feeling that he has been ostracized. *Soluti*

Once Steve, Dave, and Bill indicate their willingness to cooperate, the foreman must take the solution to Jack and gain his approval. Only after he approves can he be brought into the group without there being the risk that the difficulty may be reopened. If Jack fails to accept the group's offer, the foreman can obtain the group's support for dismissal action. Whether or not this becomes necessary depends greatly upon the foreman's skill in handling the matter.

There are many instances where problems of insubordination are unintentionally aggravated by the actions of the supervisor and could have been altogether prevented. Such instances frequently occur when a supervisor takes cooperation for granted. There are numerous conditions under which this assumption is unjustified, such as when cooperation implies inferior status or some other form of unequal sacrifice. In most work situations there are tasks which are assigned to persons of low status in the group and through this association they become degrading. In addition, almost every group acquires or develops certain values which form the basis for determining the status of the individual members. A supervisor who is alert and sensitive to the status factors in the situation can thus avoid many actions which might lead to serious misunderstandings. *recommendation*

Despite a supervisor's best efforts to prevent problems of insubordination there are times when such problems arise, and when they do it is necessary to view the employee's refusal as a new problem which must be given first consideration. This implies an understanding attitude and respect for the employee's feelings. Such conditions will remove the pressure from the employee sufficiently so that he can express his own feelings and gain relief from them, thus enabling the supervisor to learn the nature of the problem. Once this has been accomplished there is usually little difficulty in working out a solution together so that the employee no longer feels compelled to refuse his cooperation.

This case may be regarded as typical of a class of problems which center around face saving. Many of the grievances and walkouts which are described as conflicts regarding overtime, disciplinary action, insubordination, safety violation, or discriminatory practices merely had their origins in these areas, but the heat and the feeling were introduced later when someone found himself in a face-saving situation.

case 11

The Problem of Overtime

I. Focusing the Problem

It is a common practice in business and industry to give preferential treatment to employees with long service, high job grades, or skills of which there is a limited supply. In some instances such special consideration is the result of organized employee pressure for security and recognition and is received by employees with varying degrees of acceptance. In other instances it represents ways by which management seeks to reward persons with desirable attitudes and to solve its own problems, but instead of being accepted by employees, it creates status problems and dissension.

As a rule, the principle of differentiating in some manner among employees is understood and accepted by all concerned and *by itself* creates no problem. However, the *manner* in which the awards of preferential status are distributed is a frequent source of misunderstanding and conflict. Usually the issues center around fairness and group membership problems. In order to meet these difficulties, it is customary for management to establish rules and regulations designed to apply equally to all. Formal procedures for insuring impartiality are ways to avoid charges of favoritism, but at the same time new problems are sometimes created because impartiality and fairness are not the same thing. The former is based on detached intellectual judgments of a legalistic nature and ignores needs and feelings of individuals. The latter is based on subjective feeling judgments, which are emotional in nature, and recognizes the unique needs of each individual.

In the New Truck Dilemma (Case 1) the problem was to determine the fair way to share a desirable thing. In this case, the problem also hinges on fairness, but men are having something taken away from them. The superior's problem is to find a fair way to share a sacrifice. A group of employees have been having overtime as a regular thing and have set patterns of living on the increased income. If the overtime is reduced, it will be felt as a wage cut and may be taken as such even though no legal or logical claim for this can be substantiated.

Another special feature about this case is the fact that two classes of people belong to a single group and as a result, a social status issue is incorporated. If the group splits into two factions, grade A and grade B workers, then the issue no longer will center around the real problem. Instead it may degenerate into a struggle to determine which faction will become the stronger and win. If this results, there is reduced cooperation and the problem of fairness, instead of being solved, becomes the source of a new and persistent problem.

In order to throw everyone's attention on the way these conflicting factors of status, potential group division, and the fair method to divide a sacrifice develop and influence each other, the Single Group Role Playing Procedure is prescribed. It is important that the various cause-and-effect relationships be analyzed.

II. Single Group Role Playing Procedure

PREPARATION

1. In order to acquaint everyone with the background of the case, the section entitled General Instructions on pages 180 f. should be read aloud by one member of the class while the others follow the text. The portion at the end in which the names, job grade, and length of service are given should be copied on the blackboard or easel so that they will be visible to everyone.

2. Seven members of the class will be needed to fill the roles in this case. The instructor should select these participants as a group and give them a few seconds to decide among themselves who is to play the role of foreman. Beginning in a clockwise direction from the position of the foreman, other members may assume their roles by taking them in the order listed on the blackboard. Each person should announce who he is and place a tag with his name on his person. The remaining class members will be observers.

3. Each participant should study his particular role and avoid reading any other role. The roles and the pages on which they will be found are as follows:

John Willets, foreman, page 182
George Hamill, page 183
Hank Davis, page 184
Pat O'Connor, page 185
Jim Jaffe, page 186
Walt Jarvis, page 187
Sam Simpson, page 188

4. The observers should read the section entitled Instructions for Observers on page 189.

5. While class members are studying their parts, the instructor should prepare the setting for the role playing scene. It is suggested that he arrange a table and seven chairs in the front of the room to represent the foreman's office. The table and one chair will be for the foreman and the other six chairs should be placed in a semicircle in front of the desk for the participants who will be crew members. If no table is available, a chair may be used to designate a desk. The arrangement of furniture should form an arc in front of the room, with the foreman's desk on the

left and a bit forward, so that the observers will be able to see the faces of most of the role players.

PROCESS

1. When the participants have finished studying their roles and are ready to begin the scene, the six crew members should enter the previously prepared office. In order to facilitate identification of the role players they should seat themselves in the same order as their names appear on the easel, starting with George Hamill in the chair at the left, next to the foreman. It should be assumed that a meeting has been called in the foreman's office and that he has not yet arrived.

2. After the crew members are all seated, the participant who plays the part of the foreman, John Willets, should enter his office and conduct himself accordingly.

3. The role playing will usually require about 40 minutes. The participants should be allowed to finish whenever possible. However, if the role playing deteriorates into stubborn wrangling and the foreman seems to have lost control of the meeting, the instructor should interrupt the scene. In such instances the participants may wish to discuss the difficulty and offer advice to the foreman. Action can then be resumed with the same foreman or a different one, depending upon the decision of the participants and instructor. Role playing should always be terminated before it becomes boring.

4. After the role playing has been completed, the instructor should move to the front of the room to conduct the analysis of the role playing. The participants should remain in their seats in the front of the room so that they retain their identity in the case.

EVALUATION OF SOLUTION REACHED

1. The participants, including the foreman, should in turn report whether they (a) disapprove, (b) approve with reservations, or (c) fully approve of the solution. They should not give their reasons at this time.

2. The observers should compare the degree of acceptance obtained for the group solution with that for a solution that might have been reached by a typical foreman.

3. The quality of the decision should be evaluated from the point of view of (a) its practicality and (b) its degree of detail or completeness. Observers should discuss these issues, whereas the role players should

remain in character and should contribute only to the extent of answering questions regarding their feelings and opinions.

4. Role players should report whether or not they agree on what the solution requires of them and what will happen when the solution is put into effect. Any disagreement on detail indicates inadequate communication.

ANALYSIS OF THE CONFERENCE PROCESS

1. The observers should scrutinize the foreman's statement of the problem to see if they can determine what he did or failed to do which caused the workers to assume a problem solving approach rather than take a defensive position. Role players should evaluate the observers' comments but be careful to confine their remarks to the initial part of the conference.

2. Should the foreman have mentioned the amount of overtime reduction that he wished to accomplish? After observers have expressed their views, each worker should indicate the amount of overtime he feels would have been fair. These responses may be totaled to determine how much of a reduction would have been acceptable to the group as a whole. The effect on the group's behavior of stating the goal should be evaluated according to the way it influences their views of fairness.

3. Conflicts within a group may arise because of factors that existed before the conference or they might be caused by the way the conference happened to shape up. The latter type of conflict should be prevented. Were there any conflicts that could have been avoided? All class members should participate in locating conflicts within the group.

4. A potential conflict between the two grade A workers was planted in the roles. What did the leader do or fail to do to prevent this from being a disruptive influence?

5. The group might separate into two factions with grade A workers on the one side and grade B workers on the other. What factors caused or prevented this conflict from becoming serious?

6. Observers should enumerate the needs and feelings of the various workers that were expressed during the discussion. The participants should then in turn report the needs and feelings they did not express by reading from their roles.

7. Some time should be spent in discussing the importance to the foreman of obtaining a knowledge of these needs before attempting to solve a group problem.

8. What part can the conference leader play in bringing the needs of various individuals to expression? Discuss by illustrating what the foreman did or might have done in this case.

9. Observers should report instances in which they feel the foreman took sides for or against some members of the crew. Crew members should supplement the observers' reports by telling how they felt about the foreman's biases.

10. Develop a list of the things the leader did to upgrade the quality of the solution. Continue the list by adding suggestions of what might have been done.

III. Materials

GENERAL INSTRUCTIONS

You are a group of six pattern makers who work under the supervision of *John Willets*. Your work is steady and pay is good. Each of you has been getting considerable overtime work during the past 6 months for which you get time and a half pay. You are divided into two groups with respect to skill and wages. Two of you (classified as grade A) have high skill ratings and do the more complex features of the job and your pay is 20 cents an hour higher than that of the others who do the more routine type of pattern work (classified as grade B workers).

The job is such that the two highly skilled workers begin a job and the rest of you carry it to completion. The grade B workers' overtime is thus dependent upon the overtime of the grade A workers. As a result of the way the jobs are divided the four grade B workers get somewhat less overtime than the grade A workers. A typical example is an average of 8 hours per week overtime for the grade A workers and an average of 6 hours overtime for the grade B workers.

Ordinarily the arrangement is to give the men in each grade as nearly equal an amount of overtime in a week as possible. If a particular individual turns down overtime in one week the next man in seniority gets the first chance at the extra overtime. If there is a slackening up of work the man with least seniority is likely to take a reduction first. Since there has been plenty of overtime work lately none of you feel you want any more. As it now works out each of you usually stays late a few evenings a week and some of you come to work for 3 or 4 hours on Saturday morning. You usually alternate the Saturday work with one grade A man and two grade B men, taking turns. It is the company's practice to pay for the evening meal when you work overtime at night. The allowance for the meal is $1.50. The company prefers that no one work more than 2 hours overtime at nights. Usually you work until 6, take a half hour off for eating and then finish work by 7:30 or earlier. The foreman of course gets most of the overtime since he has to stay with the men when they work late and also comes every Saturday.

The names of the men, their grade, and their years of experience are as follows:

John Willets, foreman   25 years
George Hamill, grade A   23 years

Hank Davis, grade A   20 years
Pat O'Connor, grade B   12 years
Jim Jaffe, grade B   10 years
Walt Jarvis, grade B   10 years
Sam Simpson, grade B   8 years

ROLE FOR JOHN WILLETS, FOREMAN

You are the foreman of the crew of pattern makers. For the past 6 months you have averaged about 10 hours overtime, which represents nearly 40 per cent extra wages for you. You have been banking this extra money and now have a good savings account. However, your wife complains that all work and no play is wearing you down. You work every Saturday morning and about 2 hours on 3 nights a week. Although you like to save money, this way of doing it is a bit rough. However, other departments depend on your work so you have to do this much overtime work to keep up with the needs.

Lately however the company has become economy minded. Although business is good the profits have declined and company officials are worried. It is recognized by management that your unit needs more overtime than others, but the other day your boss told you of a ruling requesting all departments to reduce overtime work. He suggested that all foremen increase the efficiency of their crews so that overtime can be cut at least 10 per cent. You told your boss this was a reasonable request. You have called your crew together to discuss the question of reducing overtime. You feel that the foremen may be judged on their crew's efficiency and therefore you are anxious to more than meet this request.

ROLE FOR GEORGE HAMILL—GRADE A JOB

You and *Hank Davis* are the two grade A workers. For the past 6 months you have been getting at least 8 hours overtime a week and this has added about 30 per cent to your income. With this extra money you have made a down payment for the purchase of a cabin you can use for hunting and fishing on weekends and during vacations. It has always been your ambition to get a place up north. If this overtime keeps up you will be able to take off a little extra time for these hobbies. You wish you could get as much overtime as *John Willets*, the foreman, and you look forward to becoming a foreman someday. Since you have the most seniority in your group this is not an idle dream.

Hank Davis takes nearly as much overtime as he can get. He really doesn't need the overtime since his tastes are rather simple. You have tried to get him to turn down more of his overtime, and let you at least cover some of his Saturday work this winter, but he won't commit himself. Long hours don't bother you and you would just as soon work as waste your evenings and Saturdays this winter. Your wife is gone a lot. She spends a good deal of time with your two married daughters who live on the other side of town so you frequently have to eat out or prepare your own meals. By working overtime evenings the company furnishes the meal and this saves you trouble and time. Some of the men don't care too much for so much overtime so they have been trying to keep up with the job and reduce the overtime. You feel that they are going to spoil things. After all you do a reasonable day's work and your overtime efforts give the grade B boys an opportunity to earn something extra. These days everybody needs an extra source of income.

ROLE FOR HANK DAVIS—GRADE A JOB

You and *George Hamill* are the two grade A workers. Lately your wife has been complaining about the fact that you work so much overtime. She also has a job and resents it if you can't spend time with her. Since the two of you make a good income you prefer not to work overtime. If George weren't such a selfish person you would give him more overtime. He's always asking you to give up overtime so he can get more, but not long ago when you really wanted a Saturday off he wouldn't help you out because he wanted to go fishing. It's a one-way deal with George so you have decided to take your share of overtime so as to keep up with the job. If George would work a little harder the two of you could keep up with the job by working no more than a couple of evenings a week. Under such circumstances you would give George all of the overtime. You prefer working Saturday mornings if you have to take overtime. This would leave your evenings free so that you and your wife could get out more. You have no children.

ROLE FOR PAT O'CONNOR—GRADE B JOB

You have five children ranging from one to ten years in age. With living expenses what they are you are dependent upon working overtime. The extra 6 or 8 hours a week at time and a half pay that you have been getting lately has increased your income so that things are now running very well. Your wife got a new coat last month for the first time in years.

Jim Jaffe has been very decent with you. When overtime needs are less than usual he turns down some of it so that you can have more. Your main worry is that the overtime won't last. You admit that you have been slowing the job down a bit to insure overtime.

You prefer taking your overtime in the evening. In this way you get your meal furnished by the company and save carfare. If you always worked 2 hours extra three or four nights a week that would be ideal.

ROLE FOR JIM JAFFE—GRADE B JOB

You don't particularly care for overtime, but the company has the custom of dividing it up evenly among the men so you cooperate to help things out as much as you can. Now and then when you have a good excuse you turn down some overtime so that *Pat* can have it. He really needs it.

You are single and enjoy your freedom. You like to have your nights free because you are active in a number of clubs. You don't mind working Saturday mornings now and then but the evening work has interfered with your other activities and it has gotten you down. Some of the fellows in your group are actually slowing down on the job so as to keep the overtime up. It seems unfair that you should be inconvenienced because others want overtime. The trouble with most people is that they are developing standards of living way beyond their class. Of course some of the fellows like *Pat* and *Sam* have heavy responsibilities but that is no excuse for making everyone work overtime.

ROLE FOR WALT JARVIS—GRADE B JOB

As anyone else you like a chance to earn a little extra money. Since you are doing the same work as *Pat, Jim,* and *Sam* you feel you should have the same amount of overtime as they do. Ordinarily *John* and *George* get more overtime than the rest of you. They sort of have a controlling position. When they work 8 hours overtime it gives the rest of you about 6 hours overtime. If they really did their job each one of them could keep two of you busy. They are no more entitled to 8 hours overtime than you are. If that ratio keeps up you're going to get the grade B fellows to slow up a bit so that each of you gets 8 hours overtime. Why should George and *Hank* get all the breaks? You know for certain that George is dragging the job out. You are sick of having him say he's doing you and the others a favor by working overtime so that there will be plenty of overtime for you fellows. He sees to it that he gets most of the overtime and he needs it least of all. It's not that you are dependent on overtime. But why should it not be divided fairly? If George and Hank can't do enough to keep up with you fellows they could let Pat O'Connor help out. He knows just as much as they do and there is no reason why such a sharp distinction should be made between grade A and grade B men. The important thing is to get the job done right.

You are married and have a five-year-old daughter. As you increase your earnings your wife can always find ways to spend the money. She likes nice things and you are glad to let her spend money when you have it. The extra earnings have made it possible for you to get a television set and some new furniture.

ROLE FOR SAM SIMPSON—GRADE B JOB

The extra overtime has been a big break for you. Your wife had twins two years ago and hasn't been well since. You still are paying off on the loan you made to pay the doctor and hospital bills and you have had a succession of doctor bills since. Now your wife needs an operation which will really fix her up. If you knew the overtime would keep up for another 6 or 8 months you would feel free to go ahead with the operation.

Although the overtime work makes it difficult for you to help out at home as much as you would like you feel that the extra money is more urgent.

The 6 hours a week overtime that you usually get is entirely satisfactory, but less than that would upset your plans. Since you have the least seniority you would be the first to be cut if overtime needs fell off. There seems little chance that the other men would let you have extra overtime since there are men with more seniority who take all they can get. So far you haven't told your troubles to anyone because your tough luck is your problem. However, it would be nice if there weren't such a rigid way of dividing up overtime. Since you have the least seniority you are not in a good position to suggest a change because the others might consider you a trouble maker.

INSTRUCTIONS FOR OBSERVERS

1. Did the leader get to the point of the discussion quickly and state the problem clearly? Would you have started the discussion any differently? Make brief notes on your observations.

2. How did the crew members react in the beginning of the discussion? Did anyone show hostility? If so, which crew member did this? Toward whom was the hostility directed? What were some reactions of those to whom it was directed?

3. Was there criticism of the foreman or the company's way for allocating overtime? If so, how did the foreman react? Did the foreman or any crew member show defensive behavior at any time? What reactions were there to this? Was the leader permissive and acceptant of differing points of view?

4. To what extent was there a free airing of feelings in the group? What did the leader do to help or hinder this? In what part of the discussion did this occur?

5. What was the solution of the group, if any? If none, what are some of the reasons for it? What is the extent of agreement on the solution? Did everyone contribute in some way to the solution? To what extent did the discussion make for improvements on the solution in the future? In what ways might this method of handling overtime problems make for greater efficiency than a solution developed by the foreman? Which method will result in better human relations?

IV. Comments and Implications

In this particular case the group is set to be on the defensive and they will stand together and protect their inefficiency as well as their overtime if criticized by the foreman. Even a mild suggestion that they increase their efficiency may be met with the charge of a speed-up. Before the crew will be ready to think constructively, the foreman must explore how they feel about overtime—both the good and the bad features. He must accept and respect these views and continue to explore for others because some of the important ones represent needs that are not so readily expressed. Often the ideas expressed first in a discussion are excuses or justifications for opinions held. Disagreements in the group should be accepted as problems to solve and the foreman should be careful not to take sides or to express personal views.

Once the needs and the feelings of the group have been expressed and analyzed, the foreman can talk about a problem the company has—that is, the need to cut costs. He can ask the group to express their views of what would be fair to everyone and keep as the objective a solution that will give everybody a more satisfactory experience with the company. If the group does not respond immediately and readily, he should be patient and above all avoid becoming defensive. Once his behavior becomes defensive, things will go from bad to worse. If the group shows a lack of interest in the problem, he can indicate a solution that will reduce costs without increasing efficiency—that of hiring an extra man and thereby cutting out 40 hours of premium overtime pay.

The crew should set its own goal of how much they can increase efficiency and this goal will be more exacting and strict than management could request or even demand because the crew would not have to fear the consequences. When someone else sets the goals, the group fears what it will lead to. The important thing for the leader to do is to see that in solving the problem of efficiency, the personal needs of the men will be given a full hearing. Individuals who appear greedy may have to be protected from the force of social pressure and face-saving opportunities may have to be created for others, but through it all the foreman must play the part of a peace maker and never act as a judge.

Examples of the way the foreman may prevent critical comments of group members from becoming sources of conflict are as follows:

   a. If George talks about taking some of Hank's overtime, in case Hank expresses a willingness to give up some, the foreman might restate George's position by saying "I think George means that he's willing to take any overtime that happens to be left over, not that he thinks he's entitled to increase his overtime while others take a cut."

b. If Walt criticizes the grade A workers for trying to create overtime for themselves, the foreman might restate his argument by saying, "Walt seems to feel that we can reduce overtime somewhat and perhaps if we can see our way clear to get a fair amount of overtime and satisfy our special needs, we may find ways to take a reduction that won't inconvenience anyone. At least you feel that some saving can be made—is that right, Walt?"

c. If George has indicated that he won't stand for a grade B worker doing grade A work, the foreman might give him a face-saving opportunity in the event that all workers favor giving Pat some grade A work, by stating, "I don't think the group wants to upgrade Pat all at once, rather they are suggesting that Pat will be a grade A worker only when he is temporarily on a grade A job. Obviously he'll need help and training and perhaps we can sometime work out together a schedule for giving him any further training he may need."

Once the group agrees to take a reduction in overtime and feels that improved efficiency can keep production up, the problem of implementation arises. This requires the setting up of a tentative schedule for a trial run. Such a schedule will show each person how the change will affect him. It is at this point that the foreman can see to it that communication has been adequate and cause the problem solving process to go into specific practices rather than remain at the level of generalization. This is the stage of carrying the discussion from policy to practice. It is important that solutions of this kind remain subject to change. Since the needs of individuals change, the decisions that satisfy needs must also be subject to change. One of the most common faults with solutions to this problem is the failure to implement the decision that the group feels it has reached.

This case is of special interest because it shows how the sharing of a hardship tends to be solved on the basis of needs rather than on the basis of least seniority. Length of service is more likely to be accepted as a method for distributing privileges than lack of seniority is accepted as a method for distributing hardship. This is one important difference in the way groups behave when they are given the freedom to solve job problems. It is common practice in companies to give the junior man low status jobs, believing that the crew wants it that way. However the crew takes this attitude only when it feels the need to defend itself. When the crew participates in decisions about changes, defensive behavior rapidly disappears.

Status in a group is one of the important nonfinancial incentives in a group and many jobs have acquired a low status rating not merely because they were routine, dirty and simple, but also because they were performed by low status employees. Jobs performed by senior workers may acquire high status by the same process.

Interviewing
the Union Steward

I. Focusing the Problem

In discussions regarding the training needs of supervisors it is generally recognized that human relations principles help a supervisor to deal with his subordinates; and a little further discussion usually reveals that the same principles will help him to deal with his associates and even his superiors. Can these same principles be applied to working with the union or its representatives? Many feel that a company's dealings with the union differ basically from its dealings with an employee. Getting along with the union is a problem of negotiation and this circumstance creates two opposed viewpoints as well as two opposed interests. Success in this kind of relationship seems to require each party to bluff, exaggerate, and make demands in excess of what he hopes to get. Many people expect to haggle when bargaining, and some people even think that failure to haggle is a sign of naïveté or weakness.

Although the number of persons involved with bargaining issues is small a large number of management personnel do have face-to-face dealings with union stewards. In the instances of conflict the steward is expected to represent a union member and the supervisor is expected to represent the company. Does the existence of these two positions require a conflict in viewpoint or is there a possibility that a mutual interest exists? Must the nature of a conflict inherently be such that one party is right, the other wrong; and that as a consequence of this kind of choice one side must win and the other lose; or is it possible that a mutual interest exists and both parties involved can gain something but not at the other's expense? Making gains is what occurs when an understanding is reached between two people.

The purpose of this case is to explore the possibilities for reaching understanding when a conflict between the union and management is in the making. Because solutions to such conflicts frequently lead to dissatisfactions, grievance procedures have been worked out in order to prevent the dissatisfaction from leading to strikes or walkouts. Experience with the present case will be relevant to the problem of determining whether legalistic approaches (grievance procedures and legislation) are more promising than human relations approaches (interviewing and conference skills) in improving industrial relations.

In the present case, an employee has been caught smoking ten minutes before quitting time despite the existence of a "no smoking" rule that is well known to the employees. The foreman has imposed the prescribed penalty of a three-day layoff for the infraction. The employee, feeling that he is being discriminated against and treated unfairly, has reported the incident to his union steward. The steward, after discussing the matter with the employee, feels that he should take the matter up with the foreman. The initial interview is thus between the foreman and the steward. On the basis of the result of this interview, the foreman or the steward will then interview the employee, Jack Stevens.

The problem can be role played using a single group, or the whole audience may be allowed to participate. The procedure described here is the one to follow for Multiple Role Playing the case.

II. Multiple Role Playing Procedure

PREPARATION

1. To give the background of the case the General Instructions found on page 199 should be read. It is best for the instructor to read them aloud while the participants follow the printed page.

2. The group should divide itself into subgroups of four members each. (Persons who are left over may act as extra observers in one or two groups. If three persons are left over a group of three persons may be used, thus omitting the role of an observer.)

3. After the subgroups have been formed and seated in groups the roles are assigned by group agreement. One member in each group is to be foreman, another member becomes the steward, a third member becomes the employee; the remaining person (or persons) serves as the observer.

4. When all persons know the part they will take in the role playing, each should study his special role. The page assignments are as follows:

Foreman, Bill Schultz, page 200.
Union steward, Joe Burns, page 201.
Machine operator, Jack Stevens, page 202.
Observer, page 203.

5. When the stewards have studied their role they should stand to indicate they are ready to enter the foremen's offices and are prepared to begin the scene.

6. When all persons playing the part of the steward have indicated they are ready by standing up the instructor will give the signal to begin. In this manner all groups will role play simultaneously.

7. The role playing will start off with the discussion between Schultz and Burns. The employee is not yet present. However, when Burns and Schultz have finished, one of them calls in the employee and handles the matter further, depending on the agreement that has been reached in the initial discussion. The observer should take the responsibility of seeing that the purpose of this second interview is understood.

8. Observers should form their own opinions as to how participants feel since their personal views will be requested later on.

PROCESS

1. When everyone is ready the instructor gives the signal to begin. Mr. Burns should step toward Schultz to indicate he has entered his office.

2. About 15 to 20 minutes will be needed for the interview between the foreman and the steward. When over half of the pairs have finished or at the end of 18 minutes, the instructor should give a two-minute warning signal and ask them to terminate the interview in the period allowed. The observers should see that their groups follow the schedule and contact the instructor if the instructions are not clear.

3. As soon as all interviews between the foreman and the steward have ended, the interview with Jack Stevens takes place. This interview will be conducted by either the foreman or the steward, depending on what was agreed upon in the first interview. In some cases, all three may want to be present. The observer should take the initiative and see that this second interview is held.

4. From 5 to 10 minutes will usually be sufficient for the interview with Stevens. If some interviews are still going on after 8 minutes, a two-minute signal should be given at the end of which time the interview should be terminated.

5. During the role playing of the scene, the easel should be prepared with the headings illustrated in Sample Table 10, page 204, so that the results can be recorded.

COLLECTING RESULTS OF INTERVIEWS

1. The observers of all groups should describe the solution reached. They should conclude by reporting whether or not they feel that the foreman and the steward reached an agreement that was mutually satisfactory. (The instructor should tally the number of "yes" and "no" responses as provided for in Line 1 of Sample Table 10, page 204.) The solutions reached may be listed elsewhere.

2. The stewards should report whether or not they intend to file a formal grievance. (The instructor should indicate the responses in Line 2 of the table.)

3. The Jack Stevens in each group should tell whether or not he is satisfied with the results of the interview between Burns and Schultz. (Indicate the responses in Line 3 of the table.)

4. Jack Stevens should next report his satisfaction with the interview

he had with either Burns or Schultz or both. (This report should be tabulated in Line 4.)

5. Each observer should report whether or not he feels that the foreman tried to understand the steward's viewpoint and situation. (Indicate in Line 5.) He should supply examples from his notes to support his opinion.

6. The observers should report whether the steward showed an appreciation for the foreman's situation. (Indicate results in Line 6.)

7. The instructor should summarize the results briefly, reflecting the views that have been expressed as to the effect of the interview on relations between the foreman and the other two men, and the extent to which the problem was helped or hindered by the types of interviews that were held.

ANALYSIS OF INTERACTION

1. Observers and foremen should express their opinions on what they saw as the foreman's problem in this interview. (The instructor should fill in items *a*, *b*, *c*, *d*, and *e* under Line B1 of Sample Table 10, depending on the nature of the report. Other items may be added if needed.)

2. Observers and stewards should report what they saw as the problem for the steward. (The instructor should tally responses to list of items appearing under Line B2.)

3. The class as a whole should discuss what the foreman might gain and also what he might lose by sticking to his decision to punish Stevens. (The instructor should accept all views and list gains in one column on the easel as illustrated under Line B3.)

4. Determine number of each kind of group member who feels that the losses will exceed the gains if Stevens is laid off. (Indicate under Line B4 of table the number of "yes" and "no" responses.)

5. The instructor should summarize the views of the group briefly, highlighting the ways in which the situation was loaded against a constructive and satisfactory solution.

DISCUSSION AND EVALUATION OF VARIOUS APPROACHES

1. Discuss the attitude and the approaches the foreman might take in order to make the interview with the steward more constructive. (The stewards should participate in this discussion to evaluate how they would react. The instructor should accept all views and summarize.)

2. Since each party in the interview is inclined to favor his solution, how

can either one of them get the interview around to the solving of the problem they are faced with?

3. Jack Stevens' objective is to escape punishment. Can each of the participants "give in" on something so that everyone will save face? Evaluate some suggested solutions.

4. Discuss the significance of the fact that many members in the crew smoke despite the "no smoking" rule. (Attitude differences will be shown, with some taking a blaming attitude toward the employees and the foreman and others taking a constructive attitude. The instructor may wish to use leading questions and probe as necessary to bring out the fact that the prevalence of smoking makes this a group problem. All viewpoints should be respected.)

5. How can the problem of smoking rule violations be presented to the crew so as to lead to problem solving? Can Jack Stevens be made an exception without fear that respect for the rule will be lost in the future?

6. If the problem is not solved and a strike eventually is threatened because of the disciplinary action, will higher management support the foreman or will they "give in," believing that the incident is not worth the trouble? Discuss.

III. *Materials*

GENERAL INSTRUCTIONS

Bill Schultz has been a foreman of a work group in a factory for the past two years. All of his 18 men work on individual machines and each has his quota of work to do for a given day. It's Bill's job to see that the men have work to do and that everybody keeps busy.

There is a company rule prohibiting smoking while on the job, and the company regulation covering this matter stipulates a three-day layoff for violation of this rule. "No Smoking" signs with the penalty stated are in plain view throughout the shop. Smoking is permitted in the wash room, but men cannot be away from the job an unreasonable amount of time. There is no obvious fire hazard.

During the past year men in other groups have been laid off for smoking and others have been reprimanded for spending too much time in the wash room. Everyone knows that men steal a smoke now and then. Whether or not a man gets caught and punished for smoking depends greatly on the vigilance of the foreman. Since Bill Schultz took over this group no one has been disciplined for smoking, although three years ago both Hank and George received a layoff.

In case a man is disciplined by a foreman he can go to his steward and protest. The usual procedure is for the steward to hear the man's side because he is responsible for seeing that everyone gets a fair deal. If he feels a man has a case he takes the matter up with the foreman. He can speak to the foreman alone or take the aggrieved man with him. If the foreman and the steward cannot reach an agreement the steward makes a written complaint. The matter now becomes a formal grievance and is handled in accordance with the procedure prescribed in the union contract. Both management and union prefer to settle disputes before they reach the formal stage.

ROLE FOR BILL SCHULTZ, FOREMAN

You have imposed a three-day disciplinary layoff on *Jack Stevens,* one of your men, for violating the "No Smoking" rule. Both the rule and the penalty for violation have been in effect for as long as you can remember and are well known by everyone, and it is accepted as one of the working rules of the company that anyone caught smoking on the job is subject to a three-day layoff.

Despite all this, you have some reason to believe that at least a few of your employees occasionally smoke on the job. However, you can't watch everyone all of the time; you have other things to do. Besides, you don't want your employees to feel that you are spying on them. Since you have been on the job, there have been no flagrant violations of the rule so that you have felt no need to make a special issue of the matter. There is no obvious fire hazard, but you have been told that insurance costs are higher when smoking is permitted in a shop. You realize that it is your duty to see that discipline and proper respect for company regulations are maintained, regardless of what you may personally think of a rule.

In this instance, you caught the man on the floor with a lighted cigaret, in plain view of several other employees, about 10 minutes before quitting time. He offered no excuses, admitting that he was familiar with both the rule and the penalty. He protested vigorously, however, when you imposed the three-day layoff, saying that he was going directly to his steward, *Joe Burns,* about it.

You are in your office now. You notice that Joe is walking across the floor toward your office.

ROLE FOR JOE BURNS, DEPARTMENT STEWARD

Jack Stevens, who is one of the men in the work group in which you are the steward, has just told you that his supervisor, *Bill Schultz,* has given him a three-day disciplinary layoff for violating the "No Smoking" rule. You are aware of the rule and you know that Jack is too. Nevertheless, in this case you feel that the penalty is entirely unfair, uncalled for, and would work a hardship on Stevens' family. Most of the other employees take a quick smoke now and then, but Schultz has not been strict in enforcing the rule.

Jack admitted he was smoking, but pointed out that he smokes less than the others. Besides, it was close to quitting time and he had worked fast to get his job finished. Jack has always been thoroughly honest with you and you are convinced that Schultz is merely trying to use Jack as an example to the others instead of handling the case on its merits. Technically, Bill may have a case. There is a "No Smoking" rule. Actually, however, no one seems to know why the rule is necessary. There is no fire hazard. The only possible excuse for it is to keep people busy working. The fact that smoking is permitted in the wash room is not a true smoking privilege since men are disciplined if they spend too much time in the wash room. Schultz is a bit new on the job and he'd better learn that he can't enforce rules just when the mood hits him.

You feel that you can best handle the matter by going to Schultz without Jack being along. You are walking toward his office now.

ROLE FOR JACK STEVENS, MACHINE OPERATOR

Bill Schultz is the foreman of your work group. He has just caught you smoking and has given you a three-day layoff for violation of a "No Smoking" rule. You know of the rule and the penalty but quite a few of the men smoke and they haven't been penalized. You actually smoke less than the others. In this type of work you feel that there is no fire hazard and consequently you don't know why the rule is necessary.

You had worked fast and finished your job ten minutes early so you had time for a smoke before quitting time. Since the foreman wasn't around, you didn't bother to go to the men's room but just leaned against a post a few feet from your machine. As soon as Bill imposed the three-day disciplinary layoff you went to your steward, *Joe Burns,* and told him your story. You just can't afford to lose three days' pay. Burns agreed with you that it was unfair and suggested that the foreman may be using you as an example. He said he felt you had a grievance case and that he would go to bat for you. He's on his way to see Schultz now.

INSTRUCTIONS FOR OBSERVERS

The following items are furnished as a guide in observing what goes on in the interviews.

1. Interview between the foreman and the steward.

   a. Did the foreman avoid arguing?

   b. Was the foreman acceptant of the steward's feelings?

   c. Was the foreman open-minded about things?

   d. Did the foreman give the impression that he wanted to do the fair thing?

   e. Did the foreman avoid a hostile or defensive attitude?

   f. Did the steward have an opportunity to express himself freely?

   g. Did the discussion become more friendly or more hostile in the second half than in the first half? Regardless of which one is true, why did things turn out as they did?

   h. Was a solution reached? What things helped or hindered reaching a solution?

2. Interview with Jack Stevens.

   a. Which man, the foreman or the steward, interviewed Stevens?

   b. Did the result of the interview between the foreman and the steward satisfy Stevens?

   c. What effect do you think this interview will have on relations between the foreman and the other members of his crew?

   d. Has the problem of smoking been solved or have new, more serious problems been created as a result of this interview?

   e. Is the prescribed three-day layoff penalty a help or hindrance to the foreman?

SAMPLE TABLE 10. ANALYSIS OF INTERVIEW WITH UNION STEWARD

(Use Table for Recording Class Data)

	Number	
	Yes	No
A. 1. Was a satisfactory solution reached?	——	——
What was the solution (verbal report)?		
2. Will a grievance be filed?	——	——
3. Is Jack Stevens satisfied with result of first interview?	——	——
4. Is Jack Stevens satisfied with how he was interviewed?	——	——
5. Did the foreman try to understand the steward's views?	——	——
6. Did the steward appreciate the foreman's situation?	——	——
B. 1. Foreman's problems:		
a. Felt his action was justified — couldn't convince steward.	——	——
b. Couldn't back down but wishes he could.	——	——
c. Caught in squeeze between employees and management.	——	——
d. Had to enforce a bad rule — no choice.	——	——
e. Talked himself into trouble.	——	——
2. Steward's problems:		
a. How to convince foreman he was unfair.	——	——
b. Must defend Stevens having given him encouragement.	——	——
c. Uphold position as steward.	——	——
d. See that Stevens got fair treatment.	——	——
3. Possible results of foreman sticking to his decision to punish Stevens:		

Gains	Losses
Stop the smoking.	Stevens may quit.
Save face.	Other employees strike.
Approval of higher management.	More undercover smoking.
	Other rules violated.
	Less cooperation.
	Lower morale.

4. Losses exceed gains	Yes	No
a. Foremen	——	——
b. Stewards	——	——
c. Observers	——	——
d. Workers	——	——

IV. Comments and Implications

The foreman's dilemma is that he is likely to feel that he cannot back down without losing face. However, if he insists that the decision stand he will probably have a formal grievance to deal with and bad relations with his crew. The steward is likewise in a face-saving position with the employees. He has gone to bat for Stevens and it is hard to back down. Thus the situation is one that can easily develop into one of heated argument in which each tells his side of the story, with neither person seeing the problem in a constructive light. This type of interview goes from bad to worse. If the foreman, instead of arguing the issue with the steward, is willing to listen, accept what the steward has to say and understand that he has a problem, he may salvage the situation even though the employee has already been told of the penalty, because a formal grievance has not yet been made. By giving the steward an opportunity to have his say, the foreman can make it clear that he is willing to be reasonable and do the fair thing and in this way improve relations with the steward. If this is accomplished the steward may be willing to look at the foreman's problem. He can point out that he doesn't want to police the job, but what could he do when he caught Stevens red-handed.

Once the situations for the foreman and the steward have mutual acceptance and understanding it is possible to discuss what can be done. If the foreman gives in somewhat by reducing the penalty or giving a warning instead, the steward can give in also by indicating that he will support the foreman on the next occasion. The foreman can more readily make an exception to a rule when he has the cooperation of the steward because the fear of being charged with discriminatory practices in the future will be reduced. In this kind of agreement, which results from cooperative problem solving, neither has to fear that the other will claim a victory, which is always a fear in face-saving problems. Any agreement that is reached should be discussed with the employee by each of them separately.

When the foreman discusses the matter with the employee he should state the agreement reached with the steward and then encourage the employee to freely express his feelings. As a result of such a discussion, the foreman and the employee are likely to understand each other's position more clearly and be willing to deal with the problem in a constructive way. Frequently the foreman will come to realize that his action was hasty or regret the hardship imposed and will withdraw the penalty. In any case, the employee will be helped to understand the foreman's position, and be more likely to feel that his problem at least has been given a fair hearing.

However, since other crew members also smoke, the problem of violating the "No Smoking" rule is most properly one for the group as a whole. The rule was initially formulated to control smoking, not to punish employees. In presenting the problem to the crew for discussion and a group decision, a solution satisfactory to all concerned usually can be developed, providing a reasonable case for the need of "No Smoking" on the job can be made. If the group accepts the rule the problem of enforcement is greatly simplified.

Higher management should also be informed of the problems faced by the foreman. It is relatively easy to pass a rule with penalties attached, because this is done in the abstract and particular people are not part of the consideration. However, when a penalty must be applied, a particular person is part of the picture and to good supervisors punishing a person is an unpleasant duty. Foremen also know that management often will not back them up if the union causes trouble. Thus, the foreman finds himself in trouble if he enforces a rule and he risks the charge of failing to support management if he does not enforce the rule. Often he solves the dilemma by not seeing the violation.

case 13

The Personnel Interview

I. Focusing the Problem

When supervisors are faced with a behavior problem, they frequently take action that leads to conflict and misunderstanding instead of problem solving. Occasionally the reason for this is that the supervisor is required to operate within a framework of rules which sometimes are arbitrary, unnecessary, or unrealistic. More often, however, needless conflict is due to certain attitudes on the part of the supervisor and a lack of skill in handling people. When the supervisor's approach is one of blaming the employee for his behavior, any discussion is likely to center on fault finding and defensive behavior rather than mutually seeking for a solution to the problem. Under these conditions both the supervisor and the employee frequently talk themselves into extreme positions so that neither one can yield without losing face.

When conflict rather than problem solving occurs between the supervisor and an employee, a third party not directly involved in the controversy is frequently consulted. This may be a steward, someone in higher management, an individual in the personnel department, or an arbitrator. Both parties usually will make sincere attempts to resolve their differences before a dispute reaches the stage of a formal grievance or before a valued employee quits or is discharged. Regardless of who the neutral or third party may be, the success or failure of his efforts to obtain a solution satisfactory to both parties will depend on the attitude and skill with which he handles the situation. It is apparent that both parties to the dispute will wish to win him over and that remaining neutral will be necessary but difficult.

This case is also used to introduce the Dramatized Case Method for role playing. A prepared script lays the background for the case and for setting up a conflict in attitudes.

In this case, a situation is created by having two persons read a script dealing with a conversation between an employee and his supervisor. During the reading of the script, a third party is out of the room. Later he interviews the employee and must discover the employee's real problem. Considerable skill is demanded of the interviewer in order to get the facts and to achieve satisfactory results for all concerned.

II. *Dramatized Case Method*

PREPARATION

1. Three members in the group are needed to play the roles. Other members are to participate as observers.

2. One of the role playing participants acts as Walt Henderson, the employee; the second, as Ken Hardy, the supervisor; and the third, as Robert Welch, the personnel director.

3. After all roles have been assigned, everyone should turn to page 212 and read the General Instructions.

4. Welch should now leave the room and study his role on page 213. It is important that he refrain from reading the script or other materials. He is to remain outside the room until preparations for his return are completed.

5. The setting for the role playing scene involving Walt Henderson and Ken Hardy can be arranged by placing a table and a chair in the front of the room. The employee, Walt Henderson, should then occupy the chair and assume he has a drawing board in front of him. He should turn to page 214 and prepare to read the part of Walt in the script. The supervisor, Ken Hardy, should also turn to page 214 and prepare to read his part in the script.

6. When everything is in order Ken Hardy should walk to the front of the room and, as he comes up to Walt's table, begin reading the script aloud.

PROCESS

1. About three or four minutes will be needed for the participants to read the script. When they have finished Ken should join the observers and Walt should leave the room and study the instructions called Additional Information for Walt Henderson on page 216. Robert Welch should be asked to join the group.

2. Observers should study their instructions on page 217.

3. The table and two chairs should be arranged in the front of the room and become the office furnishings of Mr. Robert Welch, Personnel Director. Walt telephoned him a short while ago and said he wanted to talk to him about an urgent matter. It is now 2 P.M. on Tuesday.

4. When the setting is completed Welch should seat himself at his desk

in front of the room. He has Walt Henderson's file in front of him and waits for him to arrive.

5. Walt is cued to come in and go directly to Welch's office. Hardy, the supervisor, remains in the room but, in case he is later involved, he should assume he has heard nothing.

6. Approximately 20 minutes will be needed for this interview. Welch should have as much time as he wishes to handle the situation, and a free hand to make arrangements for any further steps to be taken. Thus he can decide whether to have Hardy come in, whether to talk to him privately, or whether he should make arrangements without consulting Hardy. If Welch brings Hardy and Walt face to face and they become involved in a wrangle in which no progress is made, the discussion should be terminated.

7. After Welch has completed the interview with Walt it may be worth while to give observers a chance to discuss the progress made before taking the next step, which may be an interview between Hardy and Welch or between Walt and Hardy. This evaluation should consist of an exchange of predictions on the outcome.

8. After a brief exchange of opinion the steps agreed upon should be role played. If Hardy is involved he should forget what he overheard.

ANALYSIS OF WELCH'S INTERVIEW WITH WALT

1. Observers should report the extent to which Welch was concerned with the situational *facts* about Walt's reason for leaving and the extent to which he was concerned with Walt's *feelings* about the matter. Examples should be cited and some agreement reached regarding Welch's approach to understanding Walt's problem.

2. Observers should express their views concerning which of these areas should have been explored more carefully.

3. What occurred in the interview to indicate whether or not Walt actually had a job offer? This point should be discussed by observers before Walt supplies the answer.

4. Everyone should report whether or not he believes the interview with Welch influenced Walt's desire to quit the company. These views should be expressed in this order: Welch, observers, and finally Walt.

5. In most instances Welch is sympathetic with Walt and attempts to induce him to stay. Discuss whether Welch conducted himself properly for a personnel man. (It is understood that his situation was a difficult one and that opinions on this question are very controversial.)

ANALYSIS OF WELCH'S INTERVIEW WITH KEN HARDY
(With or without Walt present)

1. What did Welch do to prevent Hardy from becoming defensive? What more should he have done?

2. Did Welch take sides with Walt, Hardy, or remain neutral? Views on this question should be expressed in this order: Welch, observers, and finally Hardy.

3. Should Welch have Walt present when first interviewing Hardy?

4. What would be the best approach for Welch to use in order to gain concessions from Hardy? Observers should discuss this before Ken Hardy explains what would have worked best for him.

EVALUATION OF SOLUTIONS

1. The solutions reached in this case should be evaluated, not only from the point of view of satisfying Walt and Hardy, but also from the standpoint of company policy and the morale of a work force. The role players should remain in character during this evaluation and leave it to the observers to supply the objective viewpoint.

2. It is quite probable that Walt will want some material concession from Hardy in order to be induced to remain with the company. The observers should discuss the inducements that could reasonably have been offered to Walt and attempt to agree on several of them. Hardy then should indicate the ones he would have been willing to give Walt. Finally, Walt should indicate the ones that would have satisfied him.

3. How can these concessions be made so that Ken Hardy will not lose face?

III. Materials [18]

GENERAL INSTRUCTIONS

Ken Hardy is a supervisor in the engineering drafting department of the Wilson Construction Company. The company employs 30 draftsmen, all of whom work in a large room. Approximately half of them are supervised by Hardy and the remainder report to another supervisor. All engineering work is under the general supervision of the department head, Mr. Johnson. The draftsmen perform such assigned duties as developing and checking written specifications and cost estimates on construction projects. In addition they use drawing boards and various complex instruments in making detailed drawings for use by the construction foremen on the job.

Walt Henderson is one of the engineering draftsmen who works under Hardy's supervision. Walt is a graduate engineer and has been with the company for 8 years. He is regarded as highly competent and is well liked by others. He is married and has a 4-year-old daughter.

Like most large concerns of this type, the Wilson Company employs a personnel manager, in this case *Robert Welch.* Welch is responsible for all hiring, job classifications, approving all pay rates and changes in pay. Employees often come to him to discuss company matters and even personal problems. He also interviews all persons who leave the company.

It is now 10 o'clock Tuesday morning. Walt Henderson is working busily at his drafting table as his supervisor, Ken Hardy, comes by:

[18] Case material is taken from Maier, Dramatized Case Material as a Springboard for Role Playing, *Group Psychotherapy,* 1953, *6,* 30–42. Permission to reproduce has been granted by Beacon House, publishers, and J. L. Moreno, the editor.

ROLE FOR ROBERT WELCH

You are head of the Personnel Department of the Wilson Construction Company. Your department does all the hiring, and must O.K. all recommendations for changes in pay rates. You have the authority to turn down recommended increases and to make changes in job classifications, and you are in a position to influence personnel policy. Your door is open to employees who want to discuss company matters or even their own personal problems. You or your staff interviews all employees who leave the company.

Walt Henderson of the drafting department has just called you and wants to see you on what he called "an urgent matter." You've asked him to come right down. Just to prepare yourself on factual matters you looked up his record. He works for *Ken Hardy,* a drafting department supervisor, whom you regard highly, and Ken has given him a very good rating. The record shows Walt Henderson to be a top-notch draftsman who turns out a lot of work. He has 8 years with the company, which is about average for the drafting room. Walt Henderson is married and has one 4-year-old daughter. As his hobbies he has listed fishing and sailing. The door opens and Walt Henderson walks in. It is now 2 P.M. on Tuesday.

SCRIPT

KEN: How's the work going, Walt?

WALT: Fine. All caught up.

KEN: Even that set of specifications of Joe's that I gave you to check yesterday?

WALT: Yep. Took it home and worked on it there so I wouldn't be too rushed today.

KEN: Well, now, I don't want you to have to be taking work home, Walt. I didn't know you were going to do that or I'd have asked Fred to help Joe out on it instead.

WALT: Oh! That's O.K. I didn't mind doing it. I knew Joe was going to have a rough time getting it all done by noon today, anyway.

KEN: What are you working on now?

WALT: Some plans for that little boat I told you I was going to build.

KEN: I see. Think you should be doing that on company time, Walt?

WALT: Well, I don't know. I've done all my own work and put in 3 hours of my own time last night to help Joe out. And besides I don't have my own equipment at home to do this drafting. What's the harm in it?

KEN: It just looks bad to be doing something like that on company time. You know that as well as I do.

WALT: Well, when I have all my work done and more, what does the company expect me to do—twiddle my thumbs?

KEN: Now let's not get hasty. We went through all this last year when you got both of us on the hot seat with Johnson over that garage of yours that you drew up here. Remember?

WALT: Sure, I remember. And I still don't think it's anybody's business what I work on here so long as my own work is done and I don't bother anybody else.

KEN: That's what you think. Now let's get this straight. Nobody's telling you what to do before or after office hours, but when you're here drawing pay you're supposed to be earning it. And I don't want another mess like the one we had on that garage of yours. Understand?

WALT: Yes, but I don't see why we have to set up such rigid rules. Just because Johnson doesn't know how much work I turn out is no reason why you should take your cue from him.

KEN: Look Walt, I'm not taking my cue from him. I didn't like the idea of your doing your own work here either, but I decided to let it pass. Then when the chief caught you at it and you didn't have the good judgment to be a bit more careful—well, you've just got the wrong attitude.

WALT: How can you say that? You know perfectly well I turn out more work for the company than anyone else. Is it my fault if you can't keep me busy?

KEN: Walt. I know you're a top-notch draftsman, but a good employee is something more than that.

WALT: Yeh—a good employee is a yes-man.

KEN: Not at all. A good employee works well with others. He's got to follow rules so that he doesn't set a bad precedent. Suppose the others brought their own work down here?

KEN: Well, make them do their job first.

KEN: How can I if they say I let you work on your personal things?

WALT: But I do company work at home and more than make up the time.

KEN: Walt, am I supposed to let you choose when and where you do company work? What a mess that would make if I had to keep track of everyone's homework. Anyway we've never asked you to do work at home. When we have more to do than you can handle during working hours we'll pay you overtime.

WALT: Ken, I'm not asking for overtime. All I want is to be treated as an honest person. I've never gypped the company out of anything and whenever the company is behind schedule I've worked like the devil to help out. Now I've got a personal problem and all I'm asking is to borrow some of the facilities. Is that unreasonable?

KEN: I can see your side, Walt, but we can't give favors to some and not to others. I've just got to make a rule and remember you've forced me into it. There will be no more personal work done during company hours. I'll let you finish this job, but that will have to be the end. I am not going to have others say I play favorites. Sorry, but that's it.

ADDITIONAL INFORMATION FOR WALT HENDERSON

Walt was disturbed by this conversation, so that noon he called his friend *Bill Alden* who told him they had an opening in the drafting department of his company (Jones Bros., Inc.). Walt asked him to check up on details. That afternoon Bill's boss, *Mr. Hansen,* called Walt and told him he was very anxious to have Walt come to work for Jones Bros. He told Walt that he would take him on Bill's recommendation and the salary he quoted was five dollars a week more than Walt was getting. From his description, the work seemed about the same as Walt was now doing. When Walt expressed interest, Hansen asked him if he could start next week. That would be next Monday. Since Jones Bros. had another applicant for the job he asked Walt if he could let him know right away. Walt asked if he could have until Wednesday morning so as to have time to talk it over with his wife. Hansen said that would be O.K. He suggested that Walt give the Wilson Company as good an excuse as he could for quitting so suddenly because he wanted to stay on good terms with the Wilson Company.

After this talk Walt thought a bit and decided it would be nice to work in Bill's office. They had often compared companies and although Walt had sometimes thought of making a change, he could find little difference between the companies. Since he had 8 years with the Wilson Company he had some seniority and retirement benefits. Now he had a reason for quitting. He knew his wife would go along with any decision. The important thing to do now was to go to the personnel office and let the company know about his decision. Walt therefore called *Robert Welch* of the Personnel Department and asked to see him on an urgent matter. Welch asked him to come right down.

INSTRUCTIONS FOR OBSERVERS

1. Walt requested the interview with Mr. Welch but Welch does not know anything about Walt's trouble with Ken Hardy. Naturally, he will explore the problem with Walt. In order to keep track of his approach, make a cross "X" in your notes for each time he probes for facts, and a circle "O" for each time he encourages Walt to talk about his feelings.

2. Note the things Walt tells about the Hardy incident and the things he holds back.

3. Walt may talk about another job offer. See if you can tell whether he actually has one. Note whether Welch pursues this point and determines if Walt has an offer and really wants to leave.

4. Does Welch discover what it will take to keep Walt? What more should he have done?

5. Note whether Welch is taking sides. This will become particularly apparent if he interviews Hardy.

IV. Comments and Implications

Welch will usually be puzzled as to why Walt wants to leave and will be skeptical about the reason given. If he listens and probes sufficiently to discover the conflict between Walt and Hardy, Welch will most often ask that Hardy be brought in to the interview with Walt on the notion that if he can get facts on both sides of the controversy he can smooth things over. However, this will almost invariably renew the argument between Walt and Hardy and produce stubborn, hostile, and defensive behavior on the part of Hardy since he is put in the position of justifying his previous action in disciplining Walt. Further, Walt will usually become sufficiently aggravated to quit. The nonconstructive emotional behavior shown will thus cause Welch to lose control over the situation and the problem will remain unsolved.

However, if Welch creates a permissive interview situation, uses the listening technique and probes for Walt's feelings, he will probably discover the real reason why Walt is considering quitting. When he gets Walt into a reasonable frame of mind, Walt usually will defer a decision until Welch can take further action by discussing things separately with Hardy. In a similar and separate interview alone with Hardy, Welch again must be permissive and encourage expression of feeling. If Welch does not take sides he usually can cause Hardy to become reasonable and to welcome a discussion of various alternative solutions to the problem. These may include less readiness to resort to making rules, discussing the problem with Johnson to obtain his cooperation, conducting a group conference with the other draftsmen as to how the problem of personal work should be handled, and the like.

After both Hardy and Walt have been interviewed separately and their hostility has been expressed, they usually are able to take a more understanding attitude toward each other. During this stage Welch can elicit their ideas for various constructive approaches that might be taken.

The practical considerations of this case are especially interesting because they raise the question of whether or not one can give a good employee special consideration without creating problems with others. Often the fear that a concession made to one employee will cause a wave of demands from others is more imagined than real. In this case it is quite possible that most of the other draftsmen did not have Walt's desire to do personal work while on the job. However, if they did have, the extent of this work could be controlled by setting some kind of limit on the privilege.

The talent a company loses when it attempts to hold strictly to a regulation is an important question to consider. As is partly true in this case, it is often the feeling of regimentation rather than the actual restriction that creates the rebellion, and sometimes it takes only a little laxity or flexibility in a rule to ease the dissatisfaction.

For example, if employees are regarded as being tardy when the time clock indicates a second or more after the hour, they tend to show resentment because no credit is given if they "punch in" a few seconds early. Might there be a zone between five minutes before and five minutes after the starting hour that is regarded as arriving on time? This kind of ruling should cause less feeling of regimentation.

If we assume that the above possibilities are impractical, and an employee clearly expects special treatment as a condition of employment, should the company consider the matter? When the employee in question is not especially desirable, the simple and practical answer is "no." When, however, a special concession seems desirable from the point of view of both the company and the employee, it may be worthwhile to consider the matter. Often it is possible to gain the consent of other employees to make an exception of a particular employee. This acceptance of a special case requires group decision. In one office a girl was given special hours for work because there were unusual circumstances in her situation that required this. Her exceptional conditions were respected by all other employees and she was given hours that turned out to be convenient for everyone concerned. No one in this office requested similar consideration as a consequence of the action.

It is quite possible that other draftsmen would have been willing to let Walt gain special privileges for doing personal work on the job, had the question been raised. The unusual amount of work that he did in the office and the fact that he took work home to make up time would have been regarded as *his* concessions. Although such practices are usually frowned upon by managers, it is perhaps desirable to reexamine some of the problems that have been neatly packaged into rules and put on the shelf.

Finally, Walt's case should be studied from the point of view of his hurt feelings. Actually he rebelled because he felt that his work was not being appreciated. Had Hardy handled Walt differently, it might have been possible to have dealt with the problem more simply. However, this was out of the question because Ken Hardy's behavior was controlled by the script.

case 14

The Promotion Interview

I. Focusing the Problem

The promotion of an individual in an organization is frequently the cause of a series of reactions and adjustments in a group, which may lead to apprehension, misunderstanding, and lessened cooperation. When one person is selected for promotion, others feel rejected or discredited, fear of change is aroused, expectations and aspirations are threatened, and differences of opinions as to the meaning of fairness are raised. Many persons may agree that the choice made is a poor one, although they might not agree on the choice that should have been made. Varied emotions and feelings may be expected to be aroused because a group includes persons who want the promotion for themselves, persons who feel that seniority is threatened, persons who are surprised by the choice made and feel that a change in policy is occurring, persons who agree with the choice but feel they must support the group reaction, and persons who fear promotion as well as fear to turn down an opportunity.

In some organizations attempts have been made to reach at least a partial solution to this problem by establishing certain policies and procedures as a basis for promotion. These include seniority, periodic merit evaluations, job sequences, and the like. While such methods tend to regularize promotion procedures they do not solve the problem of adverse feeling reactions; rather they remove the surprise element and in a sense make it possible to ignore the feelings because at any given time they are less acute in the group.

Some companies attempt to deal with the feelings by interviewing candidates. Among these methods is the procedure of beginning the selection with a reasonably broad field of possible candidates. Then, prior to announcing a promotion, all who were considered are interviewed with the objective of gaining their acceptance.

Obviously the effectiveness of such a method for preventing misunderstandings and overcoming undesirable feeling reactions depends considerably on the attitude and skill of the interviewer. In informing all persons who may be considered eligible for promotion that a particular person has been selected, an interviewer must be prepared for various reactions. An important question is whether he should have prepared himself to meet all possible objections. Further, what methods might be followed which will avoid undue disappointment for the individual not selected as well as the mixed feelings of the person who is chosen? Are there ways for conducting the interview so as to obtain acceptance and support of the decision that is made by higher management or must one sacrifice acceptance if this prerogative is to be protected?

The following case deals with an interview in which problems of this kind arise. It provides an excellent opportunity to demonstrate the values of certain interview principles and techniques as well as chances to practice the skills necessary for applying the principles effectively.

The Single Group Procedure for role playing is described for this case in order to give the group members an opportunity to test their sensitivity to the feelings aroused. Since all observers will view the same performance, a detailed discussion and analysis of cause and effect in behavior is possible. Persons playing the roles will be the center of attraction, and the person playing the part of the foreman may anticipate that his performance will be discussed in some detail. It is expected and hoped that he will make mistakes because it is from these that the importance of fine skills becomes apparent. He may be consoled by the fact that no one to date, including the authors, has turned in a perfect performance and it is hoped that he will welcome criticism and discussion of his behavior as a learning experience for everyone. As a matter of fact, it is not the person but the role and the situation that is to be analyzed.

II. Single Group Role Playing Procedure

PREPARATION

1. The description of the situation and the background facts given on page 225 should be studied by everyone. The instructor may wish to read aloud while the class follows the text.

2. Two role players are needed: one to play the part of Smith, the foreman; the other to play the part of Cole, the skilled worker. It is best for the instructor or class to suggest the persons who are to play the parts. The person chosen to act the part of the foreman should not be a volunteer, because a volunteer may feel he must put on a good demonstration; rather he should be a person who wishes to learn from his own mistakes and will not be too self-conscious. If the group has worked together on other cases, almost anyone will satisfy the above qualifications. The role of Cole is an interesting one, but since the person playing his part is the interviewee, his feelings rather than his skills will be the subject of scrutiny. He should feel free to act naturally. The remaining class members will act as observers, whose task it is to discover the cause-and-effect relationships between the events that transpire.

3. The person selected to be Mr. Smith should turn to page 226 for his role instructions; the person acting as Mr. Cole will find his role instructions on page 227; and observers should study their instructions on page 228.

4. While the roles are being studied, the instructor should prepare the setting for the scene by placing a table and two chairs in front of the room to represent Mr. Smith's office furniture. The table and chairs should be placed so that the observers can see the faces of the role players during the scene.

5. When the participants are ready to begin role playing the instructor should signal Mr. Smith to take his place at his desk. Mr. Cole should enter the office a few moments later and begin the scene.

PROCESS

1. Role playing in this case should be allowed to proceed for 15 or 20 minutes without interruption.

2. Should the role playing result in mutual frustration and bickering so that no progress is made, the scene should be interrupted. The cause of the difficulty should be discussed but care should be taken not to reveal

information supplied in the roles. It is Smith's problem to dig up the facts and feelings.

After a little discussion observers should feel free to give advice on procedure and the role players should feel free to reject or try out any of the many pieces of advice that are given. If it is desirable to delete any part of the interview or even to start over, this should be permitted.

3. In the event progress is made and no interruption seems to be in order the foreman should be allowed to terminate the interview in his own manner. If an interruption or two has been made, he should be asked to resume and terminate the interview as seems best when dealing with a problem employee.

OBSERVERS' REPORTS AND ANALYSES OF FINDINGS

1. The observers should report whether they think (a) Smith feels better or worse about Cole as a result of the interview, and (b) Cole feels better or worse toward Smith than he did before.

2. Each participant should report whether he feels better or worse toward the other person than he did before the interview.

3. In the event the interview has created new misunderstandings rather than accomplished good communication, it may be well to discuss the value of promotion interviews. If it is concluded that such interviews have value, providing they are skilfully conducted, the group may wish to explore this problem.

4. Smith should describe why he thinks Cole feels as he does about the promotion. (For the time being, Smith should not be enlightened regarding the accuracy of his description.)

5. Observers should discuss why the interview turned out as it did. The discussion should cover the following points for the purpose of pointing up the essential interviewing skills.

a. Did Smith get to the point of the interview quickly or did he beat around the bush? Discuss consequences of each approach.

b. Did Smith come to the interview thinking he knew how Cole would feel about things and why he would feel that way? Discuss whether preconceived notions as to Cole's feelings would make any difference either way.

c. How good a listener was Smith? Who did the most talking?

d. What aspects of the situation did Smith fail to get Cole to express?

e. Did Smith fail to follow leads which would have helped him discover the true nature of Cole's objections to Adams? What were they?

6. Cole should report some of the things that prevented him from being more frank with Smith and the things that caused him to tell as much as he did. He should describe some of the things he liked and some of the things he didn't like about the interview. Observers should feel free to ask Cole about his feelings.

7. Smith should report the kinds of decisions that faced him; what Cole did that helped or misled him; and what he would do if confronted with a similar problem in real life.

8. The question of whether a foreman should interview before making a final decision should be discussed. Relevant issues are: (a) could Smith have made a wiser decision by talking to Cole first; (b) would he have been more openminded if he had discussed the problem before making up his mind; and (c) would he have been less inclined to distort the facts if he presented the problem to Cole before rather than after the decision?

DEVELOPING AN INTERVIEW PLAN

1. Assuming that an interview must be conducted under the conditions of this case, how should Smith present the problem to Cole? A list of possibilities should be prepared and evaluated. Some of the approaches might be tested by trying them out on Cole and noting his reactions.

2. Develop a list of the various ways in which Smith can recognize Cole for the contributions he has made to the company.

3. Suppose Cole makes certain favorable remarks about Brown. Should Smith respond by thanking him and encouraging a fuller expression of opinion; should he defend his decision; or should he try to change the subject?

4. Suppose Cole makes sly remarks about Adams that differ from the beliefs of Smith. Should Smith defend Adams, draw Cole out and respect his views, or try to change the subject?

5. At what stage in the interview should Smith tell Cole about his decision?

6. An outline of the procedure should be developed that will serve to summarize the group's efforts. (The outline should be viewed not as the only or best method, but as one that the group is willing to regard as a distinct improvement over present industrial practice.)

III. Materials [19]

SITUATION AND BACKGROUND FACTS

Mr. Smith, a foreman, was asked to recommend one of his 12 men for a position of a foreman which had just opened up in another part of the plant. He was requested to recommend a man who not only would qualify, but one who had the ability to go higher in the organization. It is the company's practice to hire and promote a certain percentage of men who have abilities beyond the jobs in which they are placed. Since it is the company's policy to promote from within the ranks this practice is necessary to insure having good men in top positions.

Smith is a college graduate, has been with the company 5 years, and has been a foreman for 2 years. Three men have records which would make them eligible for promotion. They are as follows:

John Adams, a college graduate with 3 years service. Adams is bright, has a pleasing personality, seems conscientious, and has been highly cooperative. Smith knows Adams very well and has spent a good deal of time with him. Adams makes a good appearance and is at ease in a group. However, he doesn't seem to have much in common with his associates on the job.

Walt Brown, a high school graduate with 6 years service. Brown is also a very satisfactory employee with a good personality. He is very popular with the men and seems to have their respect. He has a lot of natural intelligence and inventive ability.

Jim Cole, a high school graduate with 12 years of service. Cole is an excellent workman. He is used for training new men and actually trained both Adams and Brown when they started with the company. He also successfully takes over the foreman's job when Smith is absent. The men seem to like Cole and have confidence in him. Although Cole is highly competent, he isn't too easy to handle. He is sure of himself and sometimes argues about the way a job should be done. He lacks a certain polish and makes mistakes in grammar. He is by no means a problem employee, but, on occasion, he speaks his mind.

Company practice requires its supervisors to interview all employees who have been considered for a particular promotion. Today Smith will interview Jim Cole.

---

[19] Role instructions are modified from a case in Maier, *Principles of Human Relations,* John Wiley & Sons, New York, 1952, 119–121.

ROLE FOR MR. SMITH, FOREMAN

After careful consideration, you decided that *John Adams* was the man for the job. You were influenced by the fact that you must choose a man with added potentialities, and feel very strongly that men must be found who can eventually fill top jobs. All three would be good foremen, but Adams could go farther, you believe. Certainly Adams was a college graduate, and that meant something. The fact that Adams was a graduate of Cornell, your alma mater, did not influence you in this choice. Since he is the only college man in your group you had no other choice.

You recognized that *Brown* has leadership ability, but not to the degree that Adams possesses it. The strong point in favor of *Cole* was his seniority, and there were no real weaknesses to point to. His personality was not bad enough to be used against him, but he did have a way of putting things bluntly. You don't feel that he would make too good an impression on your superiors.

You therefore recommended Adams; this recommendation has been accepted, but it has not been officially announced. Further, you told Adams about it confidentially, largely because you were so pleased that your recommendation was the one that was accepted upstairs. Before the promotion is announced you feel you must interview Cole. Next you will interview Brown. This is company policy.

You have arranged an interview with Cole. Your goal is to get Cole to accept your recommendation. You do not want to create bad feeling in Cole because you must still work with him, and besides Cole is your best worker.

ROLE FOR JIM COLE, SKILLED WORKER

You have heard through the grapevine that a new job is opening up. You feel you have a chance at it, but you aren't too confident you will get it since you have been passed up a few times already. Nevertheless, you have, on occasion, taken *Smith's* place as a foreman and so have some reason to believe you may be considered. However, you do not feel too qualified for such an assignment. You are happy in what you are doing and like actually doing rather than directing. You take pride in your skill. If a position for supervisory work is opening up, you feel that the best qualified man is *Brown*. In your book, Brown has everything to get ahead in the company. You fear that Brown may not get the job because you strongly feel that college men are favored, and in addition he lacks seniority.

As for *Adams*, you feel that he is an apple polisher and worse. He hangs around the boss and, you believe, talks about ideas he got from you when he was being trained. Since Adams is in good with the boss he has spent less time with the men, and you feel that Adams no longer is as friendly as formerly. You feel that Adams has changed since he got in good with the boss. Maybe it's natural since they both went to Cornell. Maybe that's the way to get ahead. You feel that promotions have not been fair and that knowing the right people is a factor in getting ahead. But you certainly don't like apple polishers. You also believe that Adams is unpopular in the group, whereas Brown is popular.

You are about to go to Smith's office for the scheduled interview. You suspect it's about the job. You fear that you may not like the results but are determined not to get into trouble over it. You consider Smith one of the best foremen you have had, but feel he isn't too experienced in the company. You don't want to get in wrong with Smith, but nevertheless you have your principles.

INSTRUCTIONS FOR OBSERVERS

There is a source of misunderstanding in this case in that Smith will assume that Cole wants the promotion himself, and he is likely to attribute to jealousy any objections that Cole raises. Actually, however, Cole has mixed feelings. He feels that Brown should get a promotion, he likes his present job, and he is strongly opposed to Adams getting a promotion because he regards him as an apple polisher. How he resolves these mixed feelings will depend, in part, upon the interview.

As observers you should take particular pains to make note of any behavior or remarks that bear on the key issues stated below.

1. What does Cole say that reveals his interest in Brown? Does Smith respond by encouraging further expression, does he disagree, or does he change the subject?

2. What does Cole do that indicates his dislike of Adams? Note all veiled hints in this direction and see if you can discover if and when Smith discovers this attitude.

3. Note all skills Smith uses to get Cole to talk, as well as all things he does that discourage frank expression.

4. If the interview gets better or worse as it progresses, take note of the cause of the change.

5. Be prepared to report on the following:

   a. Does Smith's estimation of Cole go up or down as a result of the interview?

   b. Does Cole's estimation of Smith go up or down as a result of the interview?

   c. What did Smith learn about Cole's attitude?

   d. What recognition did Smith give Cole?

   e. What was said that Cole might take as criticism of his work or his attitude?

Note: In discussing this case it is important not to reveal Cole's attitude as furnished in these instructions. The discussion should be confined to behavior evidence and not depend on inside information.

IV. Comments and Implications

The interviewer is placed in a difficult situation in this case, partly because we have made a decision for him which he may not personally support and partly because it may not be his practice to make decisions without consulting his men. The minor incident of bad taste shown by Smith in telling Adams about his promotion can be overlooked because Adams said nothing to Cole and no harm came from this indiscretion. Since real life situations often confront supervisors with actions or decisions that are not of their own making and which they must support, it is important for them to learn how to deal with problems that are imposed on them from the outside. Although prevention is an admirable goal, it is well to be skilled in making the best of the remaining problem situations that were not prevented. Recognizing the imposed difficulties written into the role as given facts, let us evaluate how best these could have been met. This does not exclude the need to discuss ways of preventing the problems that occurred in this case.

The case is likely to demonstrate dramatically the importance of discovering the interviewee's viewpoint or attitudes as early as possible. If Smith assumes that Cole wants the job for himself, all of his prepared sales points become sources of irritation instead of favorable influences. This is a basic weakness in the "selling" approach: it presumes a particular need. Smith must draw out Cole and find out how he feels about his own future, how he feels about past promotions, and how he feels about this particular one. To learn these things he must be willing to accept as reasonable and understandable any opinion Cole expresses. He need not agree with him, but he must understand him.

It is reasonable for Smith to accept and appreciate Cole's remarks about Brown, and he can thank him for the information as well as indicate that Brown was considered and will be even more seriously considered in the future because of Cole's high evaluation. He can also thank Cole for information about Adams, indicating that this is a side he may have overlooked, thanking him for drawing his attention to the weakness, and asking for a description of any further weakness that seems relevant. He can then ask Cole to remark on any good points he knows about Adams. Usually the opportunity to freely express the bad traits of Adams makes Cole feel more generous toward Adams.

Cole should be told at the outset that he was considered for the job and will be considered for others. Recognition for being a qualified candidate, and no criticism for any weaknesses, should characterize the introductory part of the interview. The actual decision should be stated as the choice that seemed most appropriate for the particular job opening. No defense beyond this is required. Rather, Cole should be given a chance to respond by telling what he thinks. The whole introduction should require only a few sentences. Small talk should be kept at a minimum because Cole wants to know what the interview is about.

In case Cole asks why his advice is being sought for something that has already been decided, there are a number of reasons that can honestly be given. Some of these are as follows: (1) Smith is sincerely concerned with how Cole feels; (2) how Cole feels in this instance can influence future promotions; (3) Smith was required to make a recommendation and now that it is accepted he is concerned with the reactions of the crew; (4) Smith wants Cole to have advance notice because he values his support; and (5) Cole trained Adams and may rightly be concerned with the progress of his trainees. One or two of these reasons may be enough to convince Cole that there is a purpose to the interview.

Little hints of dissatisfaction may be followed up by (a) permitting pauses to be long enough to be uncomfortable; (b) reflecting the feelings expressed (i.e., "You feel that we favor college men in this company"); (c) showing concern for the feelings Cole expresses; and (d) asking general exploratory questions about Cole's feelings (i.e., "How do you mean that?"). Smith must be very sensitive to the feelings hinted and must avoid intellectualizing or asking Cole to justify opinions. He must assume that there are feelings behind the remarks and believe that Cole will feel better if he can express what he feels.

Cole may need comfort and recognition from time to time. He should derive comfort from the fact that he was considered, from the fact that his views are sought, and from Smith's respect for his feelings. He can be recognized and praised for (a) his ability to substitute as foreman; (b) his job skills; (c) his contribution to training; (d) his faithful service to the company; and (e) the esteem in which the crew holds him. To indicate that Adams has said many good things about him and his ideas would be welcome information to Cole.

Smith should never feel that he must defend his choice. It may even be advisable, on occasion, that he entertain the possibility that he may have been wrong and state that he is glad to hear an opposed viewpoint. This behavior is no admission of error, rather it gives Cole an opportunity to save face and to entertain the possibility that there may be two or more sides to the question. Together they may then discuss ways by which each can benefit from the knowledge and viewpoint of the other.

This interview is representative of interview situations in which there is a rank difference between the interviewer and the interviewee. On the one hand, the person with inferior rank sees the person with superior rank as a threat or as having opposite interests, unless pains are taken to reduce this tendency. On the other hand, the person with superior rank is inclined to judge his inferior and assume that he is biased or uncooperative, unless he spends considerable effort in exploring the subordinate's attitude. Interviews involving rank differences, therefore, invariably incorporate a source of misunderstanding and complicate the problem of communication. The first step in developing constructive and cooperative attitudes is to discover and understand the attitudes that exist. This requires the interviewer to come into an interview with an open mind and perhaps even unprepared, because his preparation may assume an attitude that *may not* exist. It is seldom that an interviewer changes a judgment that he brings into the interview. Some persons playing the role of Smith persist in believing that Cole really wants the job himself.

Whether or not interviews of this kind should be conducted will obviously depend on the skills of the interviewers. It is perhaps apparent that a company policy requiring such interviews could do as much harm as good. One way of approaching the difficult problem of communicating the issues in the promotions that are made is to invite participation in evaluations from peers and even to include self-evaluations. Another approach involves inviting all interested parties to apply for the posted opening and then to submit to tests and interviews. This gives persons with seniority an opportunity to suggest others or to turn down an opportunity by not applying. There are many persons who do not want a particular promotion but feel they have been overlooked by not receiving an offer. Sometimes they are embarrassed by the remarks of friends who tell them they have been treated unfairly. For them to say they didn't want the job is to appear to cry "sour grapes." Opportunities to gain recognition and to save face are needed by persons with seniority, and the above suggestions may offer some possibilities in these directions.

case 15

Bill Edwards,
the House Service Worker

I. Focusing the Problem

Certain objects or events act as incentives for all persons. It is seldom that a raise in pay will not serve as an inducement to perform even the most unpleasant tasks. Pride is another universal need that causes people to respond to group pressures. In the case of the storm window assignment (pages 161–173), it is probable that anyone who found himself in the face-saving situation of Jack would have quit a good job rather than accept the assignment the foreman wished to give him. A knowledge of the general principles of motivation can contribute greatly to making jobs more attractive or less unattractive to employees in general.

In considering job motivation, however, one must also consider the ways in which people are different. What may serve as a strong incentive for one person may leave another unmoved. Even the same person's motivation will change from one day to the next. A hungry boy will work for food but a well-fed lad may respond more readily to a pat on the back than to food. An assignment that might be seen as a reward for one individual may be taken as punishment by another. We often overlook potential ways of motivating people because we do not know their particular needs. This aspect of motivation study requires an understanding of individual persons and a supervisor must be taught to be sensitive to differences between them if he is to succeed more fully in really treating people as persons. As companies grow larger and supervisory responsibilities increase, there is less time available to learn about each person so that one must learn more from the few visits one does have.

Learning to know what different employees like and expect from a job is only one side of the picture. One must also discover particular dislikes, and even learn the intensity of these if one is to understand persons who have strong negative reactions.

This degree of knowledge about an employee may sound like a large order and it should be added that no management could require this degree of attention for each employee. However, there are saving considerations. One is that all employees do not require this specialized consideration, and, as indicated above, employees are alike in many ways and standard considerations are fairly adequate for them. The supervisor need merely to be sensitive to situations in which the personalized considerations are required. Even when he performs these activities it is perhaps only fair to say that he is performing his job at a level beyond the call of duty.

The second consideration is that the time spent on any one occasion may yield understanding and insights into an individual's make-up that will help the supervisor deal effectively in the future with this person and others like him. Sometimes a misunderstanding extends over a period of years and even though the time lost on one occasion may be brief, the total time for many such occasions may exceed the time that would have been needed for a careful interview at the outset.

The third consideration is a selfish one. Regardless of how justified a supervisor is in his expectations and evaluations of his employees, he has an unpleasant experience when one of his employees disappoints him. If he knew more of the feelings and needs of the person who is causing him a problem, he would feel less disturbed himself. Thus one of the important rewards for knowing such individuals as persons is that it makes supervision and the management of employees a more satisfying experience. When one knows why an employee is late for work one is inclined to be less irritated by his action.

The present case deals with an employee by the name of Bill Edwards who will be asked to take an assignment much like the one in Case 10. The setting and the job are different. Whether a similar or different approach should be used is not revealed. The case is set up for Single Group Role Playing but opportunities to involve the observers are provided so that further development of skills in sensitivity and new insight into behavior problems can occur.

II. Single Group Role Playing Procedure

PREPARATION

1. Two persons are needed to play the roles: one to serve as Henry Spring, the superintendent, the other as Bill Edwards, a handyman. The instructor should divide the class into two parts and select a role player from each half. Each half of the class should try and identify with the role player from his section and act as observers as well.

2. The Background Instructions, on page 237, give the setting of the case and should be read by everyone. The instructor should ask one class member to read aloud while the others follow the text.

3. The role for Henry Spring will be found on page 238. It should be read by the person selected to play this role and the group of participants who identify with him.

4. The role for Bill Edwards on page 239 should be read by him and by the half of the class that identifies with him.

5. Observers should keep notes on behaviors and statements they consider significant. They should also record the things that the person playing the opposite role does to hurt or irritate them. Observers, however, should not interrupt the role playing.

6. When everyone has studied his part, the instructor should arrange a table in front of the room so that Bill Edwards can go through the business of sanding the top of the table while on the job.

7. Henry Spring should be in readiness to approach Bill and begin role playing when the instructor signals.

PROCESS

1. Bill Edwards should go to work on the table in front of the room.

2. When the scene is set, the instructor should give Henry Spring the signal to approach Bill Edwards.

3. Role playing should proceed until a decision satisfactory to each is reached. This may require more than 30 minutes and some help from the observers.

4. If Henry Spring seems to be having difficulty, he should be allowed to interrupt the role playing and discuss the problem with the observers who have read his role. Other observers should not enter into this discussion. Henry Spring should feel free to accept or reject any advice given. After

a brief discussion, role playing should proceed, with Bill Edwards assuming that he has not heard the discussion. In order to resume role playing, Henry Spring should take the liberty to briefly summarize some aspect of the interview or ask to have any part deleted. He should then proceed with a question or statement of a problem to again get the interview under way.

5. If a decision is reached to discharge Bill Edwards, the observers, who are familiar with his role, should be asked if they consider the decision wise. If they feel that the foreman has been insensitive to certain cues or leads dropped by Edwards, these oversights should be pointed out to Henry Spring.

6. Role playing should be resumed in order to give Mr. Spring a chance to test the suggestions.

7. When a decision is reached or when no further progress is made as a result of discussion during the interruptions, the role playing should be terminated.

ANALYSIS OF THE NEEDS OF BILL EDWARDS

1. Observers who identified with Henry Spring should report what they have learned about Bill Edwards' special needs, attitudes, or feelings. (The instructor should tally the observations on the blackboard.) Persons who identified with Bill Edwards should not participate.

2. Bill's behavior should be evaluated in terms of these needs in order to determine whether they clarify his apparent stubbornness, evasiveness, or reluctance to talk. All class members should participate in this evaluation. (Persons who identified with Bill Edwards should be careful not to reveal any information about Edwards that Henry Spring failed to uncover.)

3. Persons identifying with Bill Edwards should discuss what Spring did to make Bill tell as much as he did and what Spring did to cause Bill not to tell more.

4. Bill Edwards should report how he felt toward Mr. Spring and what caused him to feel as he did.

5. Although Bill seemed stubborn and uncooperative, what reasons are there for regarding him as a desirable employee?

6. How might Mr. Spring have come to the conclusion that Bill had a special problem even if he did not reveal what it was? List the things that Bill did or said in the interview that could cause his boss to respect his attempts to avoid putting up the storm windows.

7. Compare the methods of listening and of questioning in discovering Bill's problem. What might have been learned from each?

EVALUATION OF POSSIBLE SOLUTIONS

1. What are the arguments for and against attempting to force Bill to put up the storm windows?

2. What are the arguments for and against discharging Bill for his conduct in the interview? (When differences in opinion occur, the instructor should determine whether these are between the two groups of observers.)

3. Suppose Bill's special problem is respected by his boss and he is to be excused from working in high places. What new problem is created by this decision?

4. How should the rest of the crew be approached in order to have them accept Bill's special treatment? Outline a plan for taking this problem to the crew.

5. If it is necessary to share Bill's secret with the crew, how should this be handled with Bill? Discuss.

6. Is Bill in need of psychiatric care? What are the arguments for and against his need for treatment?

III. Materials [20]

BACKGROUND INSTRUCTIONS

The offices, mills, and shops of the Eastern Paper Company cover a wide area at the edge of a small city. Some of the buildings are old and are now occupied by certain service departments that have no need for a specialized structure or floor plan. One of those buildings is a wooden two-story structure occupied by the House Service Department, which is managed by *Henry Spring*. Twelve skilled handymen work for him.

The house service crew is called upon (*a*) to do maintenance work of a minor nature, such as repairing doors, chairs, chutes, docks, etc.; (*b*) to do a variety of carpentry jobs, such as installing shelves, making cabinets, and handling minor remodeling projects; (*c*) to refinish office furniture; and (*d*) to perform the smaller paint jobs, such as painting the building and inside walls of the structure they occupy. Jobs that can be moved to the house service building are performed there, but the men have to leave the building for most of the jobs.

The scene today takes place on the second floor of the house service building. Henry Spring, the superintendent, has a job he wants *Bill Edwards* to do. Edwards is busy sanding a desk top.

Bill has worked for the company for 9 months. He is 28 years old, is married and has two children.

[20] Role instructions are modified from Maier, *Principles of Human Relations*, John Wiley & Sons, New York, 1952, 116–117.

ROLE FOR HENRY SPRING, SUPERINTENDENT

You are in charge of a crew of men who do house service work, and you try to make assignments to fit a man's ability and status. You have a new man, *Bill Edwards,* who has been with the company for 9 months. He is a responsible worker and seems happily married. When you hired him you couldn't get too much information from him about his background. He isn't too talkative about his past, but he's a pleasant fellow and you want to give him a fair trial. You have been quite pleased with him because he is very handy and has considerable proficiency in cabinet work and refinishing furniture. He also seems to get along fairly well with the other men, but you feel he sometimes tries to get others to do his work. The other members of the crew have been with you for 4 years or more and you think you have good morale. You have always tried to be fair.

It has always been your practice and that of the company to give certain recognitions for seniority. The man with more seniority is given more overtime work if he wants it. Further, undesirable jobs which usually are simple and routine are given to the man with least seniority.

One of the routine jobs is that of washing and putting up storm windows in the small building you occupy. There are 24 windows, 12 on the first floor and 12 on the second. This work has always been done by the man with least seniority. Joe Drake did it for 4 years. You are about to ask Bill Edwards to do the job.

ROLE FOR BILL EDWARDS, HANDYMAN

You do repair jobs including carpentry, cabinet work, refinishing tables, and painting. You are a good repairman and like carpentry and painting, but could not go into either of these trades because you are afraid of high places. You had to leave several good jobs for this reason. You figure that in house service work you can avoid high places and still do the type of work you like best. So far you have not had to do work that involved your fear. On one occasion you had a job that required the use of a step ladder. This made you nervous but not panicky, so you were able to cover up.

You are ashamed of this fear and have never mentioned it to your associates. It has been very inconvenient and has greatly interfered with your selection of a vocation. At last, you feel, you have found a job that permits you to use your skills without exposing your fears.

You are happily married and have two children, a boy of two and a girl of four.

You are anxious to get ahead in the company and so far you feel that the boss approves of your work. You have managed to hide your fear of high places from your boss and hope he never finds out because it might endanger your chances of getting ahead. Abnormal fears aren't things that people understand and you might be considered a neurotic.

IV. Comments and Implications

The fact that the job assignment in this instance is like that for Case 10 introduces a note of similarity between them, but here the similarity ends. The problems are entirely different because the reluctance to accept the job assignment has a unique cause in each instance. A supervisor who tries to generalize from one case to the other may discover that one cannot generalize conclusions regarding personal problems.

When the fact of Bill Edwards' fear of high places becomes known, Henry Spring no longer considers him to be uncooperative or insubordinate. Instead he feels that Bill's behavior is justified and that he should not be asked to work in high places as long as he does not use his special problem as an excuse to get out of doing his share of the undesirable work. In other words, most people accept a *good* excuse, although controversy may arise over what constitutes a *good* excuse. However, in most instances where there is such disagreement, it hinges on inadequate knowledge. Perhaps if we always knew a person's *real* reasons we would be more inclined to accept his behavior as justified.

In role playing this case, Henry Spring may not discover Bill's fear of high places. As a consequence, he is at a loss as to what to do, and not infrequently he feels that Bill Edwards is not behaving like a real human being. Certainly his behavior is not average, but this is because he has a special problem. Perhaps all persons have special fears or unique needs and hence have personalized problems at one time or another; and one does them an injustice when actions or decisions do not respect these.

A supervisor who can discover or who can be aware of personalized needs or problems in employees improves his ability to motivate them and increases his ability to be fair in his evaluation of them. In the present case the supervisor has the difficult assignment of discovering Bill Edwards' problem. One may wonder why employees don't tell their problems freely and thus make the process of understanding them less difficult. The answer to this is that supervisors as well as other people tend to judge rather than understand their fellow men. When one judges, one usually uses oneself or some average person as a standard and as a result a person with an unusual problem is not likely to receive a favorable judgment. Persons with problems learn to hide traits or actions or experiences judged unfavorably, and account for their behavior by supplying explanations (excuses) that they think will be acceptable to the judge. Thus Bill Edwards usually gives a series of excuses, and may even demonstrate considerable intellectual agility in telling the supervisor why he should not put up storm windows. He must be evasive without actually showing insubordination and this sometimes becomes difficult when the supervisor presses his case.

Before Bill Edwards will discuss his fear with the supervisor he must be convinced that Mr. Spring is trying to understand him rather than judge him. Any threat or any talk about what the other men may have done when they had the least seniority casts the supervisor in the role of a judge.

If, however, the supervisor indicates that he feels sure that Bill has a strong reason for not wanting to put up the storm windows and if he explains how he can use Bill's ability to better advantage provided he knows the reason for his behavior, he may cause Bill to confide in him. His manner of accepting Bill's attitude at the outset and his disinclination to use his authority will tend to cause Bill to feel that his job is secure. Thus the supervisor's initial behavior may determine to a considerable degree the extent to which Bill will share his problem.

The supervisor may also discover Bill's problem by interpreting his behavior. If Bill generally is willing to do menial tasks and yet shies away from tasks that have as the common element "working in high places," he may deduce the difficulty. If he suspects either epilepsy or fear of high places, a few good questions about job choices would settle the matter in his mind. Thus the supervisor can respect Bill's problem even if Bill never mentions it.

How is one to know when Bill has a good excuse and is not merely trying to avoid his share of work? The distinction between these two possibilities becomes apparent from Bill's over-all behavior. Usually Bill indicates how much he likes the company and the other fellows; he volunteers to do extra work, even menial work; and he offers to do certain parts of the assigned job. His cooperative and friendly general manner are inconsistent with interpretations of stubbornness, laziness, defensiveness, and selfishness. As soon as the supervisor discovers that Bill's behavior seems inconsistent with the demands of the situation, he may conclude that there is more to the problem than appears on the surface. If Bill indicates that he will quit before he puts up the storm windows, the supervisor has further reason to know that he does not have all the facts, because in terms of what is known, such extreme behavior is inappropriate.

If and when the supervisor learns Bill's problem, he still has his own problem to solve, that of getting the storm windows put up. He must now give the assignment to someone else, but this cannot be done in an arbitrary manner. The group has been following a particular practice in job assignments and any deviation from this pattern must be accepted by them if trouble is to be avoided. It is likely that a group of men will respect Bill's problem, especially since they have accepted him and like him. This means that Bill must be willing to have his personal problem discussed by the group. If Bill is reluctant to permit this, one might conclude that he is in need of counseling. Usually Bill sees the point and consents to let the supervisor take the problem to the rest of the crew for a decision. When a group of persons is asked to play the role of workers and are asked what should be done with the assignment in the light of Bill's unusual fear of high places, they invariably decide to give Bill some other job and volunteer to take over the storm window job on the basis of a plan they develop in discussion.

Fears of the kind shown by Bill, known as phobias, are not uncommon. Phobic fears are characterized by being highly intense, bordering on panic, and being quite unrelated to the degree of danger involved. They are also highly specific, the more common ones being terror of specific animals (e.g., snakes, spiders, etc.), small enclosures, and high places. Many phobias are cured or relieved but the need for curing them depends on the degree to which they interfere with one's life. Bill Edwards seems to have good adjustment in general so that he can be a valuable employee even if he does not seek a cure.

The case of Bill Edwards is an example of a class of individuals who require special treatment and consideration. There are many employees of this kind and some good ones are lost because job routines do not permit the flexibility that is needed to allow deviations from standardized procedures.

The method for discovering special needs or problems in employees is, in general, the same regardless of the need. Many, however, do not require the patience, understanding, and listening skills that Bill Edwards' required, since some of them can be readily divulged. The cue for recognizing an individual in need of special consideration is the appearance of behavior that is out of proportion to the situation. A woman who becomes hysterical when her child is run down by a car is behaving appropriately to the situation, but a woman employee who becomes hysterical when she cannot have the afternoon off is behaving inappropriately. There is more to the latter's problem and to her request than meets the eye.

Special privileges can be granted to certain employees only when the company is not inconvenienced and when other employees accept the special treatment of a particular employee as fair to them. For example, it might be convenient for a company to permit one office clerk to work from 8:30 A.M to 5:30 P.M. while the regular hours are 8:00 A.M to 5:00 P.M., but yet be reluctant to grant the privilege because of the possibility that other employees might then want to set their own hours. However, if other employees agreed to this special arrangement because the employee had a special problem, there would be no danger that employees would accuse the company of favoritism. In order for an employee to obtain this kind of treatment, however, she would have to have an acceptable reason and not abuse her privilege. A girl who had difficulty getting up in the morning and was frequently tardy would probably be turned down if she wanted later hours, while a widow who had to drop a child off at school might receive special consideration. If Bill Edwards' problem were of his own making or if he inconvenienced others too much, the group might not adjust to his needs, and the supervisor would then have to conclude that Bill could not meet the job requirements.

case 16

The Personnel
Adjustment Problem

I. Focusing the Problem

There are many problems in human relations that are quite easy to handle in their early stages but that become progressively more serious when allowed to continue. However, even supervisors who are well aware of this fact frequently put off taking the necessary action until the seriousness of the situation forces them to do so. In many instances, supervisors are too preoccupied with other problems to be aware of minor problems of employees. In other cases they lack the sensitivity necessary to detect undercurrents of difficulty. In still other situations supervisors are aware that certain problems exist but put up with the conditions until they become frustrating and then take punitive actions that aggravate the difficulty. In addition there are supervisors who are aware of problems but are reluctant to take action because they are lacking in skill and hence feel uncomfortable and unsure of themselves in meeting problem situations. This is particularly true when supervisors are sensitive to the feelings of others yet know of no way to deal effectively in face-to-face situations with employees whose behavior must be corrected because of the problems they create. Frequently the necessary steps are delayed until a salvage operation is about all that can be attempted.

The question then arises of whether attitudes and skills that are effective in dealing with problems as they occur are also useful for salvaging situations that have been allowed to deteriorate beyond the usual point for constructive action. If the methods can be demonstrated as workable under these conditions, then they should be highly effective under the usual and more favorable circumstances.

The Personnel Adjustment Problem concerns an employee who has been on the job for two months. She was hired as a private secretary on a three-month probationary basis. So far her supervisor has not discussed her work or progress with her. However, just prior to leaving on a one-month vacation, the supervisor asked his assistant to discuss things with her. Ordinarily the assistant exercises no supervision over this secretary but does act for his superior when the latter is absent.

The case calls for considerable competence on the part of the interviewer with respect to the proper attitudes and skills to use. Because the case creates many opportunities to discuss cause and effect relationships it is recommended that the Single Group Role Playing Procedure be used. In this manner all persons will observe the same events.

II. Single Group Role Playing Procedure

PREPARATION

1. All group members should become familiar with the background of the case by reading the section entitled Background Information on page 249 to themselves while the instructor reads it aloud.

2. The instructor should select two members from the group to play the roles. The role for Virginia Clark on page 250 is assigned to one of the participants, and the other participant will play the role of Paul Williams, found on page 251. The remaining members of the group will be observers, and their instructions are on page 252.

3. The participants should study their own roles in preparation for the scene. They should avoid reading the role for the other person. The observers also should study their materials.

4. While all members are preparing for the role playing, the instructor should turn to page 253 and read Section IV, Comments and Implications.

5. After the instructor has read his materials he should prepare the setting for the role playing scene by arranging a table and two chairs in the front of the room to represent Paul Williams' office. The table and one chair is for Williams and the other chair is for Miss Clark. The chairs and table should be placed in such a way that the observers can see the faces of the role players during the scene.

PROCESS

1. When the participants are ready to begin role playing, the one who will be Paul Williams should enter his previously prepared office and sit at the desk. After he is seated, the participant who will play the role of Virginia Clark should enter and as she approaches Williams' desk the role playing should begin.

2. Usually about 20 minutes will be needed for the role playing. The participants should be permitted to finish except when the interview deteriorates into conflict with no progress being made. If, after 15 minutes or so, no progress is made, the scene should be ended. Frequently the interviewer will reach a dead end in the interview and want to try it again, or one of the observers may wish to attempt the interview. In such cases, the wishes of the group should be followed whenever possible.

3. After the role playing has been completed, the instructor should move to the front of the room and begin the discussion of the scene.

ANALYSIS OF RESULTS OF INTERVIEW

1. What do the observers think of this interview? To what extent did the situation improve or become worse?

2. How do the observers think Virginia Clark feels about things? Is she bitter and disappointed or does she feel she has been fairly treated? (The observers should support their views with concrete behaviors they observed. Their sensitivity to Virginia's feelings can then be checked by asking the participant who played Virginia Clark how she felt.)

3. How do the observers think Williams feels about the outcome of the interview? To what extent might he experience frustration or defensiveness? In what ways, if any, might this have been a success experience for the interviewer? (The observers should again supply behavior evidence from Williams to support their opinions. These reactions should be checked with the participant who role played Williams.)

4. Which one talked the most? How did this influence things?

5. The instructor should summarize the views of the group briefly as to the success or failure of the interview.

DISCUSSION OF METHOD USED

1. How did Williams begin the interview? What effect did his manner have on subsequent events?

2. How well was the purpose of the interview stated? In what ways did Williams' manner of stating the issue influence the reactions of Virginia? Examples should be listed.

3. To what extent was Williams permissive? Should there have been more expression of feeling?

4. What did the interviewer learn during the interview? To what extent did he use what he learned to advantage in problem solving? How could he have done this better?

5. What were Miss Clark's real feelings about herself and her work?

6. What was her real problem in changing jobs? What did the interviewer do to help or hinder acceptance of the change?

7. The instructor should highlight the points brought out in the discussion, and reflect as accurately as possible the views of the group, regardless of whether he personally agrees with them or not.

DEVELOPING AN INTERVIEW PLAN

1. What should be the attitude of the interviewer in this situation?

2. Should Williams try to justify the actions of his superior, Mr. Drake, in any way? (This question will frequently bring out attitude differences. The authors believe he should not defend Mr. Drake: first, because Drake is in error, and second, because to do so will only generate further resentment in Miss Clark and serve no constructive purpose. However this does not mean he should criticize Drake in any way. There is a good neutral ground to occupy.)

3. How can this interview be handled so as to save Miss Clark's pride? (If the interviewer is friendly and acceptant and encourages Miss Clark to tell how she feels about her present job, she may be more likely to tell him that she feels inadequate for the job and therefore be more willing to accept a transfer.)

4. What things can the interviewer do to get Miss Clark to accept the change? Could she be caused to suggest solutions herself?

5. The instructor should summarize the points brought out, highlighting the ways agreed upon for handling the interview successfully.

GENERAL DISCUSSION OF PRINCIPLES AND APPLICATIONS

1. List some of the conclusions we can draw from this case.

2. List things that can be done to avoid problems of this sort.

3. Link applications of principles discussed to other cases.

III. Materials

BACKGROUND INFORMATION

Virginia Clark is private secretary to *Mr. Drake*, the personnel director of a large university. She was hired two months previously as a replacement for a girl who had resigned to get married after two years on the job. The position is an important one and calls for an individual with (*a*) poise and competence, (*b*) ability to grasp quickly the details of office correspondence and files, and (*c*) maturity sufficient to handle appointments and deal with various members of the administration and faculty. In accordance with the personnel policies of the university, Miss Clark was hired on a three-month probationary basis, with the understanding that if her work proved satisfactory, she would be employed on a permanent basis.

In addition to Miss Clark, there are three other girls in the office, all rather young and inexperienced. These three girls work under the supervision of *Paul Williams*, the assistant director of personnel who has been on this job for the past six months. Mr. Williams is responsible for the day to day operations of the personnel office, including (*a*) the interviewing and referral of job applicants to the various administrative and clerical vacancies in the university, (*b*) arranging for transfers, and (*c*) maintenance of personnel records. As assistant personnel director, he acts for Mr. Drake in the latter's absence.

Mr. Drake has just left on a month's vacation. Prior to leaving, he asked Mr. Williams to have an interview with Miss Clark and discuss how things were going with her. Miss Clark is about to enter Mr. Williams' office.

ROLE FOR VIRGINIA CLARK

You are private secretary to *Mr. Drake,* the director of the personnel office of a large university. You were hired two months ago to replace a girl who had held the job for two years and was very capable at handling it. The job is an important one; it involves a detailed knowledge of the office correspondence and filing system, as well as handling appointments, dealing with important members of the university administration and faculty, and other duties requiring both poise and capability.

The other girls in the office are also fairly new and inexperienced and none of them can do much to help you in learning the office routine, the location of various documents, and so forth. So you are quite overwhelmed by all the details of your new job, and it has taken you some time to get at all familiar with the office routine. Furthermore, you are very shy in dealing with people, and find it hard to get accustomed to all the personal contacts you have to make with visitors, job applicants, directors of other offices, and so on. You feel you are a conscientious and willing worker, but that you cannot cope with all your new responsibilities, especially since no one in the office is able to help you.

Mr. Drake, your boss, is a very busy man. He is always nice to you, and never criticizes anything you do. However, you sense vaguely that he is in some way displeased with you, and you try extra hard to make a good impression on him and please him in everything you do. You have been trying hard to increase your typing speed, thinking that he recognized that you had not had a great deal of practice. Most girls type faster than you, but with more practice you will catch up.

Although you were hired on a three-month probation period, with the understanding that you would be hired permanently only if your work proved satisfactory, you feel that you have been doing the best you could during the past two months, and, since your boss has never criticized you, you are puzzled as to why, as soon as your boss has left on a month's vacation, his assistant, *Mr. Williams,* calls you in his office.

ROLE FOR PAUL WILLIAMS

You are the assistant director of the personnel office of a large university. You have had this job for six months now, and are very anxious to please *Mr. Drake*, the director of the office, who is a man whom you admire greatly. During the past two months Mr. Drake has talked to you several times about the inefficiency and ineptitude of his new secretary, *Miss Virginia Clark*, and you have heard other complaints about her from others in the office and from outside visitors. She is not only very awkward in dealing with people, but she is also a very poor stenographer, whose work has to be corrected and done over almost all the time.

Because Mr. Drake is very kindhearted, he has not felt able to criticize his own secretary, and has often asked you to see to it that her work was done over again, without her knowledge, by one of the other, more capable, stenographers. Mr. Drake feels that Virginia is extremely sensitive, and he is reluctant to criticize her or to tell her frankly that she is incompetent, since he is afraid of the emotional effect this might have on her. However, he realizes that in a job as important as hers, it is necessary to have a girl who is capable and efficient, and so he has asked you to find him a new secretary, and to find a job in one of the other university offices to which Miss Clark can be transferred.

You have lined up a job for Miss Clark at the registrar's office, where the salary is only slightly lower, and the duties involved are much less demanding. You feel she would be much happier in this other job, but you now have the problem of telling her that you do not want her to stay on in your office. Since you know she will become very upset by something like this, you feel you have a difficult problem and you want to handle it without either damaging the girl's self-confidence or making yourself and your boss appear arbitrary and unreasonable. She is about to come to your office for an interview.

OBSERVER'S INSTRUCTIONS

The following outline is furnished as a guide for observing and evaluating the interview.

1. In what ways did the interviewer show a friendly and helpful attitude?

2. How well was the purpose of the interview stated? In what ways did Miss Clark react? Were her reactions the sort that might be expected?

3. Was the interviewer on the defensive at any time? If so, why did this occur? What effect did this have on the interview? Did Williams attempt to justify Drake's actions? If so, in what way did this hinder things?

4. Which one talked the most, the interviewer or the person being interviewed?

5. How did the solution, if any, come about? If there was no solution reached, why was this?

6. How do you think Miss Clark feels about this interview? To what extent does she accept the idea of a transfer? In what ways did the interviewer help or hinder acceptance?

7. What were some of the skills the interviewer used that helped things? Which ones might he have used to better advantage?

8. How might future problems of this sort be prevented in this situation?

IV. Comments and Implications

In this case the interviewer will usually find himself in serious difficulty early in the discussion. There are many possible errors that can lead to failure, but probably the most frequent one is for the interviewer to be vague in stating the purpose of the interview and speak in generalities. This creates suspicion and anxiety in the person being interviewed and produces hostile reactions.

Another common error is for the interviewer to announce bluntly that he has found a different job for the individual. This is neither an explanation nor a statement of a problem but is a solution that the interviewer is attempting to impose or sell and which he hopes will be accepted. Such an attempt will also worsen the situation since this is an abrupt action which the employee had no part in planning. As a rule, the employee will see this is a crude attempt at manipulation and will show strong resentment. Further, she will quickly sense the various moves that have been made and view the interviewer as the hatchet man for his superior. At this point, the interviewer himself will usually become defensive and will often make the situation worse by attempting to justify both his actions and those of his superior. Thus any approach that stems from an attitude of defensiveness or manipulation on the part of the interviewer will almost invariably result in failure and aggravate the situation further.

However, the interviewer can adopt a permissive and acceptant attitude and indicate to the employee at the outset that he wishes to explore with her how she feels about her work at this point in the three-month probationary period. By doing this he will facilitate understanding and free expression of views. This will help the employee to speak freely without feeling the need to cover up her deficiencies and feelings of inadequacy in the work. After she has expressed these feelings she will usually be more receptive toward exploring other positions and may like the idea of transferring to a less demanding job. Under these conditions it would be unnecessary for the interviewer to bring up her unsatisfactory performance in the present job. Should she resist a change it would become necessary to explore how she is handling her job as a whole, but the previous establishment of a friendly atmosphere will do much to cause the interviewer to be seen as helpful and so facilitate acceptance of a change. Further, it is not necessary to take final action during this interview because there is still a month of the probationary period remaining. However, if the interviewer can bring about a satisfactory solution during the interview, this can be to the advantage of everyone concerned.

Problems which reveal undue delay in action by the supervisor can arise for a variety of different reasons. Most often they come about when supervisors are made to focus their attention on getting the work out instead of creating optimal conditions for their employees to work in. Such an approach tends to be self-defeating in that it diverts the supervisor from effective functioning in the role of a helpful representative of management and instead makes him appear as a judge or critic. In being close to his employees through friendly contacts of both a formal and an informal nature, an alert and sensitive supervisor can anticipate many human relations problems and deal with them before they become serious. In doing this he will also create an atmosphere of frankness in dealings with employees so that neither they nor the supervisor need feel uncomfortable over correction of deficiencies. The difference between an employee's resentment at being corrected and his appreciation for being helped to do better is largely a matter of the attitude and skill of the supervisor, and these can be developed through training.

case 17

The Parasol Assembly
Bottleneck

I. Focusing the Problem

Management in business and industry is well aware of the fact that success or failure frequently depends on the quality of solutions which are developed for the various problems that arise. Companies will often go to great lengths to recruit and train promising individuals for management positions, the expectation being that such individuals will deal with the problems in an intelligent and effective manner.

Within the framework of current management practices, many decisions are made by supervisors as operating heads of the various organization units. Problems that cut across different functions are customarily solved in formal or informal conferences between the individuals concerned. Frequently staff experts are brought in to contribute technical information or other highly specialized knowledge on the problem.

These approaches to problem solving raise the question of whether the various resources of talent and trained personnel in the company are fully utilized in the most effective manner, or whether there are other procedures by which the quality of thinking that is brought to bear on a problem can be upgraded. If so, what are the procedures for accomplishing this? In what ways does the type of supervisory leadership influence solution quality? What leadership functions can a supervisor perform in order to help rather than hinder a good solution?

Some answers to these and a number of related questions are already available from research findings. It has been demonstrated, for example, that the interacting members of a group obtain correct solutions to certain problems more readily than a similar number of individuals working independently.[21] The favorable result of interaction appears to be mainly one of more critical evaluation of suggestions and ideas. The introduction of a leader into a group also has a strong favorable influence on the quality of problem solving,[22] in that a person with the correct answer will be given the opportunity to influence the majority of the members. In the absence of a leader, the contribution of a minority with the correct answer tends to be lost. It has further been shown that a leader who has creative ideas and skills can upgrade solution quality by diverting individuals away from blind alleys in their thinking and causing them to explore in new directions for the solution.[23] Still other studies indicate the importance of democratic attitudes in the leader's ability to improve the quality of solutions.[24]

For industrial and business management these findings suggest that the necessary methods are available to management for achieving solution quality of a high order in a greater number of instances. However, these methods also require certain attitudes and skills which are not prevalent in management but which can be developed through training and practice. The purpose of the Parasol Assembly Case is to provide a demonstration of an effective approach to problem solving and indicate the attitudes and skills required of the leader. It is designed to illustrate the application of these methods and skills by means of an industrial problem. The case furnishes a problem for which there are various solutions, one of which is clearly superior to others. Individuals working by themselves rarely develop the superior solution. However, a group under the leadership of a person who possesses the proper attitudes will frequently develop this solution. As skill factors of the leader improve, there is a further increase in the frequency with which groups develop the superior solution. Thus the case furnishes an excellent demonstration of the superiority of group efforts at problem solving over the efforts of individuals. At the same time it highlights the importance of proper attitudes and skills on the part of the leader.

The problem concerns a crew of seven men who work on a circular

[21] Marjorie E. Shaw, A Comparison of Individuals and Small Groups in the Rational Solution of Complex Problems, *Amer. Jour. Psych.*, 1932, *44*, 491–504.

[22] N. R. F. Maier and A. R. Solem, The Contribution of a Discussion Leader to the Quality of Group Thinking: The Effective Use of Minority Opinions, *Human Relations*, 1952, *5*, 277–288.

[23] N. R. F. Maier, An Aspect of Human Reasoning, *British Jour. of Psych.*, 1933, *24*, 144–155; H. Guetzkow, An Analysis of the Operation of Set in Problem Solving Behavior, *Jour. Genl. Psych.*, 1951, *45*, 219–244.

[24] A. R. Solem, *The Influence of the Discussion Leader's Attitude on the Outcome of Group Decision Conferences.* Unpublished doctoral thesis, Univ. of Michigan, 1953.

assembly line. The crew members differ in ability for the job. Since the line is paced by the slowest member, and since production is low, the problem for the leader and the group becomes one of improving the situation.

It is recommended that only the Single Group Procedure be used in role playing this case so that specific skill points can be discussed in detail.

II. Single Group Role Playing Procedure

PREPARATION

1. Eight members of the group are needed to play the roles. One participant will be the foreman and the remaining seven will be the members of his crew.

2. Persons who do not participate as role players will either act as observers or play the part of consultants. A group of approximately four persons is needed as consultants, whereas the number of observers need not be limited. It is desirable, however, to have enough observers to permit a critical discussion later on. (In the event that the class is small the consultant group should be eliminated.)

3. All persons should turn to page 262 and read the section entitled General Instructions.

4. The instructor should designate one participant as the foreman, Hal Benton, and assign the crew-member roles to the other seven participants.

5. All participants should study their roles. The foreman, Hal Benton, should read his role on page 264. The roles for the crew members are on pages 265 to 272. All should study their parts carefully so that it will be unnecessary for them to refer to the written material during the scene. They should avoid reading any role except their own.

6. Observers should turn to page 272 and read the Instructions for Observers.

7. Consultants should turn to page 273 and read the Instructions for Consultants.

8. When all group members are studying their materials the instructor should draw on the easel the diagram of the assembly shown on page 262. This will help everyone to visualize the work place during the discussion.

9. The setting for the role playing scene should be arranged to represent Benton's office. This can be done by placing a table and eight chairs in the front of the room, arranging them so that the table and one chair are for Benton's use and the other seven chairs, forming a horseshoe figure in front of Benton's desk, are for the crew members.

PROCESS

1. Consultants should move to the end of the room away from the role playing scene and begin working on their solutions to the problem in ac-

cordance with their instructions. The observers should be seated where they can readily observe the role playing scene.

2. The participants who are crew members should enter Benton's office and seat themselves in the previously arranged chairs in the same order as shown in the diagram on page 262. This seating arrangement will assist role players to call each other by name.

3. After the crew members are seated, the foreman should enter his office and begin the scene.

4. Role playing will usually take approximately 45 minutes. Participants should be allowed to finish the scene whenever possible. However, if the discussion breaks down and no progress is made after 20 or 30 minutes, the scene should be interrupted. Observers should freely offer the foreman advice on how to proceed. The foreman should consider the suggestions and use any he feels are helpful. The instructor should then delete any parts of the discussion that led to difficulty and request the role playing to proceed from any point agreed upon in discussion.

5. Role playing should be carried to some natural stopping point. A unanimous agreement to try something, a majority decision, or a decision imposed by the foreman are typical stopping points.

6. Consultants should be asked to return to the class as a whole and join the discussion.

DISCUSSION OF SOLUTIONS REACHED

1. The group's solution should be summarized for the benefit of the consultants.

2. Consultants should present their solution for comparison.

3. Foreman and workers should indicate what they like and dislike about the consultants' solution.

4. Observers should comment on basic differences in the solutions. Such factors as complexity, concern for the feelings of the workers, and practical considerations should be compared in the solutions.

5. Even though consultants were given the viewpoints of the workers it is unlikely that they expected the superior workers to help out the less capable ones. Compare the solutions in terms of the degree to which superior workers were required to work according to their abilities.

6. What are some of the problems of getting acceptance of a solution offered by consultants?

ANALYSIS OF FOREMAN'S HANDLING OF DISCUSSION

1. How did the leader begin the discussion? From his statement of the problem, what would you infer concerning his attitude toward the group? Was his primary interest to increase production or improve the job for his crew? Observers should comment on these issues and all members should join in the general evaluation.

2. Did the crew react constructively to the problem in general, or did they feel pressured by the leader? What did the leader do to produce the reactions shown by the crew?

3. In what ways did Joe make the leader's situation more difficult? Should the leader protect Joe from pressure by other crew members? In what ways would defending Joe influence the discussion as compared to not defending him? Role players, especially Joe, should contribute their evaluations of the opinions expressed.

4. What did the leader do to help or hinder the crew members in expressing their feelings about the work? To what extent was he acceptant of complaints or criticisms from the crew? (To be helpful the leader should invite comment and criticism and accept it. Complaints will usually involve not having enough to do, being bored, and the pace being too fast.)

5. Did the leader learn about George's real feelings on the matter? After observers have discussed this question, George should read his role to the class.

6. To what extent did all crew members share in the discussion? What did the leader do to encourage full participation? What might he have done differently? (Unless the leader draws out silent members, some crew members are likely to dominate the discussion, thus reducing full participation.) After discussing the matter, the persons who talked the least during role playing should tell why they didn't talk more.

7. Where did the solution come from? To what extent was the final solution a group product? In what ways does the solution improve the job for the crew members? What will be the effect on productivity of the crew's participation in reaching the solution? (Good solutions are usually the product of pooled thinking in the group, and improve the job. By improving the job, production will be increased.)

8. In what ways could the foreman capitalize on the complaints and differences of opinion in the crew to improve problem solving? What would be some effects on solution quality of exploring the various complaints and the ideas suggested? What are some things a leader can do to bring out

many different approaches to the problem? What advantages would these have?

9. In what ways can we apply the results from this case to our own problems? (This question should be explored by the use of a few specific situations that the group members can contribute.)

III. Materials [25]

GENERAL INSTRUCTIONS

Visualize a sub-assembly situation in which seven men, working in a circle, assemble a part of a car (carburetor or instrument panel, for example). The article enters the circle at one point, and each person adds his

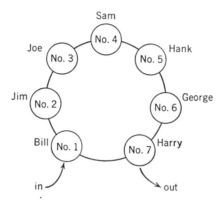

Figure 4. Positions of men in parasol assembly team.

pieces and pushes the unit to the next worker who adds his elements. When the unit leaves the circle, it is a completed part product. This work arrangement is diagrammed in Figure 4.

Suppose there are four such "parasol" sub-assembly stations, each one supervised by a foreman. Suppose further that Station A assembles 85 units per day; Station B, 80 per day; Station C, 60 units per day; and Station D, 50 units. It is a fact that Station D previously assembled 60 units. The foreman was dissatisfied with the production and reprimanded the group. Following the reprimand production fell to 50 units a day.

The assembly work is simple and requires a minimum of training for each step. The aptitude requirement is primarily good finger dexterity. The materials for each assembly position are located in bins that are kept supplied by material handlers. Thus each worker has his essential material at his elbow. The job has been analyzed by time-and-motion experts so that the positions are of equal difficulty. Pay is based on hourly rates.

[25] Role instructions are taken from an article by Maier, The Quality of Group Decision as Influenced by the Discussion Leader, *Human Relations,* 1950, 3, 155–174. Permission to reproduce the roles has been granted by the editors of *Human Relations.*

The total factory production is dependent upon receiving the required number of assembled units from these four stations. The production is now so low that the factory production as a whole has had to slow down. The desired quota is 300 parts per shift for the four stations combined.

We are concerned with Station C, producing at the rate of 60 units. The work piles up at the position of *Joe Brown*. The unit must pass through him (position 3), and he always has several piled up waiting for him. Foremen on nonproduction jobs are not willing to accept Joe as a transfer. Joe is a man of 60 with 30 years of service in the company. Emphasis on improving production has brought his deficiencies to light.

ROLE FOR HAL BENTON, FOREMAN

You are the new foreman in Unit C and have been instructed to get production up. The job has been analyzed by time-and-motion study men and the amount of work at each position is practically the same. The number 3 position (*Joe's* position) is, however, slightly easier than the others in that one less motion is required. Undoubtedly the previous foreman put Joe there to reduce the bottleneck. You have received training in the procedure of solving problems using the crew's participation and are going to try to work out your problem by this method. You therefore have stopped the production line for a discussion. You understand that what you do is your problem. You cannot pass Joe off to another foreman. You find Joe a likable person and it is your impression that Joe gets along well with the other men in the unit.

ROLE FOR BILL, NO. 1 POSITION

You find you can easily do more work but have to slow down because *Joe* gets behind. In order not to make him feel bad you hold back. You don't want to get Joe into trouble.

ROLE FOR JIM, NO. 2 POSITION

You and *Bill* work closely together and you are usually waiting for your part from Bill. This waiting for the part is more prevalent in the later part of the day than in the beginning. To keep busy you often help out *Joe* who can't keep up. However, you are careful not to let the foreman catch you helping Joe because he might let Joe go.

ROLE FOR JOE, NO. 3 POSITION

You work hard but just aren't as fast as the others. You know you are holding things up, but no matter how you try you get behind. The rest of the fellows are fine boys and have more energy than you do at your age.

ROLE FOR SAM, NO. 4 POSITION

Joe has trouble keeping up and you sometimes grab Joe's part and finish it for him when the boss isn't looking. Joe is a bit old for the pace set and he feels the strain. For you the job is easy and you feel the whole job is slowed down too much because of Joe. "Why couldn't Joe be given less to do?" you ask yourself.

ROLE FOR HANK, NO. 5 POSITION

You feel a bit uneasy on this job. There isn't enough to do so you have to act busy. If only *Joe* could speed up a bit. Why don't they move him out of the group? Is the company so blind that they can't see where the production trouble is?

ROLE FOR GEORGE, NO. 6 POSITION

You are able to keep up with the pace but on the last assembly job you were pressed. Fortunately *Joe* is slower than you are so he keeps the pressure off of you. You are determined that Joe not be moved off the job. Somebody has to protect people from speed-up tactics.

ROLE FOR HARRY, NO. 7 POSITION

You get bored doing the same operations over and over. On some jobs you get variety by working fast for a while then slowly. On this job you can't work fast because the parts aren't fed to you fast enough. It gets you down to keep doing exactly the same thing over and over in slow motion. You are considering getting a job some place where they can keep a man busy.

OBSERVER'S INSTRUCTIONS

The foreman's attitude, his skill in sensing feelings and ideas developed in the discussion, and his ability to act on the basis of what he learns will mainly determine the success or failure of the discussion. Be especially alert for how well he adapts to new developments.

1. Observe how the leader begins the discussion and what this indicates concerning his attitude.

2. Note the favorable and unfavorable reactions from the group members. Take note of what the leader did to cause the type of reactions he got.

3. Did everyone participate? What did the leader do to help or hinder participation?

4. Make a list of what the leader learned of how the men felt about the way the job was going. Note the ways he used this information to help problem solving.

5. On what things did the crew members disagree? What did the foreman do to use the disagreement as a basis for getting at the main problem? What was this main problem?

6. Who suggested the solution? Was the initial idea altered or improved in any way by the discussion? How did the leader help or hinder this interaction?

7. What were some indications that thinking in the group went in circles or got into a rut? How could the leader get the crew to get out of a single line of thinking and try different approaches?

INSTRUCTIONS FOR CONSULTANTS

Assume you have been asked to solve the bottleneck problem for Hal Benton. In order that you can better understand his situation, read over his role instructions on page 264. Assume further that you have interviewed each of the men and have gained an appreciation of the way they see things. Read the role instructions for crew members on pages 265–271 for this information.

In the light of the facts of the situation and the information on the way the men feel, prepare a practical solution to the bottleneck problem. It is hoped that you can come up with a unanimous decision.

IV. Comments and Implications

In this case the question of whether the situation will become better or worse will be determined mainly by the leader's approach in the first few minutes of the discussion.   Failure is almost certain if the leader takes a complaining or critical attitude toward the crew, or states the problem as one of low production.   This will produce defensive reactions and hostility toward the leader.   Frequently some crew members will blame Joe for the poor showing of the group and other members will protect him.   This will tend to split the crew into two opposing factions and lead to a breakdown of the discussion.   In either case the situation will almost always become worse instead of better.

However, if the leader's attitude is one of consideration for the crew and he shows a helpful interest in making the job run better, sincere attempts to solve the problem will occur.   Instead of showing negative reactions, the crew members will be constructive and cooperative and will look for ways to improve the situation.   In one way or another such methods will involve removing the pressure on Joe.   The most frequent type of solution will be one in which fast employees will find some way to help Joe with his work.   This willingness of the fast workers to help Joe is a distinct gain and is something that management could not ask its employees to do.

However, helping Joe is not sufficient to clear up a bottleneck.   As soon as the one slowest worker is helped or eliminated, a new one is created.   In this case George is just able to keep up.   If production increases he will need help and it is for this reason he may resist any suggestions to help Joe or to get rid of Joe.   It follows then that a solution that deals also with George's problem will be better than one that deals only with Joe's.

In addition to the various conventional solutions for helping out those who need help, there is an inventive rotation solution.   According to this plan, all members move to the next position in the line at regular intervals, e.g., every hour.   This improves the job in many ways.   Boredom is relieved by the change in work (both positions and pace may change) and by the goal introduced because of making a move at the end of a predetermined time.   Joe is no longer a bottleneck problem because his unfinished work becomes distributed over all the positions on which he works.   All crew members can set their own pace and make up the left-over work they find in the position they inherit.   Finally, the assembly line is no longer paced by the slowest man; instead it operates at a rate equal to the average of the entire crew.

In order to obtain this solution, it is generally necessary for the leader to demonstrate considerable skill in discussion leadership, in addition to having the proper attitudes toward his crew. The pattern followed by the leader should be one in which a free, permissive atmosphere is created from the outset; his main concern being the problem in the crew, not the inadequate production. If the leader will invite discussion of problems and difficulties and list these on the easel there will be a basis for discussing ways of improving the job. This will lead away from nonconstructive blaming of Joe and produce various ideas for reducing boredom, fitting the pace of the line to individual abilities, keeping the crew together, and so on. Exploration of different ways for solving these problems tends to lead to new thinking and this is necessary for obtaining the inventive solution and seeing to it that its merits are recognized. However, the leader must be permissive at all times as well as sensitive to the feelings in the crew. Further, he must protect Joe and show that he would like to keep the crew together. Full participation must be encouraged by questions from the leader and he must be capable of adapting to new developments in the discussion when they arise.

The ability to ask good questions so that the crew members are caused to abandon blind alleys in thinking and look for new ideas is an important aspect of the leader's contribution to the quality of thinking. Questions about (a) ways to relieve boredom, (b) methods whereby a work pace can be found that will fit everyone's interest, (c) the uses that can be made of variety, and (d) how one changes his pace for different times of the day help to move discussion into broader channels. Summarizing progress and points of difference and agreement also seems to move discussion into new territory.

In performing the functions described above, the leader can frequently upgrade solution quality to a marked degree. This case therefore can furnish an excellent demonstration of the ways in which a leader who is sensitive to needs and feelings and possesses skills in discussion leadership can produce superior results. If he has good ideas himself it will help him to ask good questions but he must not push the group into his way of thinking. It is better to accept a lesser quality solution than to persist in trying for the best.

For obtaining good solutions to management problems, methods which are democratic in nature and place the supervisor in the role of a helpful representative of management, not a policeman or a driver, would appear to have clearcut advantages. Even with a minimum of skill, a leader with helpful attitudes can obtain solutions of good quality and a high degree of acceptance. When trained leadership skills are added there is a further upgrading of solution quality and acceptance. Methods for solving problems which upgrade the thinking of employees or management members beyond the level of their efforts as individuals and, in addition, have acceptance of high quality solutions virtually built in are the goals of research in management.

case 18

The Evaluation Interview

I. Focusing the Problem

When a supervisor conducts merit evaluation interviews with his subordinates the result is often the creation of ill feelings and misunderstanding rather than improved relations and employee development. Frequently the subordinate feels there is undue emphasis on deficiencies and in protecting his interests he becomes defensive in his manner. When the superior, as a result, feels impelled to justify his point of view his behavior similarly becomes defensive. The result is that the interview situation frequently becomes one in which conflict and new problems are produced, rather than one in which solutions to existing problems are achieved.

A common cause of the difficulties encountered is the difference in frames of reference of the supervisor and his subordinates with respect to over-all performance. The supervisor's situation, on the one hand, is one which tends to make him sensitive to deficiencies in job outcomes because these create problems for him; he is likely to take adequate performance more or less for granted. The employee, on the other hand, will be aware of the little extras he does and is likely to interpret poor results as due to inadequate assignments, poor training, or someone else's failure to cooperate. Thus the evaluation interview situation tends to be one in which the divergent views are highlighted in such a manner that understanding is hindered rather than promoted.

Because difficulties are encountered in interviews of this kind there is a reluctance for superiors to "let employees know how they stand." When a company program requires periodic evaluations there is a marked tendency for supervisors to suppress the unfavorable evaluations. In this instance the purpose of the evaluations is defeated. The success or failure of an employee developmental program largely depends on the skill with which employees are interviewed by their superiors.

The purpose of this case is to develop sensitivity toward communication problems in this type of interview. For this reason the Single Group Role Playing Procedure is recommended. If the objective were to give practice, the Multiple Role Playing Procedure would be desirable.

II. Single Group Role Playing Procedure

PREPARATION

1. Two members from the group are needed to play the roles. The remaining members will participate as observers.

2. Two persons should be selected, one to role play the supervisor who conducts the evaluation interview and the other to role play the employee interviewed. (It is unwise to use volunteers because they may experience failure and have a face-saving problem.)

3. The General Instructions on pages 283 f. should be read by the observers and participants alike. The organization chart shown in Figure 5 should be consulted to learn the names and positions of relevant persons.

4. The participant who will conduct the interview should study the role of George Stanley given on pages 285 f., while the participant who is to be interviewed should study the role of Tom Burke on pages 287 f. Both should study their roles carefully so that they can play them without referring back to the written material.

5. In the meantime the observers should turn to page 289 and read the Instructions for Observers.

6. The setting for the role playing requires a table in front of the room to represent the interviewer's desk, and two chairs arranged by the desk in such a way that the participants can talk with each other comfortably and still have their faces visible to the observers.

PROCESS

1. When everyone is ready, George Stanley should enter his office and sit at his desk. A moment later Tom Burke should enter the office and the scene begins.

2. The amount of time needed to complete the interview will vary somewhat but from 20 to 30 minutes usually will be adequate. The interview should be carried to the point of completion unless an argument develops and no progress is evident after ten or fifteen minutes of conflict.

3. If an interview is ending too quickly various alternate approaches suggested by observers may be tested briefly.

EVALUATION OF THE INTERVIEW

1. Was mutual understanding increased or decreased as a result of the interview? (When the supervisor emphasizes weaknesses, there invariably will be misunderstanding and hard feelings; if he listens and is acceptant, understanding will be improved.)

2. Did Burke go up or down in Stanley's estimation, as a result of the interview? (If good communication occurs in the interview Stanley will come to think more highly of Burke. If an argument arises, Stanley may think less well of Burke.)

3. Is Burke's opinion of Stanley better or worse as a result of the interview? (When Stanley is permissive and acceptant, Burke is likely to think better of him. If Stanley rejects Burke's feelings, or is critical, Burke will usually think less of him.)

4. Will Stanley alter his judgment about the merit rating of Burke as a result of the interview? (If Stanley comes to understand Burke's side of the problem Stanley would probably rate Burke higher in several respects after the interview. If misunderstanding arises, there would probably be no change or even a lower rating.)

5. Who talked the most, Stanley or Burke? (If Stanley succeeds in drawing out Burke, Burke will do most of the talking.)

6. Will the interview have favorable or unfavorable effects on Burke's future motivation? (When Stanley is acceptant of Burke's feelings and gives recognition to his performance and ideas, motivation will be helped. If Burke feels his efforts are unappreciated or that his ideas are not accepted, motivation may be hindered.)

7. In what ways was Burke's motivation influenced (helped or hindered) by the interview? (List the actions of Stanley that affected Burke's motivation.)

8. How many interviewers would have avoided all of the pitfalls present in this type of situation?

METHOD USED BY THE INTERVIEWER

1. How did Stanley begin the interview? (In general it is desirable that the reason for the interview be stated in the first minute or so and this should be done in a friendly atmosphere.)

2. What opportunities were there for Stanley to have been more permis-

sive and acceptant of Burke's feelings and ideas? (Skill in encouraging free expression of ideas and feelings and avoiding argument is essential.)

3. What are the things the interviewer learned and did not learn from Burke? (Burke's role instructions are reexamined; items relevant to the evaluation may be listed.)

4. Did the interviewer use leading questions to explore Burke's views and feelings or did he explore mostly for facts? (The use of general questions at the outset and more specific ones left for later on when defensive reactions have disappeared is recommended. The amount of questioning and kinds of questions to use will depend on how freely and explicitly Burke expresses himself. The interviewer must be guided by his sensitivity to Burke's feelings.)

5. To what extent was each of the three stated purposes of the interview (see Stanley's instructions) accomplished?

6. What were the things observers liked about the way the interview was handled and how would they do things differently? (This discussion will bring out any points not covered by the previous discussion. The interviewee should be consulted to see if his feelings support the observers' opinions.)

DEVELOPING AN INTERVIEW PLAN

1. How should an interview of this kind be started? (Consideration should be given to (a) preliminary remarks, (b) how and when to state the reason for the interview, and (c) the use of open-ended or broad questions such as "How are things going with you?".)

2. Discuss in what areas of the work Stanley can give recognition or praise to Burke. (Those aspects of the work that are going well and are not giving difficulty can be discussed at this point.)

3. What are the best ways for getting Burke to talk freely about problems or things that give him trouble? (The place to use the listening technique and other permissive approaches that an interviewer may employ should be determined.)

4. How can the supervisor in such interviews make it clear that he wants to be helpful? (Consider such matters as who should volunteer the existence of difficulties, the ways in which improvements may be made, and the kind of help that is to be forthcoming.)

5. How can the supervisor ask questions without seeming to cross examine and question an employee's ability?

6. How accurately can employees evaluate their own performance? (Compare self-evaluations of poorly and well adjusted individuals. Which

are most likely to overestimate or underestimate their own performance? Which will tend to cover up deficiencies, and which will be most on the defensive if criticized?)

7. What type of interview situation will make a person feel most free to discuss his shortcomings?

8. What conclusions about evaluation interviewing can be drawn from this case? (A list of the contributions made by the group may be written on the blackboard.)

III. Materials [26]

GENERAL INSTRUCTIONS

George Stanley is the electrical section head in the Engineering Department of the American Construction Company. The work in the department includes design, drafting, cost estimates, keeping maps up to date, checking

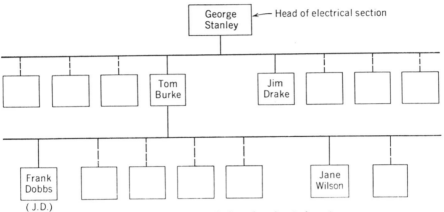

Figure 5. Organizational chart for electrical section.

standards and building codes, field inspection and follow up, etc. Eight first-line supervisors report to George Stanley. The duties of the supervisors are partly technical and partly supervisory. The organizational chart for Mr. Stanley's section is shown in Figure 5.

Company policy requires that all section heads interview each of their supervisors once a year, the purpose being

(*a*) to evaluate the supervisor's performance during the year,
(*b*) to give recognition for jobs well done, and
(*c*) to correct weaknesses.

The company believes that employees should know how they stand and that everything should be done to develop management personnel. The evaluation interviews were introduced to serve this purpose.

[26] Roles and instruction are taken from a laboratory exercise in Maier, *Psychology in Industry*, Houghton Mifflin Co., Boston, 1955, 561–564. Permission to reproduce this material has been granted by Houghton Mifflin Co., publishers.

Tom Burke is one of the supervisors reporting to Stanley; today we will witness an evaluation interview conducted by Stanley with Tom Burke.

Tom Burke has a college degree in electrical engineering and in addition to his technical duties, which often take him to the field, he supervises the work of one junior designer, six draftsmen and two women clerks. He is highly paid as are all of the supervisors in this department because of the high requirements in technical knowledge. Burke has been with the company for 12 years and has been a supervisor for 2 years. He is married and has two children. He owns his home and is active in the civic affairs of the community in which he lives.

ROLE FOR GEORGE STANLEY, SECTION HEAD

You have evaluated all of the supervisors who report to you and during the next two weeks will interview each of them. You hope to use these interviews constructively to develop each man. Today you have arranged to interview *Tom Burke,* one of the eight first-line supervisors who report to you. Here is the information and his evaluation as given in your files.

Thomas Burke: 12 years with company, 2 years as supervisor, college degree, married, 2 children. Evaluation: Highly creative and original, and exceptionally competent technically. His unit is very productive and during the 2 years he supervised the group there has been a steady improvement. Within the past six months you have given him extra work and he has gotten this done on schedule. As far as productivity and dependability are concerned, he is your top man.

His cooperation with other supervisors in the section leaves much to be desired. Before you made him a supervisor his originality and technical knowledge were available to your whole section. Gradually he has withdrawn and now acts more as a lone wolf. You've asked other supervisors to talk over certain problems with him but they tell you he offers no suggestions. He tells them he's busy or listens disinterestedly to their problems, kids them or makes sarcastic remarks, depending on his mood. On one occasion he allowed Jim Drake, one of the supervisors in another unit, to make a mistake that he could have forestalled by letting him know the status of certain design changes which he knew about and had seen. It is to be expected that supervisors cooperate on matters involving design changes that affect them.

Furthermore, during the past six months he has been unwilling to take two assignments. He said they were routine, that he preferred more interesting work and he advised you to give the assignments to other supervisors. To prevent trouble, you followed his suggestion. However, you feel that you can't give him all of the interesting work and that if he persists in this attitude there will be trouble. You cannot play favorites and keep up morale in your unit.

Burke's failure to cooperate has you worried for another reason. Although his group is highly productive, there is more turnover among his draftsmen than in other groups. You have heard no complaints as yet, but you suspect that he may be treating his men in an arbitrary manner. Certainly if he talks up to you and other supervisors, he's likely to be even more that way with his men. Apparently the high productivity in his group is not due to high morale, but to his ability to use his men to do the things for which they are best suited. This method won't develop good drafts-men. You hope to discuss these matters with Burke in such a way as to recognize his good points and at the same time correct some of his weak-nesses.

ROLE FOR TOM BURKE, SUPERVISOR

One junior designer, six draftsmen, and two women clerks report to you. You feel that you get along fine with your group. You have always been pretty much of an idea man and apparently have the knack of passing on your enthusiasm to others in your group. There is a lot of "we" feeling in your unit because it is obvious that your group is the most productive.

You believe in developing your men and always give them strong recommendations. You feel you have gained the reputation of developing your employees because they frequently go out and get much better jobs. Since promotion is necessarily slow in a company such as yours, you feel that the best way to stimulate morale is to develop new men and demonstrate that a good man can get somewhere. The two girls in your unit are bright and efficient and there is a lot of good-natured kidding. Recently one of your girls, *Jane Wilson*, turned down an outside offer that paid $35 a month more, for she preferred to stay in your group. You are going to get her a raise the first chance you have.

The other supervisors in *George Stanley's* section do not have your enthusiasm. Some of them are dull and unimaginative. During your first year as supervisor you used to help them a lot, but you soon found that they leaned on you and before long you were doing their work. There is a lot of pressure to get out production. You got your promotion by producing and you don't intend to let other supervisors interfere. Since you no longer help the other supervisors your production has gone up, but a couple of them seem a bit sore at you. *Frank*, your junior designer, is a better man than most of them and you'd like to see him made a supervisor. Since the company has some dead wood in it, Stanley ought to recognize this fact and assign to such units the more routine jobs. Then they wouldn't need your help and you could concentrate your efforts on jobs that suit your unit. At present, George Stanley passes out work pretty much as he gets it. Because you are efficient you get more than your share of these jobs, and you see no reason why the extra work shouldn't be in the form of "plums." This would motivate units to turn out work. When you suggested to Stanley that he turn over some of the more routine jobs to other supervisors he did it, but he sure was reluctant about it.

You did one thing recently that has bothered you. There was a design change in a set of plans and you should have told *Jim Drake* (a fellow supervisor) about it, but it slipped your mind. Drake was out when you had it on your mind and then you got involved in a hot idea that Frank, your junior designer, had and forgot all about the matter with Drake. As a result, Drake had to make a lot of unnecessary changes and he was quite sore about it. You told him you were sorry and offered to make the changes, but he turned down the offer.

Today you have an interview with George Stanley. It's about this management development plan in the company. It shouldn't take very long, but it's nice to have the boss tell you about the job you are turning out. Maybe there is a raise in it; maybe he'll tell you something about what to expect in the future.

INSTRUCTIONS FOR OBSERVERS

1. Observe the manner in which Stanley begins the interview.

   a. What did the interviewer do, if anything, to create a permissive atmosphere?

   b. Did the interviewer state the purpose of the interview early in the session?

   c. Was the purpose of the interview stated clearly and concisely?

2. Observe how the interview was conducted.

   a. To what extent did the interviewer learn how Burke felt about the job in general?

   b. Did the interviewer use broad, general questions at the outset?

   c. Did Stanley criticize Burke?

   d. Was the interviewer acceptant of Burke's feelings and ideas?

   e. Which one talked the most?

   f. What things did the interviewer learn?

   g. Did Stanley praise Burke?

3. Observe and evaluate the outcome of the interview.

   a. To what extent did Stanley arrive at a fairer and more accurate evaluation of Burke as a result of the interview?

   b. What things did Stanley do, if any, to motivate Burke to improve?

   c. Were relations better or worse after the interview? If worse, why did this occur?

   d. In what ways might the interviewer have done a better job?

IV. Comments and Implications

The interviewer will usually begin the interview by praising Burke for certain aspects of his performance, such as his originality, productivity, and technical competence. Since this is a form of recognition for good work and involves no area of misunderstanding the early part of the interview will generally proceed quite smoothly.

However, there are several areas of Burke's performance which Stanley is led to interpret in an unfavorable way. If Stanley proceeds with the interview on the basis of this interpretation he is likely to make a number of criticisms of Burke which will seem unjustified to Burke. When Burke is caused to feel that he is being treated unfairly he will become defensive and even hostile. When this occurs the interview will lead to further misunderstanding and bad feelings toward each other.

In order to conduct this interview satisfactorily it is necessary for the interviewer to create a permissive atmosphere so that Burke will feel free to express his ideas and feelings about things. In this way Stanley will learn Burke's frame of reference toward various aspects of the work and he should discover that many of Burke's actions can be put in a more favorable light. He is then unlikely to make unjustified criticisms and put Burke on the defensive. Thus the first thing Stanley must learn is how Burke views his performance.

In general, the best way for the interviewer to proceed is to begin the interview with a general question as to how things are going. This will help to create a favorable atmosphere and will enable the interviewer to find out Burke's frame of reference with regard to the work in general. Frequently Burke's comments will furnish leads to explore further later on.

Following the over-all discussion, the interviewer should lead into a discussion of the things that Burke feels are going well for him. These aspects of the job are not only easy for Burke to discuss, but give the interviewer a good opportunity to praise him for the things he has done well.

After an exploration of the things that are going well, the next area of discussion should center around the things that are causing Burke some difficulties. By listening and being acceptant, the interviewer will learn the problems as they appear through Burke's eyes. Further, there will be no feeling on Burke's part that he must try to cover up deficiencies or defend his actions if he finds that Stanley wants to help him.

In the final phase of the interview, mutual understanding and problem solving will be helped if the interviewer will ask Burke for his ideas as to what the interviewer, as his supervisor, or the company can do to help Burke with his problems. This not only produces constructive, problem solving behavior but, by inviting Burke to express his ideas and develop solutions to his problems, Stanley will motivate him to carry out the solutions.

Even if all of an employee's deficiencies are not discussed in one interview this should not be disturbing, if the objective is to develop an employee. It is obvious that a person who has many faults will not correct them all after one interview. The hope is to get some improvement after each interview. If the objective of an interview is to warn an employee rather than to develop him, the above discussion is deficient.

case 19

The Progress Interview

I. Focusing the Problem

Periodic interviews by supervisors with their subordinates can be one of the most effective ways for management to develop subordinates and to promote good communication. This type of interview may serve both to clear up existing misunderstandings and to prevent others from arising in the future.

However, the potential values of progress interviews for this purpose are seldom realized in practice. Sometimes this is due to a lack of knowledge and skill in interview methods. More often the failure to obtain full value from interviews is due to the interference of diverse attitudes. Thus superiors frequently approach the interview situation with certain preconceived notions and judgments. When this is the case, it is unlikely that the interviewer will attempt to learn how the other person views things. Instead of discovering the frame of reference of the person being interviewed and permitting expression of feelings when necessary, there is a tendency to proceed on the basis of the previously formed evaluations. Prior judgments about a person's progress are likely to be one sided, and when this is true such interview procedures almost invariably lead to misunderstandings.

Another frequent cause of interview failure is a lack of understanding of the nature of frustration reactions. When an individual shows hostility, defensiveness, undue stubbornness, or other symptoms of frustration, the interviewer tends to react in various inappropriate ways, such as using logic or facts to change the subordinate, resorting to the use of the force

292

of his authority to pressure the person, or becoming frustrated himself. Such methods tend to increase misunderstanding rather than remedy it, and if the interviewer becomes frustrated, he loses control over the situation altogether.

In order to successfully handle the interview situation where feelings and evaluations of another person may be involved, it is necessary for the interviewer to encourage free and full expression of these feelings and opinions. If he does this he will learn the views of the other person and at the same time will help the individual to think more constructively about his own situation. Further, the interviewer himself will then be able to react in a more problem solving and understanding way to the new developments in the interview.

In the present case, the interview is part of an executive development program in a company and is concerned with evaluating the potential of an individual for promotion purposes. The interview is fairly difficult and makes considerable demands on the knowledge, skill, and attitudes of the interviewer in order to do it successfully and to substantially improve things.

When possible, the instructions should be assigned to the role players for study and preparation a day or more prior to the interview. If this is done and the interviewer is reasonably well qualified, the case frequently becomes an excellent demonstration of nondirective counseling procedures.

The Single Group Role Playing Procedure is used for this case because it permits an intensive analysis of the effects of small but significant details in the interview process.

II. Single Group Role Playing Procedure

PREPARATION

1. Two members from the group are needed to play the roles. One of the role players is to be the interviewer, Walter Pearce; the other role player is James Smith, a chemist in one of the departments who will be interviewed about his progress in the company.

2. The remaining persons in the group will serve as observers.

3. All group members read the section entitled Background Material on pages 296 f. The leader should write on the easel the scheduling of positions held by Smith during his ten years with the company.

4. The two role players should study their roles so they can play them without referring to the written material. They should study their own parts only and avoid reading the role for the other person. Pearce's role is on page 298 and Smith's role is on pages 299 f.

5. Observers should turn to page 301 and read the Instructions for Observers.

6. The setting for the role playing can be prepared by placing a table and two chairs in the front of the room to represent Pearce's office. The furniture should be arranged so that the observers will be able to see the faces of the role players during the interview.

PROCESS

1. Pearce should take his place first and sit at his desk. After a brief pause Smith should enter Mr. Pearce's office for the scheduled interview.

2. The time needed for the interview will vary considerably. Usually from 25 to 35 minutes will be required. The role players should be permitted to finish whenever possible. If a stalemate develops and no progress is made, the role playing should be interrupted and the problem thrown open for discussion. The observers should offer suggestions and attempt to help Pearce overcome the difficulty. The interview can then be resumed and picked up from any point agreed upon in the discussion. Several interruptions may be made if the interviewer wishes help.

3. The role playing should be terminated by Pearce.

ANALYSIS

The results of the interview will vary considerably depending on the attitude and skill of the interviewer as well as on his personality. In most instances the results will be either distinctly favorable or unfavorable with little chance that an intermediate or neutral result will occur. For this reason general discussion questions, indicating the areas to explore, are furnished and these may be expanded or omitted depending 'upon their appropriateness.

1. Will Smith quit or, if he stays, will he do a good job? Did Smith behave unrealistically about his progress? Is he unreasonable about what he wants from the company? Is he satisfied with the outcome? (Different views about these questions should be explored and discussed.)

2. Did Pearce get at the real reason for Smith feeling as he does? Were all feelings explored? What evidence is there that further expression of feelings would be desirable? How could Pearce have brought this about?

3. What did Pearce learn in the interview? Did new problems arise? If so, what were they? What did Pearce do to help problem solving? What things might he have done differently? What more might he have learned?

4. Did Smith's attitude become more favorable or less so during the interview? In what ways did Pearce's actions contribute to this?

5. Was Pearce's attitude influenced in any way during the interview? If so, in what way? In what ways did Pearce's attitudes help or hinder problem solving?

6. Did Pearce alter any previous plans he may have had for Smith? To what extent should he do this? If Smith's attitude is to be improved, what must he be given? Pearce should report his side of the question and Smith should then give his views.

7. A list of arguments for and against giving Smith the double promotion should be developed through discussions.

8. Is the company policy of moving men around in jobs a wise one from a human relations standpoint? What might be some of its more important advantages? What problems might it create? What could the company do to minimize the disadvantages and retain most of the advantages?

9. Is it possible that other college recruits besides Smith have difficulties due to the company's training policies? What clues does the interview with Smith furnish with respect to other trainees? What steps might Pearce take to prevent problems of this nature?

10. What conclusions can we draw from this case? How might we apply the principles derived from this case to our own jobs?

III. Materials [27]

BACKGROUND MATERIAL

The American Consolidated Chemical Company has chemical plants located in various sections of the country. The main plant is located in Detroit and important branches are at Houston, Texas; St. Louis, Missouri; St. Paul, Minnesota; and Cleveland, Ohio. All of the products are manufactured in Detroit but each of the branches specializes in making chemicals that either utilize local raw materials available in the locality or which have a concentration of outlets there. Thus the Cleveland plant manufactures products needed in the Cleveland area and the Houston plant manufactures products which utilize petroleum derivatives.

Since the Detroit plant makes all of the products an experienced man can be moved from Detroit to any of the other plants. When a vacancy opens up in a particular department in Detroit it is possible to fill the vacancy by choosing a local man or by bringing in one from a branch that produces the product that corresponds to the one made by a particular department in Detroit. Thus there has been a great deal of movement within the organization and since the company has been expanding, opportunities for promotion have been good. Generally speaking, morale has been quite satisfactory.

Walter Pearce is the assistant to the Vice-president of Personnel and is located in Detroit. One of his duties is to keep track of the college recruits each year and from these select the men for promotion and development in higher management. Mr. Pearce is about to have an interview with *James Smith,* a college graduate who was brought into the company 10 years ago. The following schedule shows the positions which Smith has held during his 10 years with the Company.

Detroit	Dept. A	1 year	Regular employee
St. Paul	Depts. A B C	2 years	Regular employee
Detroit	Dept. A	1 year	Foreman
St. Louis	Depts. B F	2 years	Foreman
Cleveland	Depts. D E	$1\frac{1}{2}$ years	Foreman
Houston	Dept. G	$1\frac{1}{2}$ years	Foreman
Detroit	Dept. H	1 year	Foreman

[27] Role instructions and background material are taken from a laboratory exercise in Maier, *Psychology in Industry,* Houghton Mifflin Co., Boston, 1955, 631–634. Permission to reproduce this material has been granted by Houghton Mifflin Co., publishers.

Promotion in the company is based upon merit but seniority is recognized by giving qualified men with seniority opportunities to advance as high as general foreman. The rank of management positions in each plant is as follows: foreman, general foreman, superintendent, department head, and works manager. Larger plants have assistants to works managers. The executive group is located in Detroit and it includes several vice presidents (Sales, Manufacturing, Public Relations, Research, and Personnel), the secretary, the treasurer, and the president.

ROLE FOR WALTER PEARCE, ASSISTANT TO THE VICE PRESIDENT—PERSONNEL

Since *Jim Smith* graduated from college and joined the company as a college recruit 10 years ago you have kept an eye on him. During his first year in the company you were impressed by his technical ability and even more by his leadership. After one year in Department A, you sent him to St. Paul where they needed a man with his training. He made a good showing and worked in Departments A, B, and C. After two years you brought him back to Detroit and made him a foreman in Department A. He did very well on this job so you considered making some long-range plans for him. Here was a man you thought you could groom for an executive position. This meant giving him experience with all operations in all plants. To do this with the greatest ease you have made him a foreman in each of the eight departments for a short period of time and have gotten him assignments in each of the branches.

During the past two years you have had some disturbing reports. Jim didn't impress *Bill Jones,* the department head at Houston, who reported that he had ideas but was always on the defensive. Since his return to Detroit he has shown a lack of job interest and the men who work for him don't back him up the way they used to. You feel you have made quite a mistake in this man and that he has let you down after you've given him good build-ups with various department heads. Maybe the confidence you have shown him and the praise you have given him during the several progress interviews have gone to his head. If so he hasn't the stature it takes to make the top grade. Therefore, you have abandoned your plans of moving him up as superintendent in St. Paul and think it best to send him to Houston where there is a job as general foreman in Department C. This won't mean much of a promotion because you have moved his pay up as high as you could while he was sort of a roving foreman. However, you feel that he has earned some promotion even if he hasn't lived up to expectations.

Of course it's possible that Jim is having marital trouble. At a recent company party you found his wife to be quite dissatisfied and unhappy. Maybe she is giving Jim a rough time. She always did seem to be a bit snobbish.

While you are waiting for Jim to arrive you have his folder in front of you showing the positions he has held.

ROLE FOR JIM SMITH, CHEMIST

You have been with the American Consolidated Chemical Company for 10 years now. You joined the company on graduating from college with a major in chemistry. At the time you joined the company you were interviewed by *Walter Pearce*, and were told that a good man could get ahead in the company. On the strength of the position you married your college sweetheart and moved to Detroit. You preferred the Houston and St. Paul branches but Pearce thought Detroit was the place to start. So you took your chance along with other college recruits. You were a good student in college and were active in college affairs so you had reason to believe you possessed leadership ability.

During your first few years you thought you were getting some place. You got moved to Minnesota and felt Mr. Pearce was doing you a favor by sending you there. After the first year you bought a home and got started on a family. During two years in Minnesota you gained considerable experience in Departments A, B, and C. Then you were offered a foremanship in Detroit and since this meant a promotion and you had a second child on the way you decided to return to Detroit. When you came to Detroit, Pearce again saw you and told you how pleased he was with your progress.

Since this time, however, you have been given a royal runaround. They tell you they like your work but all you get are a lot of lateral transfers. You have been foreman in practically every department and have been moved from one branch to another. Other fellows that came to the company even after you joined have been made general foremen. They stick in a given department and are working up while you get moved from place to place. Although the company pays for your moves, both you and your wife want to settle down and get a permanent home for your children. Why can't people be honest with you? You find yourself told what a good job you are doing and then the next thing they do is get rid of you. Take for example *Bill Jones*, the department head at Houston. He acted as if you had done him a favor to go there but you can tell he isn't sincere. Since you've gotten to know him you can see through him. From little remarks he has dropped you know he's been saying some nasty things about you to the home office. It's obvious that the Houston man is incompetent and you feel he got rid of you because he considered you a threat to his job.

Your wife realizes that you are unhappy. She has told you she is willing to live on less just to help you get out of the company. You know you could hold a superintendent's job, such as *George Wilson* got, who joined the company when you did, and he was just an average student in college. As a matter of fact if the company were on the ball they should realize that you have the ability to be a department head if George is superintendent material.

Pearce has asked you to come up and see him. You are a bit nervous about this interview because the news may not be good. You've felt him to be less friendly lately and have no desire to listen to any smooth manipulations. Last night you and your wife had a good talk about things and she's willing that you should look around for another job. Certainly you've reached the end of your patience and you're fed up with any more of his attempts to move you around just because someone is jealous of your ideas.

INSTRUCTIONS FOR OBSERVERS

Walter Pearce has learned on good authority that Jim Smith isn't living up to his expectations. For the last two years reports on Smith show him to have a rather poor attitude although before this time the reports on him had been highly favorable. Since Pearce had given Smith a lot of breaks, having given him company-wide experience and many raises in pay, it was quite a disappointment to him when Smith failed to live up to expectations.

Smith, on the other hand, feels that he has been given a runaround. He now perceives his many moves as proof that certain people are trying to get rid of him. Although he received promises of a good future in the company he feels forgotten since he has seen others promoted.

Armed with these two differing viewpoints or attitudes concerning the many jobs Smith has held, one may either expect the misunderstandings to be discovered or to be further increased. Some of the crucial points to observe in the interview are listed below.

1. Note how Pearce begins the interview. The opening statement might encourage Smith to talk about things that bother him, cause him to go on the defensive, make him wonder what the interview is about, etc.

2. Make a two column list of things Pearce does and says (*a*) that indicate he is permissive and trying to understand, and (*b*) that show him to be critical or in disagreement with Smith.

3. Observe whether or not Pearce seems to change his viewpoint and in what way. Keep track of the events that cause such a change.

4. Make a note of the things you think Pearce learned from the interview as well as the opportunities for learning that he might have missed.

5. What do you think of the solution? How will Smith react? Do you think Pearce is aware of the way Smith feels? (Since you have been given some data on both sides of the question you are in a better position to evaluate what is going on than is Pearce.)

IV. Comments and Implications

This case is difficult to handle because a source of misunderstanding is planted in the roles and unless it is discovered fully, the misunderstanding is likely to grow. A common error is for Pearce to show his disappointment in Smith in various ways ranging from criticism to faint praise, and then tell Smith he is going to give him a promotion anyway by making him a general foreman at Houston. Smith probably will be disappointed with this, since he is likely to see this promotion as too little and too late, and the job is located at the one place he does not want to go. Pearce, in turn, is likely to further the misunderstanding by taking the view that Smith considers himself too good for this assignment. Thus Pearce and Smith may frustrate each other so that the interview degenerates into recrimination and conflict. Frequently, Smith will decide to quit the company.

Aside from failing to discover Smith's frame of reference at the outset, Pearce will frequently commit the error of misinterpreting the feelings Smith expresses during the interview. Thus he may react to Smith's hostility by showing his own authority or he may feel that Smith is unjustifiably sorry for himself. Occasionally, Pearce will try to question Smith concerning his marriage or give him unwanted advice, either of which will deepen the misunderstanding.

The third and perhaps the hardest difficulty to overcome is for Pearce to change his attitude during the interview. He has concluded that Smith has been doing below-standard work and this conclusion is likely to prejudice him. Instead of recognizing that Smith's attitude was caused by certain misunderstandings he is likely to blame him for not being more tolerant.

In order to conduct a successful interview, Pearce must get Smith to express his feelings about his work with the company. To accomplish this he must be a good listener and be acceptant and respectful of Smith's feelings. Only after Smith has had his say will he be prepared to show constructive behavior. Pearce's attitude toward Smith is likely to change because when he discovers Smith's view of things he will be able to see why Smith's job performance has deteriorated. Usually this will cause Pearce to reconsider his previous decision and offer Smith the job of superintendent at the St. Paul plant instead of the job of general foreman at Houston.

This two-step promotion is perhaps essential to correcting Smith's attitude and rekindling in him the job motivation and confidence in the company he once had. However it is difficult for Pearce to grant because he has a mental set to offer Smith the job of general foreman. Since Smith has developed an unfavorable attitude toward the company, Pearce is likely to be conservative and want to wait until the attitude has improved. Thus there is a strong tendency to withhold the very thing that is needed to cure the attitude.

Often employees develop poor attitudes because of certain disappointments they have experienced in the company. Accidentally being overlooked in promotions is a common cause of such disappointments. Later on when the employee's capabilities are discovered, promotion is denied because a poor attitude is discovered. Waiting for the attitude to spontaneously recover is too much to expect. If the company made a mistake by overlooking a prospective supervisor, can it be expected to correct this oversight by a promotion later on? Successful promotions of this type have been made but it is important that each case be studied separately. Bitterness developed through an unhappy marriage would not be removed by promotion and it might lead to placing emotionally unstable individuals in managerial positions.

case 20

The President's Decision

I. Focusing the Problem

One of the important measures of good management is the ability to make wise decisions. This is true in small everyday operating problems as well as in major policy determination. Sometimes such decisions can be made on the basis of existing facts known to the individual who makes the decision. The axiom to get the facts, weigh them, and then decide holds for these situations. At other times the available facts may be quite incomplete or one cannot wait to get the facts and then inferences, opinions, and other subjective factors influence the decision. When the problem is highly complex or the relevant factors are beyond the knowledge and ability of the responsible person, it is customary and wise to utilize the advice of various staff services in the company. Engineers, accountants, lawyers, psychologists, and other technically trained personnel frequently satisfy the need for specialized knowledge. However, even when experts are used, the responsibility for the final decision and the consequences of its success or failure rests with the line supervisor who makes it.

When the situation is such that the decision can be based on fact or inference, it usually happens that one set of facts or judgments will outweigh the others. In such instances the final solution usually emerges from an exploration and weighing of alternatives. Decision-making under these conditions therefore is essentially an intellectual, problem solving process.

However, in many instances management decisions are not based on logic and facts alone, but upon feelings of people as well. This is true whether it involves a supervisor giving the day off to a girl whose mother is ill, or a policy decision regulating coffee privileges.

The feeling and emotional factors often become paramount in such cases and when this occurs the decision may go contrary to the facts of the situation. This is usually the case when frustration is present, when there are strong attitudes toward the subject under consideration, and when factors in the situation threaten the position or pride of the decision maker. Many such decisions are made on the basis of prejudices, face-saving needs for certain individuals concerned, attempts to protect a management prerogative, and fear of change.

Persons who are responsible for making decisions not only must avoid being misled by emotional considerations, but they must know how to effectively use the aid of subordinates. It is easy for the boss to accept the suggestions of his subordinates when their suggestions are in agreement with his views, but when their suggestions are in opposition to his views, he must make a difficult choice. It is human to fail to give opposed views a sympathetic hearing and it is therefore difficult for a boss to recognize when he is wrong or biased. If he refuses to be swayed by others he will be regarded as a stubborn person, but if he is easily swayed by them, he might make poor decisions. When a leader is held responsible for his decisions and must pay the price when things go wrong, should he be expected to share the decision-making with subordinates? If he refuses to share this function he not only fails to develop subordinates, but he eventually loses out in the quality of the suggestions that are made. Subordinates soon cease offering the kind of suggestions that get turned down; as a result they spend their time trying to figure out what the boss would like them to suggest, instead of attempting to arrive at good solutions to problems.

The success or failure of a decision not only depends upon the objective merits of the decision but also upon the degree to which persons who must execute the decision are willing to accept it. A second-best decision that is accepted might prove more productive than a perfect decision that is disliked. The success of decisions, therefore, depends upon both their quality and their acceptance. Persons responsible for decisions must concern themselves with the problem of how to protect their quality without sacrificing their acceptance.

This case, which deals with a president's decision, will introduce many of the complications and conflicting forces discussed above. The possible outcomes may vary in the kind of decision reached as well as in the degree of acceptance achieved. Since the factors making for the different outcomes should be isolated and analyzed the Single Group Role Playing Procedure is presented. In this way all persons can discuss a common set of events. If one wished to test the extent of variation in outcomes, it would be desirable to use the Multiple Role Playing Procedure.

II. Single Group Role Playing Procedure

PREPARATION [28]

1. Four persons are needed to play the roles. One participant will play the role of John Ward, president of the company, and the other three will be the vice-presidents. They are: William Carson, in charge of manufacturing and product development; James Jackson, in charge of sales; and Russell Haney, in charge of personnel and industrial relations.

2. The remaining persons in the class will serve as observers.

3. All group members are to read the Background Information on pages 309 f. The instructor should write on the easel the name, position, age, and years with the company, of all four participants.

4. The participants are to study their roles. The role for Ward is on pages 311 f.; Carson's role is on pages 313 f.; the role for Jackson is on pages 315 f.; and Haney's role is on page 317. Each participant should study his part so that he can role play without referring to the written material and should avoid reading any role except his own.

5. Observers should turn to page 318 and read the Instructions for Observers.

6. The instructor can prepare the setting for the scene by placing a table and four chairs in the front of the room to represent the furniture in Ward's office. The table and one chair will be for Ward's use and the other three chairs, arranged in a semicircle in front of Ward's desk, will be for the vice-presidents. The furniture should be arranged so that the observers will be able to see the faces of all four men.

PROCESS

1. When all participants are ready, Ward should enter his "office" and sit at his desk. After a few moments the vice-presidents should enter, one at a time, and seat themselves so that Carson will be at Ward's left, then Jackson next to Carson, and Haney at the end, on Ward's right.

2. Ward will wish to greet each man as he enters and show him to his seat.

3. When everyone is seated, Ward should lead into the discussion topic as he wishes.

[28] When planning permits, role assignments for this case should be given before the meeting of the class in order to permit the persons to study the roles carefully.

4. Approximately 30 to 40 minutes will be needed for role playing.

5. Participants should be permitted to finish whenever possible. If conflict develops and persists so that no progress is made after 20 minutes, the role playing should be interrupted and the problem thrown open for general discussion. Role playing should be resumed after the president feels he has gained enough hints to proceed. If he prefers, another person can be asked to play the part of President Ward.

EVALUATION OF THE SOLUTION

1. Discuss the merits of the solution from the point of view of the future of the company and determine the extent of agreement among the observers. Compare the opinions of observers, vice-presidents, and President Ward. In case these opinions differ, each role player should feel free to introduce any relevant information that was given in his role to see if the new facts will alter the opinions of the observers.

2. Discuss the merits of the solution from the point of view of President Ward. Did he get good advice from the vice-presidents?

3. What are Mr. Ward's prospects of being retained by the Board of Directors in case the solution doesn't result in marked improvement?

4. Discuss the part the vice-presidents will play in making the decision a success and in giving Ward the support he needs to retain his job.

ANALYSIS OF THE CONFERENCE

1. Did Ward give the vice-presidents an opportunity to solve the problem he faced or did he give them a somewhat different problem? After some discussion, Ward should describe why his situation caused him to act as he did.

2. Should Ward have given his side of the problem or should he have confined the discussion to company matters as much as possible? Compare views of participants and observers.

3. Which participants persisted in discussing matters from their points of view? What could have been done to get everyone working together?

4. How did the specialized factual information that different conferees possessed get integrated into the discussion? Was there an interest in getting facts or did Ward attempt to suppress facts?

5. Stubbornness, aggression, and childish behavior indicate frustration. Enumerate the examples of these behaviors that were evidenced in the discussion and evaluate how they were handled.

DISCUSSION OF WARD'S SITUATION

1. How many observers would have taken the advice of the vice-presidents given in this instance had they played the part of Ward? How many would have declined the advice? List the arguments in favor of each position.

2. What would happen if a president's decision always was the joint decision of the vice-presidents? Discuss the favorable and unfavorable aspects of such a philosophy of leadership.

III. Materials

BACKGROUND INFORMATION

The ABCO Electrical Manufacturing Company produces various parts and subassemblies for the radio, television, and other electronics industries. The factory is located in Philadelphia and there are sales offices in several of the eastern cities in or near the major market area. During the war, the company also operated a government-built plant in Kansas City for supplying equipment for military aircraft. However, this operation was abandoned in 1946 when numerous military orders were cancelled and this plant was bought shortly thereafter by one of the larger electronics manufacturing companies.

Two years ago the company went through a major management reorganization, brought about by five years of increasing losses in its operations and a steadily diminishing share of the market. The previous top management group were extremely conservative in their outlook and methods, and for many years had operated on a small share of the market as suppliers to the radio and broadcasting industries. During the war they made a good showing as a result of increased business and profits from military orders, most of them on a cost-plus basis. Following this period there was marked growth in the electronics industry generally. At the same time new problems were created for the smaller producers such as ABCO by the unusually rapid technological developments and strong competition from the larger companies in the field. The company's inability to compete for large-volume business has made it necessary to depend more and more on specialty orders. Although the unit-profit margin on such orders is somewhat larger, the shifting demands of this type of market call for unusual flexibility of manufacturing processes and procedures and a highly alert, aggressive sales force in order to maintain demand for regular lines and push the sales of new products. Similarly, product development and engineering ingenuity are at a premium in order to meet competition, provide for economical changeover from one product to another, and achieve quick solution of a variety of complex production problems. In addition, it is necessary for the production employees and foremen to adapt to frequent job and methods changes without requiring undue training time or becoming disturbed about things.

It was the inability of the previous management to adapt to these changing conditions that led to the reorganization of the company and the installation of a new top management group. Following are the names of the present group of senior officers of the company together with a summary of their previous background and experience:

John Ward, president of the company. Ward is 49, has been with the company twelve years, first as an accountant, then as controller for five years previous to being promoted to his present position two years ago. He is a college graduate in accounting and a CPA.

William Carson, vice-president in charge of manufacturing and product development. Carson has an electrical engineering background and was hired into the company fifteen years ago as a potential management man. He had progressed to general foreman of the night shift at the time he was sent to Kansas City as superintendent. When the Kansas City plant was closed he returned to Philadelphia as plant superintendent and was promoted to his present position two years ago when Ward took over as president. Carson is 45.

James Jackson, vice-president in charge of sales. Jackson came to the company five years ago from the position of assistant sales manager for one of the divisions of a larger company. He is the only holdover as vice-president from the previous management, having been brought in to set up a sales organization and attempt to recapture lost accounts and widen the market for company products. Jackson started in sales work from business administration school. He is 46.

Russell Haney, vice-president, personnel and industrial relations, is 39. Haney was hired as personnel director for the Kansas City plant during the war and came to Philadelphia in 1946 in a similar capacity. Previously, personnel functions had been the responsibility of the office manager. Haney remained as personnel director until his promotion to the vice-presidency two years ago.

ROLE FOR JOHN WARD, PRESIDENT

You are president of the ABCO Manufacturing Company and have held this position for the past two years. In your previous position as controller you advised the president on various fiscal and policy matters, and gained a close knowledge of the inner workings of the company. As president, your duties are much broader and more complex. You now have final responsibility for policy formulation and execution in such diverse fields as procurement, manufacturing, sales, finance, product development, personnel, public relations, and various other aspects of business operation. Thus to a large extent the progress of the company and your own success or failure as president depend on your making wise decisions. You get a certain amount of credit when things go well but you also take the rap when they go wrong.

One of the most difficult problems you have had to deal with since you became president is whether to expand operations. Within the company and among your close business associates there are conflicting views on the matter. Those who are opposed to expansion contend that real estate and building values are seriously inflated and that the costs of new equipment are out of line. A further argument is that the television and other electronics sales are highly sensitive to economic conditions. Since company reserves are low, you would have to obtain the necessary funds through stock sales or mortgage loans and the present financial condition of the company does not place it in an advantageous position for such financing. Further, it would be some time before returns from expansion would begin to pay off to any great extent and an early business slump could wreck the company.

At the same time there are a number of people in the company who favor immediate expansion. However, all of them tend to see things in terms of their own particular area of the business and none are in a position to have a broad, over-all perspective on things. Nevertheless, in casual discussions of the matter they have come up with some impressive facts and arguments in favor of setting up a new plant. One contention, for example, is that the present 4-story, 30-year-old building is not adapted for modern straight-line production methods. Not only is it expensive to heat and light but it lacks the flexibility needed for efficient change-overs to meet the production requirements of various orders. In addition, it has been necessary to turn down two or three large orders in the past because of insufficient capacity to meet production deadlines. Then there is the further contention that a lack of growth is damaging to morale and that good men tend to become discouraged and leave to go with larger or faster growing companies where opportunities are greater.

Over the past several months you have tried to keep an open mind to both points of view and despite the risks of expanding you were becoming convinced that on a long term basis expansion was the better course to follow. True, you have been making headway toward getting the company back on its feet, but as things are it is a slow, uphill struggle. Nevertheless you felt that under the unfavorable circumstances you were making as satisfactory progress as could be expected.

Despite your best efforts over the past two years, the board of directors informed you late yesterday that they had voted to give you one more year in which to show some results or else resign. You had known previously that certain members of the board were becoming impatient. However, this action was totally unexpected and came as a real shock. Obviously, expansion is out of the question if results have to be shown within a year. It would take longer than that to make the necessary financial and other arrangements to construct a new plant and get it into operation. The only possible course of action is to play it safe and hope for the best. With a few good breaks and strict belt-tightening throughout the organization, it may be possible to demonstrate the desired results within the deadline set by the board. Certainly this is not the time to take chances. Your decision not to expand must be announced immediately. As a first step, you have called a meeting of your three vice-presidents for 3 P.M. Your purpose is to check with them to see whether anything has been overlooked in arriving at your decision. It is now 3 o'clock and time to begin.

ROLE FOR WILLIAM CARSON, VICE-PRESIDENT, MANUFACTURING AND PRODUCT DEVELOPMENT

You are the vice-president of the ABCO Company in charge of manufacturing and product development. When you moved into this job from plant superintendent two years ago you had high hopes of streamlining operations and have been able to accomplish a good deal. For years the previous management had refused to spend money on manufacturing facilities and instead followed a penny-pinching practice of patching and fixing and making you do the best you could with inferior, outmoded equipment and methods. Through your influence with *Ward* you have been able to make a number of changes in layout and methods. By careful shopping around you have been able to get good buys on several pieces of second-hand but fairly modern equipment. In addition, you have set up a new product development laboratory. This is a must if the company is to compete with the larger companies and their staffs of research people, both in bringing out new products and in working out designs so as to simplify manufacture. The company is slowly getting back on its feet and in large part this is due to the reduced unit costs you have been able to achieve in manufacturing.

However, you have gone just about as far as you can in this direction, and what is needed now is a new modern plant. The present 4-story building was satisfactory for its purpose 30 years ago but with newer integrated assembly line procedures all operations should be on one floor. The layout of the present building is awkward for moving things along from one process to the next and creates a lot of needless delay in changeovers when you have new orders to fill. Also it is costly to light and heat and the construction isn't strong enough to support some of the new heavy equipment on the upper floors where you can use it to the best advantage. Repeatedly you have urged Ward to expand into a new modern building and purchase new equipment, and although he has always given you a fair hearing you cannot get him to commit himself. Ward is a good accountant but he doesn't know the manufacturing end of the business too well and he seems to be a fence rider. This may be because he was not experienced in administrative work before he became president. As controller he learned company operations from a fiscal angle but he merely advised the former president and did not have to make the final decisions himself. Now that he is on the firing line and has to stand or fall on his own judgment he seems to have difficulty in making up his mind about things. You have given him the best advice you can and you want to help him move things along faster, but he has to make up his mind to expand or else the company will no longer be able to meet competition.

Ward has called a meeting with you and the other two vice-presidents in his office for 3 o'clock today. He has these meetings at fairly frequent intervals. You don't know what he has on his mind but you hope he has finally agreed to go ahead with the new plant. Almost anything would be an improvement over the one you now have.

ROLE FOR JAMES JACKSON, VICE-PRESIDENT, SALES

You are vice-president in charge of sales and came to the ABCO Company 5 years ago. Previous to that you were one of the assistant sales managers of a division of one of the large electrical manufacturing companies. Stepping into the vice-presidency of the ABCO Company meant quite an increase in salary and responsibility and it seemed that here was a real opportunity to do a good job and make a name for yourself. Five years ago the company had no real sales organization and was losing ground rapidly. Thus one of your first moves was to build from the ground up in an effort to recapture the market and expand further. This took a lot of work and you had a struggle to win over the old management to your ideas. Now there are sales offices in most of the principal eastern cities where ABCO products are in demand by manufacturers and a fairly strong organization has been built up. The reorganization two years ago had its advantages in that John Ward gave you more freedom to operate than you had enjoyed previously. In some ways he is doing a fair job as president but seems to be rather unimaginative. He always gives your ideas a fair hearing but in the end he seems to shy away from new advertising campaigns. During the past two years he has taken the steam out of some of your best promotional ideas by simply delaying action on them until too late. One of the things you have been pushing, for example, is an expansion of plant facilities. This would give you a big advantage because in the past year you have lost several big orders when *Carson* said he couldn't possibly meet the deadline set by the customers. There may have been something to what Carson calls "unreasonable deadlines" in one or two instances; however, it begins to look more and more as though Carson isn't fast enough on his feet to make the necessary changeovers in manufacturing and Ward refuses to push him. Carson seems to be Ward's fair-haired boy. With a new modern plant there could be no more excuses and you could take advantage of the breaks when big orders come in. It would help a lot too if those in charge of product development would get to work. They have been set up for two years now and despite the ideas for new things that your salesmen have been funneling in to them they haven't shown any progress. A small company like this must frequently have new and better products to put on the market if it is to compete for new markets. That way the newspapers and trade journals give you a lot of free publicity and the salesmen have a chance to get a foot in the door of potential new customers. The main thing, however, is to get a new plant so that larger orders can be handled. Turning down the big ones as you had to do several times in the past is what hurts, and it demoralizes your sales force.

Ward has been receptive enough to your arguments for expansion and there has been increasing evidence lately that he is ready to take action on the idea. Today at 3 o'clock there is to be a meeting in his office with you and the other two vice-presidents. Apparently Ward is about to announce plans for the new plant because his secretary told you over the phone that Ward wanted you to review in your mind all of the pros and cons on the matter of expansion prior to coming to the meeting. You are on your way there now.

ROLE FOR RUSSELL HANEY, VICE-PRESIDENT, PERSONNEL AND INDUSTRIAL RELATIONS

You are vice-president in charge of personnel and industrial relations, and have held this position since you moved up from the job of personnel director a year and a half ago. All of the usual personnel services, such as recruitment, hiring, promotions, training, and contract negotiations, are handled through your office. On a policy basis, you have set up your office to serve three main functions. One is to prevent as many personnel problems as possible and assist the supervisors with those that arise. Second, you advise the president, *John Ward*, on personnel matters. Third, you are responsible for maintaining a competent work force that gets along well with each other and does a good job.

One of the things you were able to get under way as personnel director was an individualized program of training and work experiences for promising young college recruits, and even though the convervatism of the previous management stymied their progress in many ways, you were able to obtain a few good men each year. Then when the reorganization took place two years ago, a considerable number of these young fellows were able to move up a notch. This left a number of vacancies at the trainee level which you were able to fill by going out to the colleges. However, you are again faced with the same problem you had previously. The company isn't growing and many of the fellows you brought in a few years back who were not ready to move up at the time of the reorganization are becoming impatient. Further, you cannot hold out much promise to new college men. At present, there just isn't any place for them to move up in the company, and there won't be any new opportunities unless the company expands its operations. Meanwhile, some of your best men are disheartened and are leaving. Competing companies are picking them off one by one. If this is allowed to continue, the management at the middle and lower levels will be second-rate again in a few years. Unless the company can offer good men some inducements to stay, there will be crippling losses in many of the key positions and the company simply cannot afford that and stay in competition. As far as you can see, expansion is absolutely essential if the company is to keep these men.

John Ward has sent word that there is to be a meeting at 3 o'clock in his office and that *Carson* and *Jackson* are also to be there. Since Carson is in charge of manufacturing and Jackson in charge of sales, this looks as though Ward may be ready to announce plans for the new plant. Unless there is some such development, it will be hopeless to try to keep your best men.

INSTRUCTIONS FOR OBSERVERS

On the basis of what you already know about the ABCO Company and the four top executives, *Ward, Carson, Jackson,* and *Haney,* you probably have formed certain impressions about the situation. Most of the things you have learned so far are factual in nature. However, you also know that these facts may be relatively unimportant except as background and that the attitudes, feelings, and personalities of these men as well as their relationships with each other may be the important things. It is important to observe the feelings about the facts that are indicated and not be misled by the actual words spoken if you are to sense the developments as they occur in the role playing. It is in developing sensitivity to feeling that one becomes a good observer. The following questions are designed to give you certain clues as to what to watch and listen for:

1. Observe how Ward opens the discussion. Does he seem at ease? Did he state a problem with all relevant facts for open discussion? Is he being open-minded about things?

2. What are Ward's reasons for calling this meeting? How do the other members react to his views? To what extent is he acceptant of their views? What evidence is there, if any, that Ward is defensive about things?

3. To what extent is this a problem solving discussion? If not, why is this? What do you think is the real problem here? What did Ward do to help or hinder the group?

4. Did any of the participants become stubborn? Why?

5. Note behaviors that indicate a member was holding back relevant information.

6. How acceptable is the decision to each of the members? Note behaviors that support your evaluation.

7. What evidence is there to indicate that fear or threat influenced the relationships of the various persons in the discussion?

IV. Comments and Implications

Ward will usually begin the meeting by announcing his decision not to expand company operations. This will produce disagreement and conflict because the vice-presidents all feel that expansion is essential and they will argue with Ward. Further, they are likely to feel that he is being arbitrary and inconsiderate of their views.

Actually, the reason for Ward's behavior is an ultimatum by the Board of Directors to show results within one year or get out. In the face of this threat Ward has decided to play it safe. In addition, he is reluctant to tell the others of the board's action because this would hurt his pride. He also may fear that if he tells the vice-presidents about the board's action they may lose confidence in him and either try to move elsewhere or maneuver themselves into competing positions for the presidency. However, if he attempts to protect his pride, the other members are likely to sense that something isn't right and feel that he is deliberately keeping them in the dark about something. As a result they will become suspicious of his motives and at the same time become resentful of what appears to be an arbitrary decision on his part. When this occurs the situation will go from bad to worse and deteriorate into one of mutual frustration. Neither side will then be capable of viewing the differences as a misunderstanding and they will therefore be unable to find anything constructive to do.

In order to handle this situation successfully it is necessary for the President to inform the group of the action taken by the Board of Directors and ask them for their ideas and help in meeting the situation. He can do this without arousing sympathy for himself if he presents the problem in situational terms and treats the ultimatum he has received as their having a year to prove themselves. By sharing the problem with his vice-presidents he can practically be assured of their cooperation and support. In doing this, he will also focus their attention on the real problem, which is to show results within one year or convince the directors that this is an unsound request. Viewed in this light the question of whether to expand is no longer the problem, but becomes merely one of several alternatives to be explored in the search for a solution to a problem created by the Board of Directors.

In essence then, the decision the president must make resolves itself into one of playing a lone hand against pressures both from above and below or sharing the problem with his subordinates in a joint effort to meet the situation. To choose the latter requires him to have confidence in the judgment of his subordinates and respect for their views. When influenced by fears and threats he is not likely to do this and instead will tend to take the very actions that will bring about his own failure and jeopardize the company.

Fear and threat are negative forms of motivation and, as such, are likely to produce avoidance reactions rather than positive explorations of new possibilities. These avoidance and timid reactions may be expressed in various ways and since they are based mainly on feelings, they generally make little sense in terms of fact or logic. Thus they tend to be unadaptive ways of reacting to the realities of the situation. Unfortunately, it is a common practice in life and in industry to use these methods in an attempt to get results. The fact that there exist alternative procedures for solving most problems does not always occur to those in positions of authority. If men in authority had no big stick with which to threaten others they could not resort to fear motivation and instead would have to use their wits. This suggests that men who possess power might have to learn to behave as if they had none if they wished to increase the tendency in their groups to solve problems by constructive thinking. Observers of conferences readily discover how the leader influences the contributions of the participants. In evaluating problem solving discussions, it is interesting to classify the various contributions into two categories: (a) the fear-produced behaviors, which at best make for cautiousness and the avoidance of immediate threats; and (b) the exploratory or forward-moving behaviors, which have to do with locating obstacles and finding ways to circumvent them. It should not be assumed, however, that all avoidance or protective behavior is undesirable. There are times when caution and avoidance are appropriate, but once the initial protective responses have been made, opportunities for positive action should be explored.

Index